CONSERVATION
TROPICAL FIELD
1

W9-BWU-153

LEMURS
of Madagascar

Russell A. Mittermeier
Ian Tattersall, William R. Konstant,
David M. Meyers & Roderic B. Mast

Illustrated by
Stephen D. Nash

CONSERVATION
INTERNATIONAL

CONSERVATION INTERNATIONAL
Washington, DC

1994

Inquiries to the publisher should be directed to
the following address:

> Russell A. Mittermeier
> Editor, CI Tropical Field Guide Series
> Conservation International
> 1015 Eighteenth Street, NW, Suite 1000
> Washington, DC 20036 USA

Library of Congress Cataloging-in-Publication
 Data No. 94-72352

ISBN 1-881173-08-9

Printed and bound in the United States of America

10 9 8 7 6 5 4 3 2 1

CONSERVATION INTERNATIONAL

Washington, D.C.
December 4, 1994

In the last five years of this century and early in the next, our species will face what may be its greatest crisis ever: the potential loss of a large portion of our planet's biological diversity. To meet this challenge head on, we will need many creative, innovative, and immediate new approaches to maintaining this critical living resource base. Foremost among these are the need for greater knowledge of the scope of biodiversity, a much enhanced appreciation of its intrinsic value, and demonstration of a whole new range of economic benefits that its conservation can provide.

Economic solutions are especially critical, since the "bottom line" drives so much of decision-making in today's world, especially in many of the developing countries where so much of global biodiversity exists. Of the many possible economic solutions, one that stands out is *ecotourism,* the rapidly growing field of nature-based tourism that focuses heavily on the biologically rich tropical countries. Ecotourism can demonstrate economic benefit more rapidly than almost any other alternative, both to national governments and to local communities, and, if carried out properly, is non-consumptive and largely benign. A number of countries have already demonstrated the enormous potential of ecotourism, foremost among them the Central American nation of Costa Rica, where it is now the number one foreign exchange earner, and it is rapidly growing elsewhere as well.

However, to reach its full potential, ecotourism needs to be based on the best available science, and, through knowledge, to instill appreciation. It is hard to get excited about a group of animals or plants if you don't know very much about them, can't identify them, and don't know where to find them; good information can make a world of difference. The vast community of bird watchers owes its existence in good part to the excellent field guides for birds beginning with the renowned *A Field Guide to the Birds* by Roger Tory Peterson, first published in 1934. Bird watchers are a dedicated lot and make up a good proportion of the ecotourism market. However, with the exception of a few other groups of animals (*e.g.*, the mammalian megafauna of the African savannas), this kind of information does not exist in a convenient, user-friendly format.

It is therefore with great pleasure that we launch this new series, entitled *Conservation International Tropical Field Guides* - to fill a largely vacant niche, to increase knowledge of and further appreciation for wildlife of the tropical world, and to help stimulate a tradition of "watching" and "life-listing" for other creatures in addition to birds. The first in this series deals with the lemurs of Madagascar, a spectacular, entirely unique group of primates found exclusively on the island continent of Madagascar, one of the world's highest biodiversity conservation priorities. We hope that you find it useful, and that it increases your interest in the many other wonderful forms of life with which we share our planet. Other volumes in this series will follow in the near future.

We thank you for your interest in biodiversity conservation and urge you to become more involved by joining our organization and working with us in this tremendously compelling cause.

Sincerely,

Peter Seligmann
Chairman of the Board and CEO

Russell A. Mittermeier
President

This book is dedicated
to
Margot Marsh
in recognition of
and grateful appreciation for
her commitment, enthusiasm
and consistent support
for the cause of
primate conservation
around the world

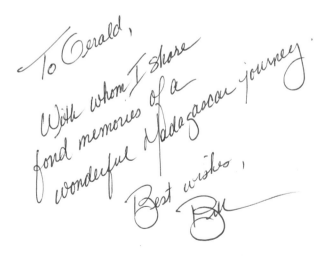

To Gerald,
With whom I share
fond memories of a
wonderful Madagascar journey.

Best wishes,

Russell A. Mittermeier
Russell A. Mittermeier is President of Conservation International, and has also served as Chairman of the Primate Specialist Group of the World Conservation Union's Species Survival Commission (IUCN/SSC) since 1977. Prior to joining CI in 1989, he was Vice-President for Science at World Wildlife Fund - US. A primatologist and herpetologist by training, Dr. Mittermeier's publications include seven books and over 200 articles, and he has conducted field work on three continents and in more than 20 countries. He received his Ph.D. in Biological Anthropology from Harvard University in 1977, and is also an Adjunct Professor at the State University of New York at Stony Brook.

Ian Tattersall
Ian Tattersall is Curator and Chairman in the Department of Anthropology of the American Museum of Natural History in New York City. A primatologist and paleontologist who has specialized in the study of lemurs since 1968, he has a central interest in systematics and has studied numerous aspects of lemur biology. He has carried out extensive field work both in Madagascar and the Comores, and is co-editor of *Lemur Biology* (1975) and author of *The Primates of Madagascar* (1982). He also holds the distinction of being the only living lemur biologist to have a lemur species named after him.

William R. Konstant
William Konstant is the Vice President for Conservation of the Zoological Society of Philadelphia and founder of the Zoo's *One With Nature* program. He has more than a decade of experience developing species conservation projects in both Latin America and Africa. He has held positions with the World Wildlife Fund-US Primate Program, Wildlife Preservation Trust International, and Conservation International, and currently serves as Deputy Chairman of the IUCN/SSC Primate Specialist Group.

David M. Meyers

David Meyers received his Ph. D. in Physical Anthropology from Duke University in 1993 based upon a comparative ecological study of the newly-discovered golden-crowned sifaka. Meyers has done extensive field research in Madagascar's eastern and northeastern forests, and is currently the Interim Technical Assistant for Conservation for the World Wildlife Fund's project in the Montagne d'Ambre protected area complex in northern Madagascar.

Roderic B. Mast

The founding Director of Conservation International's Madagascar Program, Roderic Mast currently serves as CI's Vice President for Madagascar and the Tropical Andes. A marine biologist and primatologist with 15 years of conservation experience in Latin America, Madagascar, and Africa, Mast's past positions include Program Officer at the World Wildlife Fund, Assistant Director of RARE, Inc., naturalist for the Galapagos National Park Service, and marine turtle researcher for the U.S. National Marine Fisheries Service and Mexican Fisheries Department. He is currently co-editor of *Lemur News*, the newsletter of the Madagascar section of the IUCN/SSC Primate Specialist Group.

Stephen D. Nash

A native of Great Britain and a graduate of the Natural History Illustration Department of the Royal College of Art in London, Stephen Nash has been Scientific Illustrator for Conservation International since 1989, producing images for conservation education and biological publications. Prior to working for Conservation International, Nash was part of the World Wildlife Fund-US Primate Program. Based at the State University of New York at Stony Brook, he is a Visiting Research Associate in the Department of Anatomical Sciences and an Adjunct Associate Professor in the Department of Art.

TABLE OF CONTENTS

ILLUSTRATIONS

Postural and Behavioral Drawings

Color Plates

PHOTO BY RUSSELL A. MITTERMEIER

Aerial view of the reed beds of Lac Alaotra, sole remaining habitat of the Lac Alaotra bamboo lemur (*Hapalemur griseus alaotrensis*) and one of the most threatened ecosystems in Madagascar.

1

INTRODUCTION

Madagascar is without doubt the world's highest major primate conservation priority, with high diversity and unmatched endemism. Madagascar is third highest on the world list of primate species diversity (in spite of being less than 7% the size of Brazil, the world leader, and roughly one-quarter the size of Indonesia or Zaire, second and fourth in species diversity), and its 32 species and 50 distinct taxa are 100% endemic. Two species, *Eulemur fulvus* and *Eulemur mongoz*, also live on the nearby Comores, but they were almost certainly introduced there from Madagascar.

At the generic and family levels, Madagascar's diversity is even more striking, with fully five primate families and 14 genera found nowhere else. Compare this to Brazil, the richest country on Earth in primate species with 69, but with only three families, none of them endemic, and two endemic genera out of 16.

Furthermore, of the 50 lemur taxa recognized for Madagascar, fully 10 are considered critically endangered, 7 are endangered and another 19 vulnerable, figures that are unmatched by any other country. In addition, one entire family (Daubentoniidae) and four genera are considered endangered, a degree of endangerment at higher taxonomic levels that not even Brazil can match, and that is of great international concern.

Looking at Madagascar's diversity in yet another way, although it is only one of 92 countries to have wild primate populations, it alone is home to 13% (32/246) of all primate species, 23% (14/61) of all primate genera and 36% (5/14) of all primate families, a great responsibility for any one nation.

Madagascar also demonstrates clearly that primate extinctions are a very real phenomenon and not a figment of the conservationist's imagination. Fully eight genera and at least 15 species of lemur already have gone extinct on this island since the arrival of our own species there less than 2000 years ago, and, as indicated in the pages that follow, many others could disappear within the next few decades if rapid action is not taken. Today, the major threats to lemurs include deforestation due to slash-and-burn agriculture, logging, charcoal and firewood production, burning of dry forests to create cattle pasture or monocultures, hunting for food and live capture of lemurs as pets.

Conservation International and the Primate Specialist Group of the World Conservation Union's Species Survival Commission (IUCN/SSC) have long recognized Madagascar as one of their top priorities, and are pleased to present this guide to facilitate field identification of lemurs, to summarize available data on their ecology, distribution and conservation status, and to stimulate further interest in the survival of these animals in their natural habitats. As should be obvious from the information presented here, one of the most glaring gaps in our knowledge of lemurs is often the most basic information on geographic distribution and conservation status. In spite of several centuries of observation and collection and more than three decades of research, we are still not clear as to the limits of distribution of most species and have largely subjective impressions of conservation status and population numbers for the majority of lemurs.

Good indicators of how little is known about lemurs are the striking cases of two new species (*Hapalemur aureus*, *Propithecus tattersalli*) being described in the last 8 years, two others, *Hapalemur simus* and *Microcebus myoxinus*, being rediscovered, and yet another, the aye-aye (*Daubentonia madagascariensis*), previously believed to be highly restricted and nearly extinct and now being found in many different parts of the island. Clearly, much more thorough survey work is needed for all species, with special emphasis on the most endangered, among them *Allocebus trichotis*, *Eulemur macaco flavifrons*, *Varecia variegata rubra*, *Hapalemur aureus*, *Hapalemur simus*, *Hapalemur griseus alaotrensis*, *Indri indri*, *Propithecus diadema candidus*, *Propithecus diadema perrieri*, *Propithecus tattersalli*, *Propithecus verreauxi coronatus* and *Daubentonia madagascariensis*. It is hoped that this field guide, by compiling available information on ecology, distribution and status in one handy publication, will encourage further research, and add to our knowledge of lemur biology in general. We also hope to use it to stimulate the growth of ecotourism in Madagascar, a potentially important source of income for the country that could provide strong economic justification for the maintenance of natural habitats.

In conjunction with this field guide, we have also published *Lemurs of Madagascar: An Action Plan for their Conservation* (Mittermeier *et al.*, 1992). This action plan includes a wide variety of projects using these beautiful and unique species as "flagships" for biological inventories, protected area management and public awareness campaigns, both to increase general interest in conservation within Madagascar and to focus greater international attention on the critical importance of this country in global efforts to conserve biological diversity. In addition, the Primate Specialist Group and Conservation International publish *Lemur News* (Mast, 1993), a newsletter that serves as a means of disseminating current information about lemur conservation within a broad and diverse international community. Since lemurs are the most attractive, conspicuous and best known component of Madagascar's wildlife, they are ideally suited to these purposes. Indeed, they have been and continue to be Madagascar's wildlife ambassadors to the world.

As with other similar publications, this field guide has been a collaborative effort incorporating the knowledge of many specialists, both in Madagascar and internationally. We are grateful to all who have contributed, in particular Roland Albignac, Joseph Andriamampianina, John Carr, Isabel Constable, Patrick Daniels, Lee Durrell, Anna T. C. Feistner, John G. Fleagle, Jörg Ganzhorn, Laurie Godfrey, Steve Goodman, Albert M. Greve, Caroline Harcourt, Alison Jolly, Bill Jungers, Andrea Katz, David Krause, Olivier Langrand, Jean-Marc Lernould, Bernhard Meier, Thomas Mutschler, Martin Nicoll, Sheila O'Connor, Jean-Jacques Petter, Serge Rajaobelina, M. Rakotomalala, Pothin Rakotomanga, Berthe Rakotosamimanana, Lala Rakotovao, Voara Randrianasolo, H. J. Ratsimbazafy, Alison Richard, Yves Rumpler, Michelle Sauther, Elwyn Simons, Hilary Simons-Morland, Eleanor Sterling, Robert Sussman, Martine Vuillaume-Randriamantena, Patricia Wright and Anne Yoder. We are grateful to these distinguished individuals, and also to *you*, the reader, for your interest in these wonderful animals and their conservation.

Principal support for this publication was provided by Conservation International, with additional funding from the Zoological Society of Philadelphia's *One With Nature* program. In-kind support was also made available by the Department of Anatomical Sciences, Health Sciences Center, State University of New York at Stony Brook, and the Primate Specialist Group of the IUCN Species Survival Commission.

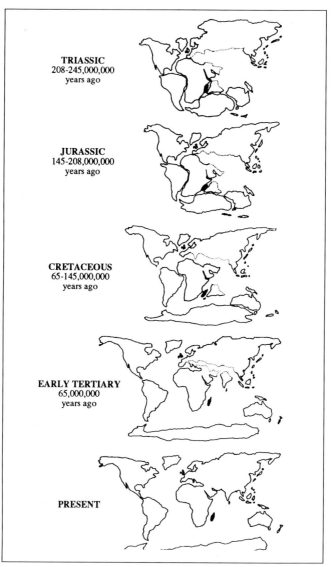

TRIASSIC
208-245,000,000
years ago

JURASSIC
145-208,000,000
years ago

CRETACEOUS
65-145,000,000
years ago

EARLY TERTIARY
65,000,000
years ago

PRESENT

Fig. 2.1: Sequence of maps showing the location of the world's continents in the past, with Madagascar in black. (D. Krause, pers. comm.)

2

ORIGIN OF THE LEMURS

Madagascar once formed part of the great southern continent of Gondwanaland. This enormous land mass began to break up about 180 million years ago into the continents and countries we know today as Africa, South America, Antarctica, Australia and India. Initially, Madagascar remained attached to Africa (and perhaps also to India), but about 160 million years ago it began to break away from its parent continent. Within at most a few tens of millions of years the island had assumed its present position some 400-550 kilometers to the east of the African coast, from which it is separated by the Mozambique Channel. This has interesting implications for the origin of lemurs. In the early days of the science of plate tectonics, the subdiscipline of geology that deals with continental drift, it seemed that we had found a simple explanation for Madagascar's faunal uniqueness. The island, it was widely assumed, had merely parted from Africa with a sampling of that continent's fauna aboard. And while Africa's fauna saw a great deal of replacement of one group by another over the course of the epochs that followed, that of isolated Madagascar did not.

The clarification of Madagascar's geological history has precipitated much rethinking about this scenario. If Madagascar has been essentially where it is for the past 100 million years or more, we cannot explain the presence of lemurs in Madagascar by an African "founder effect" (which probably does explain the presence of some of the older members of the island's biota). It was not until the dawn of the Age of Mammals, some 64 million years ago, that the primates seem to have begun their diversification, and primates comparable in evolutionary level to the lemurs are not known in the fossil record until the beginning of the Eocene epoch, some 58 million years ago. Of course, there is a problem here in that there is virtually no mammalian fossil record in Africa for the first half of the Age of Mammals, and none whatsoever from Madagascar until subrecent times. However, even if certain key events in mammalian evolution took place in Africa a little earlier than in the northern continents from which fossil records are available, we have no choice but to conclude that the ancestors of today's lemurs reached Madagascar by a sea crossing from Africa.

Large, matted clumps of floating vegetation are routinely washed down major rivers and out to sea, sometimes with unwilling mammalian and other passengers aboard. There are plenty of cases in which this is the only plausible mechanism for getting terrestrial mammals to isolated places which they have somehow managed to reach. Despite the breadth of the Mozambique Channel, Madagascar's lemurs appear to represent one more such case, and this, of course, raises questions of its own. For example, the lemurs have generally been viewed as a rather inferior, "lower" kind of primate. Compared to today's African "higher" primates - the apes, humans and cercopithecoid monkeys - lemurs generally have smaller brains compared to their body sizes, have less perfect grasping hands, and retain a primitive dependence on the sense of smell that has been greatly reduced among the more visually-oriented higher primates. In this, the lemurs more closely resemble the Eocene ancestors from which we are all descended than do the higher primates, and to that limited extent they can be regarded as evolutionarily more conservative despite the fact that they form a remarkably diverse group. However, if crossings of the Mozambique Channel today are in theory no more difficult than they were back in the Eocene, how have the supposedly competitively inferior lemurs managed to hold the Madagascar fort against more advanced newcomers? Or was the crossing of the Mozambique Channel in fact achieved against such overwhelming odds that only once was it ever accomplished by primates - coincidentally earlier rather than later in the Age of Mammals?

One inclines towards the latter explanation, at least until one further factor is added in. The implication of recent analyses of relationships among the members of the primate suborder Strepsirhini, to which the lemurs belong, is that at least two crossings of the Mozambique Channel may have been involved (detailed discussions of this question may be found in Tattersall [1982] and Schwartz and Tattersall [1985]). It seems that one group of lemurs - the cheirogaleid dwarf and mouse lemurs - may be more closely related to the strepsirhine primates of Africa - galagos, bushbabies and pottos - than they are to their fellow lemurs of Madagascar. If this is the case, at least two crossings of the Mozambique Channel are indicated. However, whether both were in the same direction - from Africa - or whether the bushbaby ancestor made the perhaps easier journey back to Africa from Madagascar is not clear.

However this question may eventually be resolved, there is no doubt that the lemurs form a remarkably diverse group, most of the diversification of which must have taken place on the vast island of Madagascar. It is also clear that, together with the galagids (bushbabies) and lorisids (pottos and lorises), they form a homogeneous suborder Strepsirhini within the order Primates.

Thirty-two species and 50 distinct taxa of lemurs are known today, but when humans arrived in Madagascar at most 2,000 years ago there were at least 15 more lemur species on the island. These now extinct forms, discussed in Chapter 4, tragically emphasize that the lemurs surviving today could face a similar fate if major conservation efforts are not put into effect.

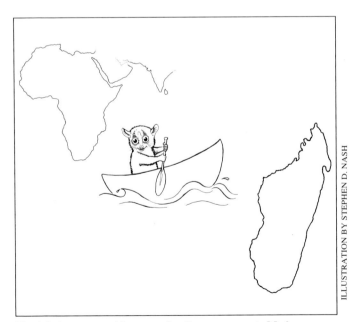

ILLUSTRATION BY STEPHEN D. NASH

Fig. 2.2: An ancestral lemur makes its way across to Madagascar.

Fig. 3.1: The "maucauco" (ring-tailed lemur) *(Lemur catta)* from the
Gleanings of Natural History (1758-1764) by George Edwards.

3

DISCOVERY AND STUDY
OF THE LIVING LEMURS

The remarkable lemur fauna of Madagascar must surely have been known to Arab and Portuguese sailors long before the seventeenth century. But the earliest reference to any lemur of which we are aware dates back to the year 1608, and was published in 1625. The vehicle was an enormous compilation of voyages, titled *Hakluytus Posthumus or Purchas his Pilgrimes*, which Samuel Purchas edited in the latter year in celebration of the early successes of the East India Company of London. In this work, Purchas included parts of an account of a visit to St. Augustine's Bay (just south of modern Tuléar) by several of the Company's ships. William Finch, one of the expedition's merchants, recorded that

"In the woods neere about the [Onilahy] River, is a great store of beasts, as big as Munkies, ash-coloured, with a small head, long taile like a Fox, garled with white and blacke, the fur very fine."

Clearly this was *Lemur catta*, appropriately described by Finch's companion Captain Keeling as "the beautifull beast."

In the following years anecdotal accounts of lemurs proliferated, among the most engaging being those of the Cornish merchant Peter Mundy, who was the first to record a lemur from the Comores. In a journal entry for 1655, Mundy described a mongoose lemur (*Eulemur mongoz*) which had been taken aboard his ship when it called at the island of Anjouan. It was

"exceeding nimble, thatt itt would skip from rope to rope...with such agilitie thatt itt seemed rather to flie than leape. And soe famigliar to every one thatt hee would leape on their shoulders, take them fast about the necks and licke their mouths and faces."

This is a most evocative description for anyone familiar at first hand with these charming primates.

Justifiably, the most famous of the early accounts of lemurs
is that of the French merchant Etienne de Flacourt, who spent the
years from 1648 to 1665 at Fort-Dauphin as "Directeur de la
Compagnie Francoise de l'Orient & Commandant pour sa Majesté
dans [Madagascar] & és Isles adiacentes." During his stay at the
island's southern tip, this remarkable man compiled an account of
Madagascar's people and natural wonders that remained definitive for two centuries. In a famous passage, Flacourt described at
least seven living species of lemurs, including the ruffed lemur
(*Varecia variegata*), the bamboo lemur (*Hapalemur griseus*), the
sifaka (*Propithecus verreauxi*), the ring-tailed lemur (*Lemur
catta*), the mouse lemur (*Microcebus murinus*), the brown lemur
(*Eulemur fulvus*), and maybe the woolly lemur (*Avahi laniger*). In
addition, Flacourt described the "tretretretre" or "tratratratra,"
which is often interpreted as *Megaladapis*, one of the largest of
Madagascar's extinct lemurs. It's perhaps worth translating
Flacourt's description of this animal in full:

> *"An animal as big as a two-year-old calf, with a round
> head and a human face: the front feet are monkeylike, and the
> rear ones as well. It has frizzy hair, a short tail and humanlike
> ears.... One has been seen near Lake Lipomami, around
> which it lives. It is a very solitary animal; the local people
> fear it greatly and flee from it as it does from them."*
> (Flacourt, 1658).

Given what we know of *Megaladapis*, Flacourt's description
is not entirely convincing, and it is anyway far from clear that
Flacourt ever saw a "tretretretre" himself. However, this may be
about as close as we will ever come to an eyewitness description
of one of the extraordinary giant extinct lemurs of Madagascar.

Throughout the seventeenth century, travelers continued to
supply accounts of Malagasy lemurs, but it was not until 1703 that
one of these primates is recorded as having reached a European
capital where it could be examined by the savants of the day. In
that year, a mongoose lemur from Anjouan was described and
illustrated by James Petiver, a London apothecary. Petiver had
some difficulty in classifying this primate, and eventually equated
it with one of the African monkeys that had been described by the
eminent anatomist John Ray.

As early as 1638, Peter Mundy had recorded seeing a lemur

that had been taken by sailors to the Indian town of Surat, so almost from the beginning these animals had evidently found their way at least occasionally onto merchant ships passing through Madagascar or the Comores. In view of this, it is perhaps rather surprising that almost 40 years seem to have passed after Petiver's description before any further published notice of lemurs appeared. This came from the pen and brush of the London illustrator George Edwards, who in 1751 described and illustrated a mongoose lemur (Color Plate 3, p. 320), which he clearly recognized as distinct from any monkey. It was, indeed, on another of Edwards' illustrations that Carolus Linnaeus, the Swedish inventor of the modern system of classifying living things, based the species description of *Lemur catta* in the definitive 1758 (10th) edition of his great work *Systema Naturae*. *Lemur* was one of only three genera into which Linnaeus classified all primates then known, and *L. catta* was the only Malagasy primate among the several species allocated to this genus.

Two years earlier, however, the French naturalist Brisson had been able to describe at least three species of what he called "Prosimia" (but which in today's terminology were undoubtedly *Lemur catta*, *Eulemur mongoz* and *Eulemur fulvus*) from specimens belonging to the Count de Réaumur in Paris, and by 1756 Edwards himself had added the "Black Maucauco" and some others to his gallery of lemurs illustrated from life. The Black Maucauco was later designated the type (definitive) specimen of *Eulemur macaco* by Linnaeus in his 12th edition of *Systema Naturae* in 1766. This animal, kept by Mr. Critington of the Royal College of Surgeons, appears to have had rather eclectic dietary tastes; while Edwards had it to illustrate, "it eat cakes, bread and butter, and summer fruits, it being in July."

It may seem a little odd that after forty years of obscurity, lemurs appear suddenly to have abounded in London and Paris in the 1750s. However, at around this time the collection of exotic animals had become something of a craze among the wealthy, and naturalists began to benefit from the trend. In Paris during the 1760s and 1770s, for example, such eminent scientists as Buffon and Daubenton were able to provide descriptions of the anatomy of several different lemur species (Fig. 3.2).

This was also the time when more substantial accounts of

Plate 320

Fig. 3.2: Depiction of an aye-aye (*Daubentonia madagascariensis*) from Buffon's *Histoire Naturelle* (1812).

lemurs and their native habitat began to be furnished by travelling naturalists. In 1771, Joseph-Philibert Commerson made his classic statement about Madagascar:

"I can announce to naturalists that this is the true Promised Land. Here Nature seems to have created a special sanctuary whither she seems to have withdrawn to experiment with designs different from any she has used elsewhere. At every step, one finds more remarkable and marvellous forms of life."

None too soon, Madagascar was finally beginning to be seen as the extraordinary home of an endemic and astonishing fauna.

Commerson, alas, failed to survive the return journey to France, although his illustrations provided the basis on which Etienne Geoffroy St-Hilaire first described the dwarf lemurs (*Cheirogaleus*) in 1812. Commerson's colleague, Sonnerat, was more fortunate, visiting Madagascar on several occasions between 1774 and 1781, and recording a variety of lemur species in the Fourth Book of his *Voyages aux Indes Orientales et à la Chine*. Sonnerat's "firsts" included illustrations of the aye-aye (later *Daubentonia*) and the woolly lemur (later *Avahi*).

The nineteenth century ushered in a period during which published references to new lemurs came thick and fast as specimens flooded into Europe. The resulting proliferation of new zoological names led to a nomenclatural thicket which later systematists were obliged to work hard and long to disentangle. From mid-century on, most lemur specimens came to the attention of museum curators in England and continental Europe through the efforts of a new category of explorers: professional collectors whose expeditions had as their primary objective obtaining of specimens for museums, menageries and cabinets. The first major foray of this kind to Madagascar was undertaken in 1864 and subsequent years by François Pollen and J. C. Van Dam of the Rijksmuseum van Natuurlijke Historie in Leiden, Holland. Pollen and Van Dam's collection from the north and northwest of Madagascar and on the island of Mayotte in the Comores still forms perhaps the central resource for systematic studies of lemurs from these regions. These collections were splendidly complemented during 1876-79 by the German collector Josef-Peter Audebert, who obtained numerous specimens from Madagascar's northeast for the same museum.

Hard on the heels of Pollen and Van Dam came the English-
man Alfred Crossley, who crisscrossed Madagascar in search of
bird and mammal specimens between 1865 and his premature
death in 1870. Unfortunately, Crossley's marvelous collections
were dispersed through commercial dealers (in whose care much
documentation was lost), but many of his specimens found a
permanent home in the British Museum, where they form the core
of another of the world's outstanding collections of Malagasy
birds and mammals.

Another cause for dispersal of unified collections during this
period was a general "postage stamp" mentality among naturalists. It was considered vastly preferable to have one specimen of
each of ten species than to have ten of one species, and this led to
the widespread trading of specimens between individuals and
institutions, as those responsible strove to maximize the breadth
of their collections, inevitably at the expense of their depth. This
activity, and the mindset behind it, did much to impede the
appreciation by systematists of the variation in external appearance that naturally occurs between individuals of the same species.

One naturalist who clearly understood the importance of such
variation was the French explorer Alfred Grandidier, who devoted his life to the documentation of the peoples and natural
history of Madagascar. His efforts culminated in the publication
of a magnificent series of volumes between 1875 and 1930.
Unfortunately, while several folios of lemur illustrations appeared (Vols. 9 & 10; see Fig. 3.3 and Color Plate 3, p. 320), only
one volume of explanatory text was completed (Vol. 6 on the
Indriidae); this is particularly regrettable since Grandidier was
rather innovative in his use of names to identify the lemurs that he
so magnificently illustrated. Confusion inevitably resulted when
later workers used his plates to identify specimens that came
before them. Compounding this is the fact that virtually all of the
collections on which Grandidier's illustrations were based appear
subsequently to have disappeared.

Several other major collections were made during the last two
decades of the nineteenth century, in the years leading up to the
French takeover of Madagascar in 1895. Notable among them
were those made by the German J. M. Hildebrandt for the Berlin
Museum, W. W. Abbott for the Smithsonian Institution and C. I.

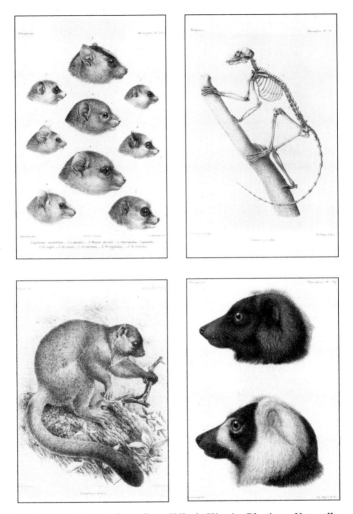

Fig. 3.3: Four plates from Grandidier's *Histoire Physique, Naturelle, et Politique de Madagascar* **(Vol. 10).**

Forsyth Major for the British Museum (Natural History). Other important contributions were also made during this period by missionaries, in particular by William Deans Cowan and other emissaries of the London Missionary Society. Back in Europe, the efforts of numerous museum systematists such as John Edward Gray and Albert Günther in London and A. Schlegel in Leiden ensured that the supply of new names kept up with that of new specimens. As a result, by the early years of this century a large number of competing nomenclatures existed for the lemurs of Madagascar.

The nomenclatural chaos of the late nineteenth century gradually gave way to a more ordered approach during the 1920s. The identifications of the many specimens collected during the Mission Zoologique Franco-Anglo-Americaine of 1929-31 (a resource divided today between the great natural history museums of New York, London and Paris) show that by this time the familiar modern nomenclature had more or less taken on its present form. This was enshrined in a landmark publication by Ernst Schwarz in 1931, which has provided the starting point for all subsequent systematic work on lemurs. Schwarz's review of lemur systematics reduced the plethora of names to somewhat fewer than are recognized today. Since Schwarz's time, only three new lemur species and a handful of new subspecies have been described - though some earlier names, such as Gray's genus *Mirza* for Coquerel's dwarf lemur, have since been resuscitated.

While a firm framework of nomenclature for the lemurs of Madagascar had thus been laid well before the middle of this century, those interested in aspects of the behavior and ecology of these primates were limited until quite recently essentially to the anecdotal accounts of nineteenth century explorers and collectors. It was not until late in the 1950s that Jean-Jacques Petter (1962) undertook a survey of Madagascar's primate fauna in which he included observations on the ecology and social groupings of a variety of lemurs at different sites on the island. Alison Jolly (1966) followed shortly afterwards with a more detailed study of the diet and social behavior of the ring-tailed lemur (*Lemur catta*) and Verreaux's sifaka (*Propithecus verreauxi verreauxi*) at the now famous site of Berenty in Madagascar's far south. Between them, these two pioneering studies ushered in a new era of research on lemur ecology and behavior, including in recent years intense concern for the conservation of these unique animals.

Several notable studies of lemur behavior and ecology were undertaken in the late 1960s and early 1970s, prior to a hiatus imposed by political events of the mid-1970s. These included the first detailed study of the mouse lemurs, *Microcebus*, by R. D. Martin (1972, 1973), and of the sportive lemur, *Lepilemur*, by Pierre Charles-Dominique and Marcel Hladik (1971), comparative studies of *Propithecus verreauxi* at sites in the northwest and south by Alison Richard (1973, 1974a, 1974b, 1976, 1978), and of sympatric *Lemur catta* and *Eulemur fulvus rufus* in southwestern Madagascar by Bob Sussman (1972, 1974, 1977); and the pioneering rain forest study of *Indri indri* by Jon Pollock (1975, 1977) at Périnet (= Andasibe). During this period, the first studies were also made of lemurs living in the Comores, the mongoose lemur, *Eulemur mongoz*, on Mohéli and Anjouan (Tattersall, 1976a, 1976b) and the Mayotte brown lemur, *Eulemur fulvus fulvus* (= *mayottensis*), on Mayotte (Tattersall, 1977).

Field activity waned in the aftermath of Madagascar's revolution from 1972-74, but since the early 1980s field studies of the lemurs have resumed with great vigor, due in part to the renewed involvement of the Duke University Primate Center under the direction of Elwyn Simons and, subsequently, Ken Glander. A notable result of this was the establishment, through the efforts of Patricia Wright, of a research base and national park at Ranomafana in the eastern rain forest. Since the mid-1980s, there has been a proliferation of studies of rain forest lemurs at that site, including research on Milne-Edwards' sifaka, *Propithecus diadema edwardsi* (Wright, 1988), the red-bellied lemur, *Eulemur rubriventer* (Overdorff, 1988, 1990), the red-fronted brown lemur, *Eulemur fulvus rufus* (Overdorff, 1990), and, of course, the first report of the previously undescribed golden bamboo lemur, *Hapalemur aureus* (Meier *et al.*, 1987).

Also noteworthy is the study site for lemurs of the southwestern deciduous and spiny forests established at Beza-Mahafaly in 1985. Detailed demographic records of *Propithecus verreauxi verreauxi* (Richard *et al.*, 1991) and of *Lemur catta* (Sussman, 1991; Sauther, 1991) have been made possible by the identification of all individuals in the main part of this reserve.

In the northwest, Jörg Ganzhorn and others (Ganzhorn and Abraham, 1991) have renewed research interest in the Ankarafantsika Nature Reserve. To the north of this, near

Maromandia, Koenders *et al.* (1985a) were able to confirm the separate identity of Sclater's black lemur (*Eulemur macaco flavifrons*), and David Meyers and colleagues (Meyers *et al.,* 1989*)* have since documented the geographical relationship between this subspecies and the black lemur, *Eulemur m. macaco*, which is itself currently the subject of several studies. Still further north, the Ankarana Massif has at last begun to attract the attention it deserves, both from zoologists and ecologists (Hawkins *et al.*, 1990) and from paleontologists (Simons *et al.*, 1990). It was on the Ankarana that Jane Wilson and colleagues (Wilson e*t al.,* 1989) undertook the first field study of the crowned lemur, *Eulemur coronatus*. Close to the northern tip of Madagascar, David Meyers (Meyers and Ratsirarson, 1989) has recently completed a detailed field study of the golden-crowned sifaka, *Propithecus tattersalli*. Finally, the island of Nosy Mangabe in the Bay of Antongil in the northeast has been the site of two pioneering studies, that by Morland (1991) on *Varecia variegata variegata* and another by Sterling (1993) on the elusive aye-aye (*Daubentonia madagascariensis*).

This brief listing of major recent studies is not meant to be comprehensive, but rather to point out how the improvement of Madagascar's relationship with the West over the past decade has resulted in an ongoing proliferation of lemur field research. It is not unreasonable to hope that within another decade our knowledge of the unique primates of Madagascar will be much more comprehensive than it is today, provided that conservation programs carried out hand in hand with research efforts are successful in ensuring their survival.

4

THE EXTINCT LEMURS

Remarkable as is the diversity of the lemurs living on Madagascar today, in numbers of species as well as in ecology and adaptation, this diversity pales in comparison with what an early explorer would have found on the island as little as a thousand years ago. Since the arrival of humans on Madagascar, fully eight genera and at least 15 lemur species have become extinct (Figs. 4.1, 4.3-4.6; Table 4.1; Color Plate 4, p. 321). This represents almost a third of all known species (living and extinct) and fully 36% (8/22) of all known genera. It is understandable that the extinct and the living lemurs have been studied in different ways and, for the most part, by different people. However, we should not let this disguise the fact that the loss of lemurs in Madagascar in geologically very recent times is a dramatic example of the kind of extinction spasm that conservationists are constantly warning us about; indeed, the surviving lemur species could fall victim to the same fate if conservationists are unsuccessful in their efforts. Earlier in this book we mentioned in passing the existence of the "subfossil" lemur fauna of Madagascar. In this chapter, we briefly describe this extinct fauna in order to convey some sense of the catastrophic loss of primate diversity which the island has already experienced, in the hope that it will make us redouble our efforts to save those that remain.

Discovery of the Subfossil Lemurs

A century ago, C. I. Forsyth Major described the first "subfossil" remains of giant extinct lemurs recovered from marshes in the center and southwest of Madagascar. Not only were these remains clearly those of lemurs much larger than any which survive today, they were equally clearly of no great antiquity (hence the "subfossil" appellation). These discoveries kicked off a flurry of paleontological activity, and by the early years of this century a host of recently extinct lemur genera and species had been described. In a review published as early as 1905, the

Table 4.1
Dental Formulae of
Extinct and Living Lemur Genera

Microcebus	
Allocebus	
Cheirogaleus	
Mirza	
Phaner	$\frac{2.1.3.3}{2.1.3.3}$
Hapalemur	
Lemur	
Eulemur	
Pachylemur *	
Varecia	
Avahi	
Propithecus	
Indri	
Palaeopropithecus *	$\frac{2.1.2.3}{1.1.2.3}$
Archaeoindris *	
Babakotia *	
Mesopropithecus *	
Archaeolemur *	$\frac{2.1.3.3}{1.1.3.3}$
Hadropithecus *	
Lepilemur	$\frac{0.1.3.3}{2.1.3.3}$
Megaladapis *	
Daubentonia	$\frac{1.0.1.3}{1.0.0.3}$

* indicates extinct genus

Upper	Incisor(s) . Canine(s) . Premolar(s) . Molar(s)
Lower	Incisor(s) . Canine(s) . Premolar(s) . Molar(s)

Key to illustrations on the opposite page:

<u>**Living Genera**</u>

		<u>**Extinct Genera**</u>
1. *Indri*	8. *Cheirogaleus*	15. *Pachylemur*
2. *Propithecus*	9. *Lepilemur*	16. *Archaeolemur*
3. *Varecia*	10. *Avahi*	17. *Mesopropithecus*
4. *Daubentonia*	11. *Eulemur*	18. *Babakotia*
5. *Hapalemur*	12. *Mirza*	19. *Palaeopropithecus*
6. *Phaner*	13. *Allocebus*	20. *Archaeoindris*
7. *Microcebus*	14. *Lemur*	21. *Hadropithecus*
		22. *Megaladapis*

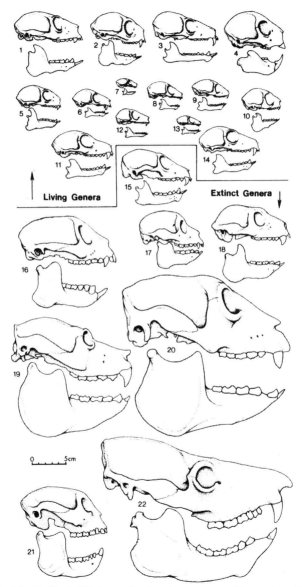

Fig. 4.1: Skulls of all living and extinct lemur genera (drawn to scale). Note the great diversity in this radiation of primates, and the enormous size achieved by some of the extinct genera.

ILLUSTRATION BY STEPHEN D. NASH

paleontologist Guillaume Grandidier (son of the explorer Alfred) was able to show that many more names than necessary had been bestowed upon the large collection of subfossil lemur bones that had been amassed by that time. However, among those names were most of the extinct genera recognized today. Despite extensive excavations during the first half of the century, notably by Charles Lamberton (1934) of the Académie Malgache, no new extinct lemur genera were recovered between the first decade of the century and the late 1980s.

In 1986, a team led by Elwyn Simons of Duke University began work in karst caves on the Ankarana Massif in the far north of Madagascar. Besides discovering at least one new genus of extinct lemur, this team has over the past several years made finds that have caused considerable rethinking of the adaptations of the extinct lemurs and of the relationships among them. It also has made finds indicating that species that still survive today, among them *Hapalemur simus* and *Indri indri*, once had much more extensive ranges.

The Subfossil Sites

Until mid-century, subfossil lemurs were known almost exclusively from the center, south and southwest of Madagascar. Now, however, the only major biogeographic region of Madagascar whose subrecent fauna remains unsampled is the eastern rain forest area. Perhaps even more importantly, the recent era of fieldwork has allowed the collection of complete or relatively complete skeletons in which skulls and the various elements of the body skeleton are positively associated. This contrasts dramatically with earlier excavations in which bones tended to be dredged up one by one from swamps and muddy marsh bottoms. Given such circumstances of excavation, the association of postcranial bones with skulls and with each other tended to be a matter of guesswork and size-matching. As it has turned out, this was not the most accurate way of proceeding.

All currently known subfossil sites consist either of marsh deposits (dried to varying extents) or of deposits washed into limestone caves or fissures. Most such sites are rich in the bones of many other vertebrates besides primates (living as well as extinct). Common among such remains are those of pygmy hippopotami, giant tortoises and the famous elephant bird

(*Aepyornis;* Fig. 4.2). Weighing perhaps a third of a ton, this flightless relative of the ostrich probably was the heaviest bird that ever lived.

All of the subfossil sites are strictly localized, and all are of comparatively recent age (Fig. 4.3). Most radiocarbon dates that have been obtained so far cluster in the period between about 2,500 and 1,000 years ago, and only one or two stretch back to the final millennia of the last Ice Age, which ended around 10,000 years ago. These are not very ancient ages by any standard, and they dramatize the fact that subfossil and living lemurs all form part of the same contemporary fauna; the extinct lemurs are in no way the precursors of those that still survive. At the same time, however, almost all radiocarbon dates do predate the documented arrival of the earliest humans on Madagascar, of which more will be said later.

PHOTO BY RUSSELL A. MITTERMEIER

Fig. 4.2: An Antandroy tribesman holding the egg of the extinct elephant bird (*Aepyornis maximus*), which weighed up to 300 kg and stood 2.5 m tall.

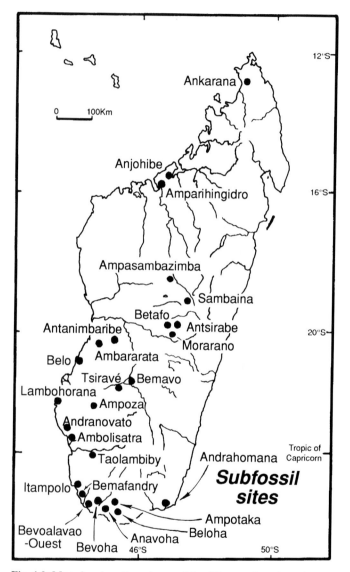

Fig. 4.3: Map showing sites where subfossil lemurs have been found.

Affinities of the Subfossil Lemurs

Of the lemur genera that are known as subfossils, at least eight are entirely extinct today. All of these extinct genera were larger-bodied than any that survive, and the closest affinities of each one, except for *Megaladapis* (a relative of *Lepilemur*) and *Pachylemur* (a very close relative of *Varecia*), lie with the living indriids. When the living and subfossil lemurs are considered together, they form an adaptive spectrum that rivals, or even surpasses, the variety achieved in the major continental areas where primates occur (the Neotropics, Africa and Asia), all of them many times larger than the island of Madagascar. In other words, Madagascar's concentration of primate diversity in recent times (and even today) was truly unsurpassed.

The eight extinct genera are listed in the outline classification below:

> Superfamily Lemuroidea
> > Family Lemuridae
> > > Genus *Pachylemur*

> Superfamily Indrioidea
> > Family Archaeolemuridae
> > > Genus *Archaeolemur*
> > > Genus *Hadropithecus*
> > Family Palaeopropithecidae
> > > Genus *Palaeopropithecus*
> > > Genus *Archaeoindris*
> > > Genus *Babakotia*
> > > Genus *Mesopropithecus*

> Superfamily Indrioidea (?)
> > Family Megaladapidae
> > > Genus *Megaladapis*

Adaptations and Habits of Extinct Lemurs

Superfamily Lemuroidea

Family Lemuridae

The only extinct lemurid genus thus far discovered is *Pachylemur*, a slightly larger relative of *Varecia* that is known from sites in central and southwest Madagascar. Skull structure is very close to that of *Varecia*, and the two probably would be classified in the same genus were it not for the relatively heavy build of the postcranial bones that have been associated with *Pachylemur*. These are said to suggest a more terrestrial way of life than that of the highly arboreal *Varecia*.

Superfamily Indrioidea

The recent discoveries in northern Madagascar have had the greatest impact on our knowledge of the extinct Indrioidea, both in terms of their relationships and their habits. For example, while it has long been known that both the archaeolemurid genera *Archaeolemur* and *Hadropithecus* and the palaeopropithecids *Palaeopropithecus* and *Archaeoindris* were reasonably close relatives of the living indriids (*Propithecus*, *Indri* and *Avahi*), it was uncertain which of the extinct families was more closely related to the extant forms. While the archaeolemurids remain relatively primitive (and thus indriid-like) in the structure of their skulls, their teeth are highly specialized and non-indriid-like, although they do retain three premolars (reduced to two in the indriids and palaeopropithecids). Conversely, the palaeopropithecids depart from the indriids and the archaeolemurids in having rather heavily built and specialized skulls, while resembling the indriids in retaining a very similar dentition. Which of this evidence should be given priority in determining relationships - that of the skulls or that of the teeth?

The answer has been provided by the new fossils from the Ankarana, and particularly by the associated skeletons among them. Studies by members of the Ankarana team, notably Laurie Godfrey of the University of Massachusetts at Amherst (who kindly provided the body-weight estimates quoted in this chapter), Bill Jungers of the State University of New York at Stony Brook, and Martine Vuillaume-Randriamanantena of the Univer-

sity of Madagascar, have produced strong evidence that it is the
archaeolemurids that are the outliers. While the new genus
Babakotia (Fig. 4.4) and the formerly postcranially poorly known
Mesopropithecus share suspensory adaptations of the body skeleton with the other palaeopropithecids, they remain extraordinarily indriid-like in both their skulls and dentitions. The
archaeolemurids, on the other hand, show a highly developed
suite of locomotor adaptations for terrestrial living. It thus seems
that a craniodentally conservative and postcranially generalized
indriid ancestor with three premolar teeth gave rise on the one
hand to the three-premolared, terrestrial archaeolemurids, and on
the other hand to a two-premolared but still postcranially generalized lineage (albeit with a good bit of suspensory behavior in its
locomotor repertoire). The latter then split to give rise to the
leaping (but still quite suspensory) indriids on the one hand and to
the hanging palaeopropithecids on the other.

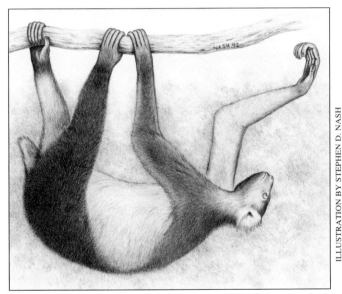

ILLUSTRATION BY STEPHEN D. NASH

**Fig. 4.4: Reconstruction of *Babakotia*, a subfossil lemur which
probably had a sloth-like lifestyle.**

Family Archaeolemuridae

Archaeolemur is perhaps the most widely distributed of all the subfossil lemurs, having been found in abundance at sites in the south, southwest, center, northwest and north of Madagascar. Its close, but more specialized, relative *Hadropithecus* is known from the south, southwest and center of the island, but is still something of a rarity. As we have seen, these medium-sized extinct genera (about 15 to 25 kg body weight, depending on the species) retain rather primitive, *Propithecus*-like skull proportions, but have very specialized teeth apart from the primitive retention of the third premolar. In *Archaeolemur*, the molar teeth resemble those of Old World monkeys in being "bilophodont" with transverse crests. The premolars are unique, being modified to produce a single longitudinal shearing blade. The upper canine teeth are reduced, and the lower front teeth are relatively upright, although they do show evidence of having been derived from a tooth comb like that of the indriids. The upper incisors are greatly expanded and are so close together that there would not have been room for a "superior labial tract" to pass between them. This is of great interest, since the tract is an integral part of the "wet nose" apparatus that is otherwise ubiquitous among the highly scent-sensitive lemurs.

Exactly what kinds of foods the specialized teeth of *Archaeolemur* were adapted to process has not yet been established, but the teeth of *Hadropithecus* look like an *Archaeolemur* dentition adapted for strong grinding. The molars are greatly expanded and are quickly worn, the posterior premolars are incorporated into the grinding surface, and the toothcomb and upper incisors are even further reduced. These developments resulted in a shortening of the face, and its deepening to accommodate heavy chewing stresses. This suite of characteristics fits well with conclusions drawn from the body skeleton of *Archaeolemur*, which has a whole set of terrestrial adaptations. *Hadropithecus* is much more poorly known, but attributed limb bones point in the same direction. The limb bones show that the archaeolemurids were short-limbed and powerfully-built, but the most telling evidence of all comes from the hands and feet of *Archaeolemur* (first found properly associated in the Ankarana), which are astonishingly short. To quote Bill Jungers, they are "almost paw-like," with the foot of *Archaeolemur* even shorter than that of *Indri*, an animal only one third its size. The new

Ankarana evidence thus reinforces earlier hypotheses that the archaeolemurids were Madagascar's equivalent of baboons (*Papio* spp.), found throughout mainland Africa. *Archaeolemur* was a more generalized form that was nonetheless committed to the ground, while *Hadropithecus* filled a niche similar to that of the gelada (*Theropithecus gelada*), a specialized terrestrial primate that feeds on grass blades and rhizomes, and on other tough, gritty foods in the open grasslands of Ethiopia.

Family Palaeopropithecidae

For many years the locomotor adaptations of the genus *Palaeopropithecus* were the subject of heated debate. This was resolved, once and for all, in the mid-1980s when a group led by Ross MacPhee, now of the American Museum of Natural History, found an associated and relatively complete skeleton in the cave of Anjohibe in northwest Madagascar. At least two species of the genus are now known, with a weight range of perhaps 40 to 60 kg. *Palaeopropithecus* has a wide distribution in Madagascar, being known from sites in the south, southwest, center, northwest and north of the island. The closely related genus *Archaeoindris* is, on the other hand, much less widely distributed, being known only from the site of Ampasambazimba on the central plateau, and even there only from rare fossils. It seems likely that this species was always very rare, and was perhaps the only Malagasy subfossil lemur to have become extinct naturally. In any event, *Archaeoindris* is distinguished by its extremely large body size, which has been estimated at 160-200 kg (as large as an adult male gorilla).

Another extinct genus, *Mesopropithecus*, has been known since early in this century from a number of crania, found in the center and south of Madagascar, that closely resemble those of *Propithecus* (this is especially true of the more lightly built *Propithecus verreauxi*). However, attributed postcranial bones were few and far between until the Ankarana group recently discovered an associated skeleton. This shows that even though its teeth and skull may be close to the living indriids, the postcranial skeleton of *Mesopropithecus* is quite different. With a body weight estimated at about 10 kg, this palaeopropithecid had elongated forelimbs in contrast to the elongated hindlimbs of *Propithecus*, and it clearly de-emphasized leaping in favor of suspensory postures. The Ankarana team also discovered an entirely new genus of palaeopropithecid, to which they gave the name *Babakotia*. This form, estimated from an almost complete skeleton to have weighed about 15-20 kg, has a very *Indri*-like skull, although it also has cranial features that recall the larger palaeopropithecids. In contrast to *Indri*, though, the forelimbs are very long, and the hands and feet are also long and adapted for strong grasping. The hindfoot is reduced, as in suspensory forms and in contrast to leapers.

According to the Ankarana researchers, *Mesopropithecus* and *Babakotia* can be viewed as stages in an increasingly specialized locomotor series that culminates in the extraordinary *Palaeopropithecus*, whose commitment to arboreal suspension is complete. Indeed, they have informally named this entire group the "sloth lemurs" because of the numerous sloth-like attributes that they share. As noted, *Palaeopropithecus* shows the most such features, and in the most specialized ways. As in other dedicated suspensory forms, joints throughout the skeleton of this sloth lemur are built for flexibility rather than for stability and strength. The exception is in the extremities, where stability is most needed when hanging below branches. The first digit is missing and the long, curved phalanges of the rest have tongue-in-groove joints that limit movement to one plane and maximize power grasping.

Although *Archaeoindris* represents the extreme of the body-size spectrum of the palaeopropithecids, it cannot also represent the extreme of suspensory adaptation. Not only would it have been difficult to beat *Palaeopropithecus* at its own game, this extraordinarily heavy form probably was far too big to spend much, if any, time in the trees. There are few potential postcranial bones known of this giant, but those that do exist suggest that *Archaeoindris* may have filled much the same niche in Madagascar that the much bigger giant ground sloths occupied in the southwestern United States before they too became extinct at the end of the last Ice Age.

Family Megaladapidae

Details of the molar teeth and various aspects of skull structure reveal that the three species of M*egaladapis* have their closest living relative in *Lepilemur*. However, in most ways, these large to very large (about 40 to 80 kg in body weight) animals show specializations that are unique among the lemurs and indeed among the primates as a whole. For example, the skull of

Megaladapis is highly elongated, to a degree found in no other primate, and the face is tilted upwards on a rather short cranial base that lies below a smallish brain. The hole through which the spinal cord exited in life from the braincase faces fully rearwards, as do the joint surfaces by which the skull articulated with the spine. In combination, these adaptations would have turned the long head into a functional extension of the neck, maximizing the radius within which this heavy animal could have cropped leaves (probably its major food source) from a single sitting position. *Megaladapis* would have eaten by employing the horny pad that presumably replaced the adult incisors that are missing in the front of the mouth; an overhanging shelf of bone above the nasal aperture also hints at the presence of a mobile snout.

The body skeleton of M*egaladapis* was no less unusual (Fig. 4.5), apparently finding its closest analogue in the marsupial koala of Australia. Its extraordinarily long hands and feet, highly adapted for strong grasping, make very clear that it was an arboreal animal. However, its arms and legs were rather short, and, in combination with its high body weight, suggest that *Megaladapis* possessed severely limited leaping abilities. Like the koala, these primates would have climbed slowly and cautiously in the trees (Fig. 4.6). Furthermore, they may well have adopted a variety of suspensory postures, perhaps emphasizing the hind limbs, since the feet were even more elongated and specialized for powerful grasping than were the hands.

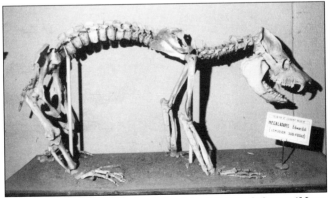

PHOTO BY RUSSELL A. MITTERMEIER

Fig. 4.5: One of the reconstructed subfossil lemur skeletons (*Megaladapis edwardsi***) on exhibit in the museum at Parc Tsimbazaza in Antananarivo. Note that this is an early reconstruction, and it may be that not all bones are properly associated.**

ILLUSTRATION BY STEPHEN D. NASH

Fig. 4.6: Artist's reconstruction of *Megaladapis edwardsi*, a subfossil lemur comparable in size to a modern female gorilla and occupying a niche similar to that of the Australian koala.

Extinction of the Subfossil Lemurs

One of the most notable results of the early discovery of subfossil sites in central Madagascar was to draw attention to the fact that this region, almost treeless today, must formerly have been forested. It was obvious that most, if not all, of the extinct lemurs had been forest-living animals, and their bones were also found in association with those of extant forms which we know to be confined to forest areas. However, the degree to which the plateau was forested when the subfossil bones were accumulating remains a subject of discussion. Early workers, especially Henri Humbert, developed the notion that Madagascar had once been entirely covered by forests, but that these were largely destroyed by fire following the arrival of humans, who cleared the land for grazing and cultivation. Others, noting that many of the southern and southwestern subfossil sites represent marshes that have to one extent or another dried out, proposed that natural drying of the climate, at least locally, had deprived the large extinct lemurs of needed habitat.

Recent paleoenvironmental work by David Burney and colleagues has shown that the forests of Madagascar have fluctuated in extent over the past several millennia. The grasslands of the central plateau are thus not entirely anthropogenic in origin, although Humbert was clearly right in identifying cutting, burning and grazing as the greatest current threats to the island's natural vegetation and thus to the habitat of the surviving lemurs. Nonetheless, substantial areas of forest habitat still support large populations of lemurs, and this points to the selective nature of the recent extinctions. The lemur species which disappeared are those which were the largest-bodied and the slowest-moving.

As Burney's work suggests, Madagascar was not immune to the environmental vicissitudes that are well known to have afflicted northern latitudes during the Ice Ages. It may well be that climatic changes in the past reduced and/or modified the habitat available to the precursors of the living and subfossil lemurs. Nonetheless, the now-vanished lemur lineages and the still extant forms had obviously survived these climatic stresses. This, together with the fact that all of the large-bodied lineages went extinct in so short a time, suggests that a novel factor was at work. In the absence of any evidence that the most recent climatic oscillations were particularly severe (they probably were not), the only evident candidate for such a factor is the appearance of humans in Madagascar.

Those lemur (and other vertebrate) species that went extinct so rapidly were both the most attractive as a food source (because of their large body size) and the most vulnerable (because of their slow-moving habits) to human predation. Furthermore, they were the species which presumably reproduced at the slowest rate and existed at the lowest population densities. In sum, the extinct lemurs were those that would be expected to succumb most readily to human hunting pressures; it is the smaller, swifter forms that have survived to the present, and 42% of the survivors are also nocturnal (21 of 50 taxa), an added measure of protection. Despite the rather sparse evidence that archaeology furnishes for direct human predation on the extinct lemurs, we can surmise with confidence that it was through human activities that these primates met their rapid end. The same is true of the threats faced by the living lemurs, except that the range of human activities placing them at risk has increased in number and complexity. These threats are summarized in the next chapter.

5

CONSERVATION OF LEMURS

Biodiversity in Madagascar

The island of Madagascar is not just important for lemurs; it is often considered the single highest major conservation priority on Earth. Its exceptional diversity and endemism, combined with the fact that much of its original forest cover and some of its most spectacular species have already been lost, make it both one of the world's most endangered "hotspots" and one of the top 12 "megadiversity" countries (Figs. 5.1, 5.2).

Madagascar's privileged position in terms of biodiversity is based on its geological history and geographic placement. The world's fourth largest island, it has been separated from all other land masses for more than 160 million years, meaning that most of its plant and animal life has evolved in isolation. This has resulted in very high levels of endemism, both at the species level and, more importantly, at higher taxonomic

TROPICAL RAIN FOREST HOTSPOTS

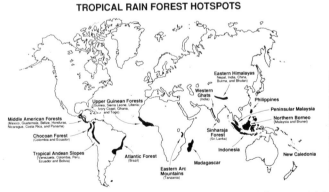

MAP BY STEPHEN D. NASH

Fig. 5.1: The world's top priority "threatened hotspots" for terrestrial biodiversity, modified from Myers (1988, 1990) and closely following Conservation International (1990). These hotspots consist largely of tropical rain forest formations (with some drier formations included as well, as in the case of Madagascar). They are characterized by very high diversity and endemism, and by high degree of threat. Many among them are down to only small percentages of their original extent, and require rapid action and intensive management effort to ensure their long-term viability.

levels, with Madagascar having numbers of endemic plant and animal genera and families rivalled only by Australia, which is 13 times larger.

Madagascar is situated largely in the tropics (between 11° 57' S and 25° 37' S) and also has very high species diversity, especially given its relatively small size (587,041 km²). For example, although Madagascar occupies only about 1.9% of the land area of the African region, it has more orchids than all of the African mainland, and indeed is home to about 25% of all African plants (Jolly *et al.*, 1984). Overall, about 80% of Madagascar's plant species are endemic, and for animal groups the proportion is usually even higher, the best example being the primates; 100% of the island nation's 32 species and 50 distinct taxa occur naturally only on Madagascar (Tables 5.1, 5.2). Two species, *Eulemur fulvus* and *Eulemur mongoz*, also live on the nearby islands of the Comores, but they were almost certainly introduced there from Madagascar by our own species.

THE MEGA DIVERSITY COUNTRIES

MAP BY STEPHEN D. NASH

Fig. 5.2. The world's top 12 *megadiversity* countries. This ranking, originally conceived of by Mittermeier (1988; see also McNeely *et al.*, 1990; Mittermeier and Goettsch de Mittermeier, 1992), recognizes that this small number of countries (12 out of a global total of more than 190, or about 6% of the world's sovereign nations) harbor and have primary responsibility for some 60-70% of the world's total biodiversity. Madagascar, with its high diversity of plants, primates, reptiles and several other groups of organisms and its very high endemism at higher taxonomic levels (genus, family), is a prominent member of this elite group.

At the generic and family levels, Madagascar's primate diversity is even more striking, with fully five primate families and 14 genera found nowhere else. Compare this to Brazil, the richest country on Earth in primate species with 69, but with only three families, none of them endemic, and only two endemic genera out of 16. In terms of species numbers, Madagascar is third highest on the world list, after Brazil and just behind Indonesia, but with five more genera than Indonesia and only two less than Brazil; this is the case in spite of the fact that Madagascar is less than 7% the size of Brazil and only 31% the size of Indonesia (Tables 5.1, 5.2).

Table 5.1
Top Five Countries on Earth for
Nonhuman Primate Species Diversity

Country	Species	Genera	Families
Brazil	69	16	3
Indonesia	35	9	5
Madagascar	32	14	5
Zaire	32	13	4
Peru	30	12	3

Table 5.2
Primate Endemism in the
Most Diverse Countries on Earth for Nonhuman Primates

Country	Species	Genera	Families	% of Species Endemism
Madagascar	32/32	14/14	5/5	100.0%
Indonesia	19/34	1/9	0/5	55.9%
Brazil	31/69	2/16	0/3	44.9%
Peru	4/30	0/12	0/3	13.3%
Zaire	2/32	0/3	0/13	9.4%

Other vertebrate groups exhibiting comparable levels of diversity and endemism include the amphibians and the reptiles. Ninety-five percent (95%) of the country's 265 reptile species and 99% of its 120 amphibians are endemic, and new species are being described on a yearly basis. However, it is important to note that high vertebrate diversity in Madagascar is restricted to certain groups like the primates, reptiles and amphibians; others are either poorly represented (e.g., rodents) or entirely absent (e.g., ungulates). Species numbers for birds (256 spp., Langrand, 1990) are relatively low, but endemism is high (105 spp.; 41%) and five bird families are endemic, a remarkably high number given Madagascar's size.

Madagascar's very high levels of diversity for certain groups, its endemism at both the species and higher taxonomic levels, and its high diversity *and* endemism per unit area all help to push this country to the top of the global conservation priority list. A hectare of forest lost in Madagascar has a greater negative impact on global biodiversity than a hectare lost almost anywhere else, the only regions of comparable importance being some of the other endangered "hotspots" like the tropical Andes and the Atlantic forest of South America, the Philippines, parts of Indonesia, and a handful of other islands like New Caledonia in the South Pacific. Unfortunately, many hectares are still being cut every year in Madagascar, and much has already been lost in recent times. The lemur extinctions discussed in Chapter 4, and the disappearance of many other spectacular species such as the elephant birds (*Aepyornis* spp.), at least one species each of pygmy hippopotamus and giant tortoise, and an aardvark are the most striking examples, but others exist as well. Only the extinctions in the Hawaiian Islands and the impact of the Europeans in Australia can match the great losses in Madagascar that have taken place over the past 2000 years. Furthermore, as discussed in the individual species profiles in the following chapter, it is clear that many of the living lemur species are at great risk of disappearing as well.

What are the threats to lemurs and other forms of life in Madagascar? In this chapter, we discuss these threats, and also what is being done to prevent further lemur extinctions, both through *in situ* conservation in parks and reserves and *ex situ* international captive breeding efforts. We provide an outlook for the future of lemurs in the wild, and comment on how their chances for survival can be improved by demonstrating their long-term economic value to Madagascar and its people. In spite of the many serious problems faced by lemurs and their natural habitats, we believe that the prospects for their long-term survival are better now than at any time in the recent past, and we are optimistic that all of the species alive today can be saved from extinction.

Major Threats to Lemurs

The specific threats to wild lemurs (and indeed to all primates) are many, and can be divided into three main categories: habitat destruction or alteration, hunting for food or other purposes, and live capture (Mittermeier and Coimbra-Filho, 1977; Mittermeier, 1987). The impacts of these factors vary considerably from species to species and from region to region, but habitat destruction is usually the major threat.

Habitat Destruction

The most severe threat to primate populations worldwide is destruction and degradation of tropical forest habitats, where 90% or more of the world's primates reside (Mittermeier, 1987). Lemurs are no exception. As mentioned earlier, it is estimated that as much as 80% of Madagascar's original forest cover has already been converted by man for extraction of precious hardwoods, fuelwood and other products, to open up land for agriculture and pasture, for mining, and for a variety of other uses.

The underpinnings of forest destruction in Madagascar are many. The human population in Madagascar is 12 million people in an area of 587,041 km^2, not very high compared to many other developing countries (and roughly comparable to the population of greater Los Angeles in an area the size of Texas). Nonetheless, it is growing annually by 3.1% with a doubling time of 25 years, definitely a cause for concern. Perhaps more telling is the fact that there are only 30,000 km^2 of arable land in a country that is 80% dependent on small-scale agriculture (rice, coffee, vanilla, spices), indicating the land-use pressures that already exist. Another factor is that the Malagasy are relative newcomers to their island, arriving there from southeast Asia, Africa, and intermediate points as recently as 1,500-2,000 years ago. Rather than evolving appropriate land-use practices over tens of thousands of years, they arrived with a mix of traditions (rice-growing from Southeast Asia, cattle-raising from East Africa) not appropriate to the delicate Madagascar ecosystems.

The rates of forest loss since the arrival of man are striking. One study by Green and Sussman (1990) compared satellite imagery with earlier aerial photographs of the eastern rain forest biome, and concluded that an average of 111,000 ha of forest had been lost each year over the 35 years from 1950-1985. This represents a 50% decline in eastern rain forest cover in just the 35 years until 1985, and an estimated reduction of these forests to 34% of their original extent. Deforestation rates for the remainder of the country have not yet been analyzed in the same way. However, they are expected to be at least as serious in parts of the southern spiny desert region and the western dry deciduous forest. Slash-and-burn agriculture, locally known as *tavy*, is a problem wherever natural habitats remain, and is probably the single greatest cause of forest loss (Fig. 5.3).

PHOTO BY RUSSELL A. MITTERMEIER

Fig. 5.3: Slash-and-burn agriculture in the western dry deciduous forest region of Madagascar, in this case the Analabe region north of Morondava in the southwest. This practice is known as *tavy* in Madagascar and is probably the single most important cause of forest destruction.

Madagascar's lateritic soils, with their low fertility, are not suited to such agricultural uses, and exposing them to the ravages of erosion in this way has already left much of the country's central plateau a lifeless moonscape of baked red earth (Fig. 5.4), giving rise to one of Madagascar's popular albeit tragic nicknames, "le Grand Ile Rouge" ("Great Red Island"). This hemorrhaging of the island's soil into its rivers and the surrounding ocean during the rainy season leaves a red ring around the island so striking that it has been observed by astronauts from space. The results of this misuse of land have been disastrous. According to a recent World Bank estimate, some $100-300 million of future potential is being lost each year in Madagascar due to this widespread erosion. Furthermore, the quality of life is not improving; a United Nations Development Program Human Development Report for 1993 ranks Madagascar 123rd out of 173 countries on a human development index that incorporates data on poverty, quality of life and national GNP.

The case of rice helps to illustrate some of Madagascar's critical land-use problems. Rice is the mainstay of life in Madagascar, and its cultivation is the primary livelihood of 70% of the country's population; indeed the Malagasy have the greatest per capita rice consumption of any country on Earth (National Geographic, 1994).

PHOTO BY RUSSELL A. MITTERMEIER

Fig. 5.4: Deforested landscape of the central plateau of Madagascar, which was once covered by a mosaic of forest and woodland savanna. In the dry season, this "moonscape" gives rise to one of Madagascar's popular names, "Great Red Island."

Paddy rice is grown in the valleys and low plains, especially in the area surrounding Lac Alaotra and the Marovoay plains of the lower Betsiboka River, while dry rice is grown throughout the country. Traditionally, about 70% of Madagascar's rice is grown in paddies (Fig. 5.5), which can be maintained year after year and have relatively high productivity (though not comparable to those of Southeast Asia). The remainder is grown as dry rice on deforested slopes. This practice is not only disastrous for lemurs and other wildlife living in the forests, it also exacerbates erosion and destroys the watershed for paddy rice in the valleys below.

In the normal *tavy* process used in dry rice cultivation, a plot of forest is cleared of its natural vegetation and that vegetation is then burned. The resultant ash provides sufficient nutrients to the otherwise poor soil to allow for a season or two of crop production. When the nutrients are exhausted, the farmer moves on to another plot, leaving the original to lie fallow and the forest to regenerate before returning, ideally 10-15 years later. In situations where population pressure is low, such shifting techniques can indeed be sustainable, but in Madagascar demands for agricultural land are so great that cultivators are frequently forced to return to their fields before forest can regenerate, or to open new plots. Average fallow time in the agricultural lands surrounding the Zahamena Nature Reserve for example, is seven years or less (F. Boltz, pers. comm.).

PHOTO BY RUSSELL A. MITTERMEIER

Fig. 5.5: Typical rice paddy in the central plateau region of Madagascar; 70% of the country's economy is devoted to rice growing.

The best example of what is happening is the Lac Alaotra region of central Madagascar, which includes the biggest lake and largest rice-producing area; there, some 3,000 ha of rice paddy are being lost each year through siltation. This siltation results from *tavy* cultivation of dry rice on the rainforest-covered slopes to the east of the lake itself and from poor maintenance of the primary irrigation system (Barnes, 1986). The same is true in the Marovoay region, where deforestation on the Ankarafantsika plateau has resulted in downstream paddy siltation. Many other examples of this problem exist in other parts of Madagascar; nationwide, shifting agriculture was estimated in 1986 to account for a loss of 200,000 ha of forest cover each year (Seyler *et al.*, 1986).

The process of forest regeneration in Madagascar is slowed by the absence of any vigorous colonizing trees such as the South American tree genus, *Cecropia* (Preston-Mafham, 1991). Repeated burning leaves behind increasingly nutrient poor soils that are eventually unable to support secondary growth other than a few grasses. These lands then fall victim to erosion, particularly if they lie on hillsides which, though inadequate for agriculture, are frequently utilized as a last resort by local farmers. It is estimated that as much as 1 million ha/year may be lost to productive agriculture through soil erosion in Madagascar (Seyler *et al.*, 1986); indeed, erosion is so prevalent that the technical term for one severe type of erosion - *lavaka* - comes from the Malagasy word that describes the immense erosion-generated gullies that scar the landscape over much of Madagascar (Fig. 5.6).

PHOTO BY RUSSELL A. MITTERMEIER

Fig. 5.6: Classic erosion in eastern Madagascar, known as *lavaka* in the Malagasy language.

Another subsistence level land use issue is fuelwood. Every year, large areas of natural forest are cut down to provide firewood and charcoal for cooking. This problem is especially severe in the southern spiny desert region, where very poor Antandroy tribesmen convert large areas of slow-growing Didiereaceae bush into bags of charcoal and stacks of firewood for sale to townspeople (Fig. 5.7). Dozens of roadside stands selling these low value products can be seen alongside the major roads throughout the southern part of Madagascar. Needless to say, such use of these globally unique forests, with 95% plant endemism at the species level and close to 50% at the generic level, is very sad indeed. Unfortunately, it also does very little to improve the lot of the Antandroy or their neighbors.

PHOTO BY RUSSELL A. MITTERMEIER

Fig. 5.7: Roadside charcoal production in the spiny desert region of southern Madagascar. This practice destroys slow-growing forests that have 95% species endemism.

In such areas, a possible solution might be the introduction of simple-to-use solar energy technology or development of alternative fuel sources - both in the towns to reduce demand for fuelwood and in the villages themselves. However, these cultures are very conservative, and new energy sources may meet with resistance, at least initially. Furthermore, the alternative fuel technologies are often either too expensive or not sufficiently advanced to provide attractive alternatives to fuelwood. A special focus on providing appropriate energy technologies in this region should be a high priority.

Yet another problem has been the cattle-raising tradition, imported centuries ago from East Africa (Fig. 5.8). There are as many cattle in Madagascar as there are people, and the effects of overgrazing, clearance of forest for cattle pasture, and periodic burning to provide the "green bite" of new grass, has been at least as bad as on the savannas of East Africa, where the negative environmental impact of cattle-raising by tribes like the Maasai is known worldwide.

In Madagascar, this problem is concentrated in the west and south, especially among the Sakalava, the Mahafaly, and the Antandroy people. Among these tribes, cattle are the principal source of wealth.

They are rarely eaten except at huge funeral ceremonies, at which time many will be slaughtered for a single event. As in East Africa, the cattle-raising people of Madagascar are very closely tied to their herds, and changing this tradition will be very difficult.

PHOTO BY RUSSELL A. MITTERMEIER

Fig. 5.8: Cattle in western Madagascar. There are as many cattle in Madagascar as there are people.

Major international develoment programs funded by a variety of bilateral and multilateral donors have also wreaked havoc on Madagascar's environment. Almost invariably, these have been grand in scope and short on careful planning, and have paid little or no attention to the environment or the local people they were theoretically intended to help. Many examples of these exist in Madagascar, as in the rest of the tropical world, and only a few will be mentioned here.

One of the best known is the paper pulp scheme for the Moramanga and Fianarantsoa areas. Initiated in the 1970s, this program resulted in the clearance of 70,000-80,000 ha of rich eastern rain forest in the Moramanga area and some 30,000 ha near Fianarantsoa to make way for pine and eucalyptus plantations. The plan was to use the pulp from these plantations to produce paper locally, but the mills were never built. The result of this devastation, funded by the World Bank, is clearly visible to the ecotourist along the road to Périnet (= Andasibe).

Two other programs involve rice production, one in the Marovoay region in western Madagascar and the other in the Lac Alaotra region.

In the Marovoay project, a dam built for irrigation purposes in the early 1980s was poorly planned, and the road accompanying it led to an unplanned immigration by small-scale farmers. This in turn resulted in forest destruction and major siltation that now threatens the original program itself. This effort was funded by the German government.

At Lac Alaotra, another poorly planned project has resulted in rice farmers migrating into the lake area. This has led to increased siltation, exacerbating that resulting from the *tavy* agriculture referred to earlier, and loss of unique reed beds; the eventual result could be the destruction of the lake itself. Aside from the lake's great value to local communities and to Madagascar as a whole, its loss would result in the extinction of at least three endemic species, including the Lac Alaotra bamboo lemur (*Hapalemur griseus alaotrensis*), found only in the reed beds of Alaotra, the Alaotra pochard (*Aythya innotata*) and the Alaotra grebe (*Tachybaptus rufolavatus*). This program was supported by French Cooperation.

The last of the development efforts that we will mention here is the QIT titanium mining program in the southeastern corner of Madagascar near Fort-Dauphin. Madagascar has some of the world's largest deposits of titanium, and this element is potentially worth hundreds of millions of dollars to the country. QIT, a large English company based in Canada and with mining interests around the world, has contracted biological surveys and environmental impact assessments in the areas of interest, mainly Mandena, Sainte-Luce and Petriky, on the coast north of Fort-Dauphin. This part has been positive. However, once again, some preliminary activities have resulted in ecological problems, *e.g.*, trails built for prospecting purposes were used by villagers, who went in and turned natural forest into charcoal. Better planning and appropriate education and training of local communities could help to avert this, but such efforts have rarely been undertaken by major development agencies.

To their credit, some of the multilateral development banks and bilateral aid agencies have begun to change their approach. The World Bank was instrumental in preparing an Environmental Action Plan for Madagascar (World Bank *et al.*, 1988), and the U.S. Agency for International Development (US-AID) has been exemplary in its biodiversity conservation efforts. Indeed, it has supported key biodiversity projects since the early 1980s, and biodiversity is a major component of its overall assistance program for Madagascar. Hopefully, this positive trend will continue in the future.

Fig. 5.9: White-fronted brown lemurs (*Eulemur fulvus albifrons*) shot for
food in eastern Madagascar.

Hunting

Worldwide, hunting is the second most important threat to primate
populations behind habitat loss. Primates are hunted around the world
as food items, as bait, for medicinal purposes, as crop pests, for their
skins and other body parts as ornamentation, as evil omens or for other
quasi-religious reasons, and often simply for sport (Mittermeier, 1987).
Generally, hunting pressure increases with the size of the species; larger
animals simply provide more meat, skin, bait or other products, while
small ones barely recompense the hunter for the cost of a shotgun shell
or the effort involved. This is probably why the lemur species that have
already gone extinct were larger than almost all of the extant taxa. Even
today, hunting pressure is likely to be a greater threat to the larger species
such as the indriids, *Eulemur* and *Varecia*, than to the smaller nocturnal
animals.

Although there is little documentation of hunting of living lemurs,
anecdotes abound. Jolly (1980) cites several cases, mainly involving
Propithecus verreauxi. Another case came to our attention in 1984,
when reports were received that Chinese workers building the road from
Antananarivo to Tamatave (= Toamasina) were paying a premium for
indri, which they considered a delicacy. Rapid action was taken to
prevent this, but it never was determined how many indris were killed as
a result. Yet another case is the recent report that a Frenchman named

Gros Michel has been supplying local Malagasy with guns and shotgun shells so that they can shoot red ruffed lemurs (*Varecia variegata rubra*) on the Masoala Peninsula. These are then sold to local Chinese merchants as a delicacy. Needless to say, such behavior is unacceptable in this day and age, and should be dealt with appropriately by the Malagasy authorities.

Another highly endangered species that is suffering from hunting pressure is the recently-described *Propithecus tattersalli*. Gold miners in the area of Daraina are apparently hunting it and it has already been wiped out by hunting in other areas in which it once occurred.

Fig. 5.9 depicts one more case of lemur hunting, the taxon in question being *Eulemur fulvus albifrons*, the white-fronted brown lemur (R. Albignac, pers. comm.).

Fortunately, along with the lemur hunting traditions that exist, there is also a strong tradition or taboo, known in Malagasy as *fady*, against hunting certain species. The *fady* varies from ethnic group to ethnic group, killing of indris, for example, being prohibited among the Betsimasaraka people of the eastern rain forest and *Propithecus v. verreauxi* being *fady* among the Antandroy and the Mahafaly of the southern spiny desert.

Methods that have been reported for hunting lemurs are similar to those used for primate hunting in other parts of the tropics, and range from nest raiding, trapping, snaring, tree-felling and stone throwing (Tattersall, 1982), to the use of slingshots, blowguns and rifles (Figs. 5.10 , 5.11). The main reason for hunting lemurs is for food, and the majority of published and anecdotal accounts of hunting cite the target animals as being the larger lemurs, especially *Propithecus* spp. or *Varecia variegata*, those which would provide the greatest amount of food. Nonetheless, small genera like *Cheirogaleus* and *Lepilemur* are regularly captured for food as well, the usual methods being trapping or simple removal of the animals from their daytime nesting sites, some of which are only a few meters above the ground.

Fig. 5.10: Snare trap used on the Masoala Peninsula to capture *Eulemur fulvus albifrons* and *Varecia variegata rubra* (1984).

Fig. 5.11: Trap used to capture small lemurs (*Microcebus, Cheirogaleus, Lepilemur*) for food in the Ranomafana area (1985).

Although most killing of lemurs is for food, one well known exception is the tradition of killing the aye-aye among the Betsimasaraka people. If an aye-aye passes through a village, this *fady* requires that it be killed immediately since it is considered an evil omen that warns of impending death or disaster. In some cases, the appearance of an aye-aye even requires that the village be abandoned. Aye-ayes may be killed for more practical reasons as well, since they apparently raid coconut and lychee plantations and are regarded as crop "pests" in some areas.

In comparison to the threats posed by habitat loss, hunting is of less concern, yet its impact is worthy of further study and monitoring. Movement of human populations is on the rise throughout Madagascar, as families search for new arable lands. Demographic shifts of this nature are often accompanied by a decline in traditional values. As food becomes scarcer and in the absence of social pressure from the community to prevent hunting, local people may be driven to kill lemurs that were once considered *fady* in a last-ditch effort to put food on the table. Alternatively, tribes without taboos for a particular lemur may move into an area with a large population of that species that is unafraid of people because the traditional inhabitants considered it *fady*. The result can be rapid local extermination of naive animals by immigrant hunters.

Live Capture

Fortunately, live capture of lemurs for local use as pets or for export is not a serious threat, even though it has been a major factor in the decline of certain species like the Colombian cotton-top tamarin (Mast *et al.*, 1993) and the African chimpanzee (Mack and Mittermeier, 1984). A few of the hardier lemur species, such as *Lemur catta*, *Eulemur fulvus* sspp., *Eulemur macaco macaco*, *Hapalemur griseus* and *Cheirogaleus* spp. are sometimes kept as pets by local people, but this is much less of a problem than in most other regions in which primates occur. Indeed, most lemur species are difficult to keep in captivity, especially folivores like *Lepilemur* and the indriids. Since they usually perish quickly, there is little incentive to keep them. One exception to this is the frequent capture of live *Hapalemur griseus alaotrensis* by villagers in the Lac Alaotra area. This practice is apparently quite common there, and is probably a major factor in the decline of this critically endangered subspecies (see discussion on pp. 152-154).

Although the reader may see an occasional lemur kept as a pet by local people, this is usually not cause for major concern (although it is illegal). Nonetheless, since there is relatively little information on this topic, we would welcome hearing from you if you do see lemurs in captivity. Data on the species in question, where it is being kept, where it originated, and how it was captured are all of interest. Information on how to contact us is given at the end of this book (p. 357).

Lemur export is also not a serious issue. Although a substantial legal and illegal reptile trade exists (Joint Nature Conservation Committee, 1993), lemur export has been prohibited for decades and has been well-enforced.   All lemurs are protected by law in Madagascar, and all species are listed in the appendices of CITES, the Convention on International Trade in Endangered Species.   Indeed, the only documented lemur exports over the past 10 years have been for scientific purposes, particularly for conservation-oriented captive breeding operations such as those being undertaken by the Duke University Primate Center and the Jersey Wildlife Preservation Trust. These programs have removed only a very small number of individuals from the wild. Hopefully, this strict control of lemur trade will continue.

Lemur Conservation Efforts

In order to ensure the survival of a representative cross-section of lemur species, a diversified approach is needed, requiring elements of each of the following:

1)   effective management of protected areas that are home to a wide variety of lemur species;

2)   establishment of new protected areas for species and   ecosystems that are not yet covered;

3)   special efforts aimed at critically endangered taxa;

4)   captive breeding programs for target species, both for possible future reintroduction and also to learn more of their basic biology and genetic management;

5)   continued and expanded research efforts to learn more of lemur ecology, behavior, geographic distribution, taxonomy, and conservation status in the wild;

6)   conservation education and public awareness efforts both within Madagascar and internationally, using lemurs as "flagship species" for their habitats;

7)   training of a cadre of Malagasy conservation professionals to carry the cause of biodiversity conservation into the future; and

8)   development of economic incentives for the conservation of lemurs and their habitats.

In this final section, we discuss these different aspects of lemur conservation, including some of the activities already underway and others that need to be developed or expanded in the near future. This section is divided into four main headings: conservation in the wild, conservation in captivity, conservation status, and incentives for lemur conservation.

Conservation in the Wild

It goes without saying that the principal focus of lemur conservation efforts has to be on the natural habitats of these animals (1-3) above) and that protected areas of various kinds are the most critical element in the largely fragmented landscape of Madagascar. It is also obvious that certain species will require more specific attention than others, either because of their critically endangered status or because they require large areas of intact forest to survive. Other species may be more adaptable and capable of surviving in altered habitats and secondary forests adjacent to human habitation. These will probably require less atention than their more demanding relatives, and, in any case, will also be beneficiaries of habitat conservation efforts for the more endangered lemurs. Among the latter adaptable species are *Microcebus, Cheirogaleus,* and some of the *Eulemur fulvus* subspecies, all of them capable of surviving in human-modified habitats. The most demanding species include many of the larger forms, such as the indri, the subspecies of *Propithecus diadema, Allocebus trichotis*, *Hapalemur aureus* and *Hapalemur simus*; these will require tracts of undisturbed habitat and special management efforts to ensure their survival. Indeed, all of the Critically Endangered Species in Table 5.3 will require species-focused management efforts in addition to maintenance of their natural habitats.

The basic system of protected areas in Madagascar was established in 1927, and now includes seven different designations based upon purpose, management, degree of protection and access. The national parks, nature reserves, special reserves and private reserves cover more than 1,000,000 ha of national territory and have been the focal points for ecosystem and species conservation activities in Madagascar (see Appendix, Figs. A.2, A.3). Protected area management in Madagascar is overseen by a National Association for Management of Protected Areas (ANGAP), other nature protection and forestry activities are covered by the Department of Waters and Forests (DEF), and the overall environmental program is orchestrated by a National Environmental Office (ONE). Following the guidelines of a National Environmental Action Plan (PAE) developed in the mid-1980s, the DEF and ANGAP has contracted the operation of several protected areas to international agencies. For example, Conservation International (CI), is working closely with ANGAP and DEF to manage both the Zahamena and Ankarafantsika Integral Reserves; the World wide Fund for Nature (WWF) is also working at Andohahela, Montagne d'Ambre, Marojejy and Andringitra Reserves; Duke University oversees efforts at the Ranomafana National Park, and UNESCO manages biosphere reserves at Mananara-Nord and Bemaraha. CARE has also become an important player in recent years, working with local and international agencies to provide development assistance to several of the protected areas. These programs are financed by a wide variety of international donor agencies including bilateral government assistance from the USA, France, Germany, the Netherlands and Switzerland, private foundations such as the MacArthur Foundation, the W. Alton Jones Foundation and many others, and multilateral development banks like The World Bank and several United Nations agencies.

Madagascar also has 267 classified forests and forest reserves which cover more than 4,000,000 ha (Conservation International, 1993), an area four times larger than the country's protected area network (see Appendix, Figs. A.3, A.4). These forests are set aside for future exploitation, and concessions are managed by DEF. The actual extent of these forests, their condition and the policies for managing them are poorly defined. However, a study has recently been completed by DEF and Conservation International that for the first time maps these forests along with the remainder of the country's protected area system. On-the-ground reconnaissance of these reserves is currently underway. This will be required to an even greater extent over the coming years to assess the biodiversity of these important areas and to determine what conservation actions are needed in them. This network of classified forests and forest reserves deserves far greater attention in nationwide schemes to protect lemurs and biodiversity in general, as do the so-called "dominial forests" (*forêts dominiales*) of the country (*i.e.*, those that are currently uncategorized).

It is also important to recognize that protected area management in Madagascar means much more than erecting fences to keep people out and lemurs and other wildlife safely inside. Strict protection of this kind clearly has a major role, but much greater integration of communities in conservation efforts is essential. Local people need to be part of the effort, and to be fully aware of the short- and long-term benefits that intact forest provides to them.

Conservation in Captivity

Although wild populations of lemurs should always be the main focus of conservation efforts, captive breeding (4) plays a key role as well. Captive colonies provide a safety net against possible extinctions in the wild, they are a source for possible future reintroduction programs, they serve a very important public awareness and conservation education function, and they should be a focal point for research into diet, reproductive behavior, handling and transport, and genetic management that complement and augment field-based research activities (Porton, 1993). Indeed, it is essential that captive and field-based conservation activities no longer be treated as separate endeavors; rather, they should be viewed as points on a collaborative continuum, the ultimate goal of which should be to ensure the continued survival of all living lemurs.

Fortunately, many lemur species are already represented in captivity. The world's largest collection of lemurs is unquestionably the Duke University Primate Center in Durham, North Carolina, USA, which houses some 23 lemur species and subspecies, including two (*Propithecus tattersalli and P. d. diadema*) that can be found nowhere else in captivity (K. Glander, pers. comm.). Other noteworthy lemur collections include those of the Jersey Wildlife Preservation Trust on the Isle of Jersey; the Mulhouse Zoo in Alsace, France; the Bois de Vincennes Zoo outside Paris, France, and the St. Louis, San Francisco, Los Angeles, San Diego, Indianapolis and Cincinnati Zoos in the United States.

Some lemur species thrive in captivity and are very well represented in collections, including *Varecia variegata variegata*, *Varecia variegata rubra*, *Eulemur macaco macaco*, *Microcebus murinus* and *Lemur catta*. Other species can be found in small numbers in a handful of collections, such as *Eulemur macaco flavifron*s, *E. mongoz*, *E. coronatus*, *Daubentonia madagascariensis*, and the two species of *Propithecus* mentioned earlier. Still others such as *Indri indri* have never been successfully managed in a captive setting.

In addition to the zoos and research collections mentioned above, IUCN's Species Survival Commission (including both its Primate Specialist Group and its Captive Breeding Specialist Group) and the American Zoo and Aquarium Association (AZA) have taken a strong interest in managing captive populations of lemurs and other globally threatened and endangered species. The AZA, in particular, has created a Prosimian Taxon Advisory Group (TAG) currently headed by Ingrid Porton of the St. Louis Zoo. The Prosimian TAG produces an annually-revised *Regional Collection Plan for Lemurs* that manages data on lemurs in captivity. It is intended to assure optimum use of captive space by collaborating institutions, to share relevant information on lemur genetics and husbandry, and to make recommendations regarding research, limiting breeding of over-represented captive species and establishment of new captive management programs for species of greatest concern.

Several international and regional studbooks for taxa like *Varecia variegata variegata* and *Eulemur macaco macaco* have been established over the past few years. These studbooks maintain records on individual animals and their genetic lineages, and they serve to monitor captive population fluctuations and genetic variability.

Also, as a result of two very significant meetings on lemur conservation held on St. Catherine's Island, Georgia in 1985 and 1986, a consortium of North American and European zoos interested in Madagascar was formed; this is now known as the Madagascar Fauna Interest Group (FIG). Madagascar FIG member institutions are committed to preserving endangered Malagasy fauna through both *in situ* and *ex situ* conservation programs, and providing technical advice and training to Malagasy institutions and specialists. The Madagascar FIG is currently chaired by David Anderson of the San Francisco Zoo, with Sukie Zeeve serving as US Project Coordinator.

Captive management techniques for primates in general have improved substantially over the past decade, mainly as a result of ongoing biological research in captive settings and in the wild. Given the attention being paid to the proper genetic management of lemurs through the use of studbooks, the Prosimian TAG, the Species Survival Plans (SSPs) of the AZA, and the efforts of the IUCN/SSC Captive Breeding and Primate Specialist Groups it is likely that vigorous captive populations of several lemur taxa can be maintained for the future.

Conservation Status of Lemurs

Since the earliest days of the modern conservation movement, the lemurs of Madagascar have been recognized as a conservation priority. In his classic work, *Extinct and Vanishing Mammals of the World*, Harper (1945) discussed 40 lemur taxa, and gives what was for the time a good account of their status. Twenty-one years later, the first volume of the *IUCN Red Data Book, Mammalia* (Simon, 1966) listed most of the then recognized lemurs as endangered or vulnerable, a total of 24 taxa in all. The 1972 version of the mammal *Red Data Book* (Goodwin and Holloway, 1972) continued to recognize the same taxa as those of the 1966 edition, with some updating of information. The 1990 version of the *Red Data Book*, an entire volume focusing exclusively on the lemurs (*Lemurs of Madagascar and the Comoros. The IUCN Red Data Book* ,Thornback and Harcourt, 1990), greatly updated the information in the earlier volumes, recognizing 16 taxa as *Endangered*, 16 as *Vulnerable*, nine as *Rare*, one as *Insufficiently Known* and four as *Abundant*. In 1992, we introduced a somewhat different rating system in the IUCN/SSC Primate Specialist Group's *Lemurs of Madagascar: An Action Plan for their Conservation, 1993-1999* (Mittermeier *et al.*, 1992), focusing on priorities for conservation action and using a weighting system that took into account taxonomic uniqueness, degree of threat and level of protection. This resulted in an analysis that recognized 12 taxa as *Highest Priority*, 11 as *High Priority*, seven as *Priority* and 20 as *Not of Conservation Concern*.

In this publication, we have carried out yet another analysis of lemur conservation status, based on the new and greatly expanded IUCN Red List Criteria. This in-depth revision of status categories began with a workshop held at the IUCN General Assembly in Madrid in 1984, and continued in a series of workshops and studies spearheaded by the IUCN Species Survival Commission (SSC) and Georgina Mace and Russ Lande, two leading conservation biologists. Their first attempt at more rigorous analysis resulted in the paper, *Assessing Extinction Threats: Toward a Re-evaluation of IUCN Threatened Species Categories* (Mace and Lande, 1991). This was then widely circulated, criticized and substantially revised, resulting in a still more extensive analysis that was presented at the IUCN General Assembly in Buenos Aires in January 1994. It is this latest version that we have used here to yet again rate the conservation status of living lemurs. The results are presented in Table 5.3, with 10 species in the *Critically Endangered* category, 7 *Endangered*, 19 *Vulnerable* and 14 considered at *Low Risk*.

These recent efforts to revise and expand the IUCN criteria have grown out of a long-standing concern that the process of assessing conservation status was too subjective and lacked the quantitative rigor needed to stand up to criticism. These new criteria have taken us a long way towards more rigorous analysis. However, the simple fact remains that a considerable degree of subjectivity is still needed to come up with status categories for lemurs and almost all other nonhuman primates. As discussed earlier in this book, we do not even know the precise limits of geographic distribution for most lemur species, and much less of population numbers or other basic biological parameters. The population "guesstimates" that we give at the end of each species profile in Chapter 6 are very rough; indeed, they are within an order of magnitude only, and even our order of magnitude "guesstimates" may be off. The

Table 5.3
Conservation Status of Malagasy Lemurs
(using the latest IUCN Red List criteria)

Taxon	Rating
Microcebus murinus	Low Risk
Microcebus rufus	Low Risk
Microcebus myoxinus	Vulnerable?
Mirza coquereli	Vulnerable
Allocebus trichotis	Critically Endangered
Cheirogaleus major	Low Risk
Cheirogaleus medius	Low Risk
Phaner furcifer furcifer	Vulnerable
Phaner furcifer pallescens	Vulnerable
Phaner furcifer parienti	Vulnerable
Phaner furcifer electromontis	Vulnerable
Lepilemur mustelinus	Low Risk
Lepilemur microdon	Low Risk
Lepilemur leucopus	Low Risk
Lepilemur ruficaudatus	Low Risk
Lepilemur edwardsi	Low Risk
Lepilemur dorsalis	Vulnerable
Lepilemur septentrionalis	Vulnerable
Hapalemur griseus griseus	Low Risk
Hapalemur griseus occidentalis	Vulnerable
Hapalemur griseus alaotrensis	Critically Endangered
Hapalemur aureus	Critically Endangered
Hapalemur simus	Critically Endangered
Lemur catta	Vulnerable
Eulemur fulvus fulvus	Low Risk
Eulemur fulvus rufus	Low Risk
Eulemur fulvus albifrons	Low Risk
Eulemur fulvus sanfordi	Vulnerable
Eulemur fulvus albocollaris	Endangered
Eulemur fulvus collaris	Vulnerable
Eulemur macaco macaco	Vulnerable
Eulemur macaco flavifrons	Critically Endangered
Eulemur coronatus	Vulnerable
Eulemur rubriventer	Vulnerable
Eulemur mongoz	Vulnerable
Varecia variegata variegata	Endangered
Varecia variegata rubra	Critically Endangered
Avahi laniger	Low Risk
Avahi occidentalis	Vulnerable
Propithecus verreauxi verreauxi	Vulnerable
Propithecus verreauxi coquereli	Endangered
Propithecus verreauxi coronatus	Critically Endangered
Propithecus verreauxi deckeni	Vulnerable
Propithecus diadema diadema	Endangered
Propithecus diadema edwardsi	Endangered
Propithecus diadema candidus	Critically Endangered
Propithecus diadema perrieri	Critically Endangered
Propithecus tattersalli	Critically Endangered
Indri indri	Endangered
Daubentonia madagascariensis	Endangered

greatest value of our estimates is that they are relative; certain taxa are clearly much less or much more abundant than others, and this, along with other criteria like taxonomic uniqueness, adaptability to human-induced habitat modification, susceptibility to hunting pressure, reproductive rate, age at sexual maturity, and presence in protected areas all need to be taken into consideration. In other words, although we now have more rigorous guidelines to assess conservation status than ever before, our assessments still include a heavy dose of subjectivity and need to be viewed with this in mind.

Incentives for Lemur Conservation

In order to achieve long term conservation objectives in Madagascar, it is essential to come up with a wide variety of incentives for the people of Madagascar to become more involved in these activities. As indicated in numbers 6-8 above, three key ingredients are developing a sense of pride among the Malagasy in their country's globally unique wildlife heritage, training a cadre of Malagasy conservation professionals to carry the cause of biodiversity conservation into the future, and, most important of all, demonstrating the concrete economic value of lemurs and other wildlife to local people and to the nation as a whole. Lemurs will be instrumental in achieving all of these goals. Madagascar's greatest shadow asset is the often unrecognized value of its wildlife and natural ecosystems, as well as the country's global reputation as a biodiversity "hotspot". Biodiversity in Madagascar exceeds all other resources in terms of potential for future sustainable economic gain in Madagascar, and lemurs are the best known symbols of this natural diversity - the "flagship" species that are the global ambassadors for all the rest of the country's wildlife.

Education and public awareness in Madagascar is a priority at all levels, from government decision-makers to city-dwellers to local people living in the remotest villages. Education efforts, using lemurs and other species, have been carried out sporadically in the past employing materials such as t-shirts, posters, stickers, pins, brochures and a variety of other products (Figs. 5. 12 - 5. 14). However, these efforts must be greatly increased and undertaken in earnest with the goal of changing attitudes toward the environment on a national scale.

Government officials need to understand that wildlife and natural ecosystems are the country's greatest asset, and should be managed for sustainable rather than one-time financial gain. By the same token, local people must be aware of the economic potentials available to them through ecotourism and other sustainable forms of resource use, as it is only with support from the grass roots that long-term conservation efforts can succeed. As just one example, a Malagasy version of this book would contribute to such education efforts, and is in fact planned for the near future.

Training is also critical for the future. Although much lemur field research has been carried out in Madagascar, there is still only a very small number of Malagasy lemur experts. A major focus on such training is a key element in any overall conservation program.

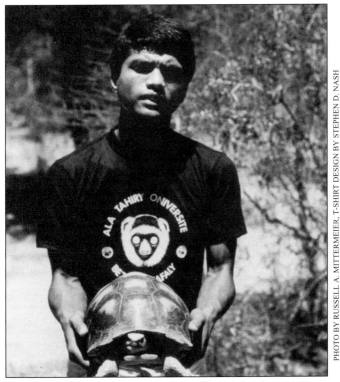

PHOTO BY RUSSELL A. MITTERMEIER, T-SHIRT DESIGN BY STEPHEN D. NASH

Fig. 5.12: A Malagasy biologist wearing a t-shirt produced by the World Wildlife Fund-US Primate Program, the design depicting a sifaka.

In economic terms, ecotourism in Madagascar has enormous potential. We believe that an ecotourism industry focusing on lemurs as the principal "flagship" species, but incorporating many other compo-

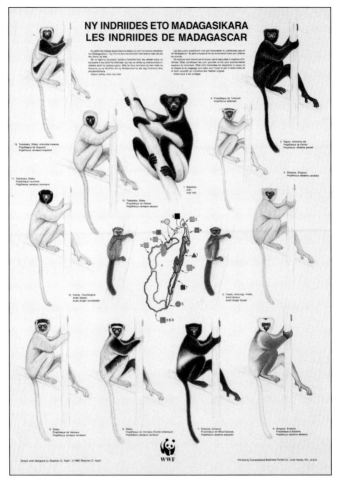

Fig. 5.13: This poster, illustrated by Stephen D. Nash, was produced in 1989 by the World Wildlife Fund-US Primate Program, and depicts all living members of the family Indriidae and their distributions.

nents of Madagascar's rich wildlife as well, could become a major foreign exchange earner for Madagascar. Indeed, the example of Costa Rica, where ecotourism is now *the* major source of revenue for the country, and that of Rwanda, where tourism based on a single primate species, the mountain gorilla, is also the number one foreign exchange earner, are models that Madagascar could well follow. Some ecotourism already exists in Madagascar, but we believe that it could be increased by an order of magnitude. Only a handful of lemur-watching sites are now heavily visited (*e.g.*, Berenty, Périnet, Ranomafana, Nosy Be, Mananara), but others could be easily developed for low-impact tourism that would generate income for local communities. Indeed, such activities would provide strong local incentive for forest conservation. Périnet (= Andasibe) provides an excellent example of this type of locally-based tourism operation. In this reserve, home to a small number of habituated indris, about 30 young guides have formed a well-organized group to provide high quality, standardized tour service. This organization, known as the *Association des Guides d'Andasibe*, is a true grassroots effort and a model that should be emulated elsewhere in Madagascar. Tourists should also recognize the importance of these local initiatives and encourage them through generous and regular support. In many ways, the future of lemurs and other wildlife depends on local people, and they should be viewed as major partners in the conservation of Madagascar's biological heritage.

Improving the lot of poverty-stricken human populations and maintenance and restoration of healthy, functioning natural ecosystems must go hand in hand. Ultimately, neither will succeed without the other. The magnificent lemur fauna of Madagascar has played and should continue to play a role in the development of solutions. These unique animals have already attracted a great deal of international attention to the environmental problems of Madagascar, resulting in substantially increased investment in many sectors of the Malagasy economy. And the international appeal of these animals will attract increasing numbers of ecotourists, bringing with them much-needed foreign exchange. If this ecotourism is well-designed and carried out with maximum care, it can account for hundreds of millions of dollars per year in national income, as it presently does in several other countries that are not nearly as unique and spectacular as is Madagascar. We hope that this book will stimulate much further interest in Madagascar's magnificent natural heritage, and contribute to ensuring its survival. You, the reader, are already making a contribution by coming to Madagascar, and we hope that you will encourage others to do the same.

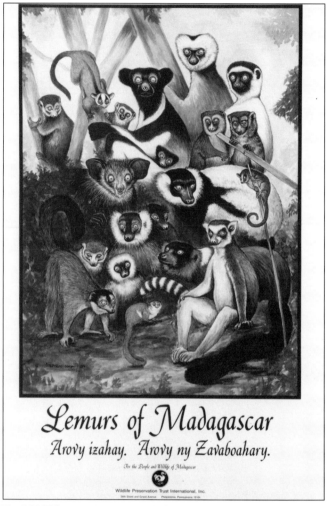

Fig. 5.14: This poster, based on a painting by Stephen D. Nash, was produced in 1989 by Wildlife Preservation Trust International and continues to be distributed to communities throughout Madagascar, along with an accompanying conservation education pamphlet.

6

THE
LIVING LEMURS

Using This Field Guide

In preceding chapters, we have discussed in general terms the ancestry, discovery and conservation of Madagascar's living lemurs. This chapter is devoted to detailed descriptions of their distribution, ecology, behavior, conservation status, and taxonomic relationships, and also provides information on identification in the field and recommendations as to where these animals can best be seen in the wild.

The reader should find this chapter informative and very easy to use. It begins with a complete listing of the 32 lemur species and 50 lemur taxa currently recognized, which are divided among five families: Cheirogaleidae, Megaladapidae, Lemuridae, Indriidae and Daubentoniidae. The next section includes a brief description of each family, its biological affinities and distinctive traits. The description of each genus within a family consists of a brief statement regarding its unique and distinguishing characteristics, as well as any relevant information pertaining to its taxonomy and explanations of the taxonomic framework used in this field guide. Also included for each genus is a distribution map, and a series of line drawings designed to acquaint the reader with typical locomotor postures and behaviors that will be useful in identifying lemurs in their natural habitats, *i.e.*, to give a *Gestalt* or "feel" for the genus that goes beyond what is provided in the Color Plate section.

Individual species and subspecies are described in detail. Each is introduced by its Latin name and most commonly used English name, followed by other English, French, German and Malagasy names. Page numbers for relevant color plates are also provided here for quick and easy reference.

The description of each species and subspecies is presented in five sections: *Identification*, *Geographic Range*, *Natural History*, *Conservation Status* and *Where To See It*.

Identification: This section includes information needed to identify the species, based upon what can be seen and, in some cases, heard in the field. Start with the genus and work down to subspecies (if any), taking special note of the geographic range which offers a useful guide to identification as well. We also mention other sympatric species with which a given taxon might be confused (if any), and suggest how to distinguish between them. Where available, data on body size and weight are given down to the species or subspecies level; dental formulae important for identifying skulls found either in the field or in museum collections are given in Fig. 4.1 in the Extinct Lemurs chapter.

Geographic Range: This section gives a verbal description of the animal's geographic range, and should be used in conjunction with the map. When trying to identify species within a given genus, one's location in Madagascar is often the best clue to species identification.   Similarly, if the species can be determined, geographic location will be a big help in determining the subspecies in question. The range descriptions and maps will both be useful here, but be aware that these simply give range limits; nowadays a given lemur will not be found in all forests within its former range. Finally, remember also that Madagascar is imperfectly known zoologically; if you wander from the beaten path, it is possible that you will make a new scientific discovery, or at least an addition to our knowledge of geographic distribution. If you are confident that you have seen a particular lemur outside the range we have specified, please let us know using the form at the end of this book; photographs plus geographic coordinates are essential in helping us to confirm identification and range extensions.

Natural History: In this section, we briefly summarize what is known of the ecology and behavior of each lemur taxon. This information will probably not be needed for identification, but it will help enhance your appreciation of the animals encountered in the field. Bear in mind that some species are better known than others, and that no lemur has been studied in all areas of its distribution and in all habitats that it occupies. In some cases, virtually nothing is known of an animal's natural history. Again, new observations are valuable; remember to record species or subspecies, map coordinates, time of year, and any other pertinent information such as forest type, plant species, and plant (or animal) parts eaten or otherwise utilized.

Conservation Status: Virtually all lemurs are under threat from different kinds of human activities. This section summarizes how severely a particular taxon is threatened, and what human activities are responsible. Remember that all lemur species are protected under Malagasy law and by international treaties, so it is essential that observers do not disturb these important animals in any way, and certainly that they *not* try to take lemurs (living or dead) out of the country.

In this section, we give a comprehensive list of all protected areas in which the lemur in question is known to occur, along with estimates of population size in the wild (within a reasonable order of magnitude) and the best available figures for captive populations. Also included is a conservation priority rating for each species or subspecies, based on the IUCN/SSC Primate Specialist Group publication, *Lemurs of Madagascar: An Action Plan for Their Conservation, 1993-1999* (Mittermeier *et al.*, 1992), and an assessment of threat (*Low Risk, Vulnerable, Endangered, Critically Endangered*) based on the latest IUCN Red List criteria (1994).

Where To See It: This section recommends the best sites on the main ecotourism circuit for observing the species and subspecies in question. It is not intended to be comprehensive, and sightings are possible in all protected areas in which a given lemur is known to occur, and in other unprotected sites as well. Indeed, we encourage visitors to explore other, less known sites, especially on their second or third trips to Madagascar, after they have learned a bit more about the country and its people. The *Where To See It* section is intended mainly for the visitor who has only a short time in Madagascar, and wants to see as many wild lemurs as possible.

Table 6.1
Classification of the Living Lemurs

Family Cheirogaleidae (Gregory, 1916)

Microcebus (E. Geoffroyi, 1828) Mouse lemurs
  M. murinus (J. F. Miller, 1777) Gray mouse lemur
  M. rufus (Lesson, 1840) Brown or rufous mouse lemur
  M. myoxinus (Peters, 1852) Pygmy mouse lemur
Allocebus (Petter-Rousseaux and Petter, 1967)
    Allocebus trichotis (Gunther, 1875) Hairy-eared dwarf
        lemur
Mirza (Gray, 1870)
    Mirza coquereli (A. Grandidier, 1867) Coquerel's dwarf
        lemur
Cheirogaleus (E. Geoffroy, 1812) Dwarf lemurs
  C. major (E. Geoffroy, 1812) Greater dwarf lemur
  C. medius (E. Geoffroy, 1812) Fat-tailed dwarf lemur
Phaner (Gray, 1870)
    P. furcifer (de Blainville, 1839) Fork-marked lemurs
        P. f. furcifer (de Blainville, 1839) Eastern
            fork-marked lemur.
        P. f. pallescens (Groves and Tattersall, 1991)
            Pale fork-marked lemur.
        P. f. parienti (Groves and Tattersall, 1991)
            Pariente's fork-marked lemur.
        P. f. electromontis (Groves and Tattersall,
            1991) Amber Mountain fork-marked
            lemur

Family Megaladapidae (Forsyth Major, 1894)
Subfamily Lepilemurinae (Rumpler and
Rakotosamimanana, 1975)

Lepilemur (I. Geoffroy, 1851) Weasel or sportive lemurs
  L. mustelinus (I. Geoffroy, 1851) Weasel sportive
      lemur
  L. microdon (Forsyth Major, 1894) Small-toothed
      sportive lemur
  L. leucopus (Forsyth Major, 1894) White-footed
      sportive lemur

L. ruficaudatus (A. Grandidier, 1867) Red-tailed
    sportive lemur
L. edwardsi (Forsyth Major, 1894) Milne-Edwards'
    sportive lemur
L. dorsalis (Gray, 1870) Gray-backed sportive lemur
L. septentrionalis (Rumpler and Albignac, 1975)
    Northern sportive lemur

Family Lemuridae (Gray, 1821)
Subfamily Lemurinae (Gray, 1821)

Hapalemur (I. Geoffroy, 1851) Bamboo or gentle lemurs
    H. griseus (Link, 1795) Lesser bamboo lemurs
        H. g. griseus (Link, 1795) Eastern lesser
            bamboo lemur
        H. g. occidentalis (Rumpler, 1975) Western
            lesser bamboo lemur
        H. g. alaotrensis (Rumpler, 1975) Lac Alaotra
            bamboo lemur
    H. aureus (Meier et al., 1987) Golden bamboo lemur
    H. simus (Gray, 1870) Greater bamboo lemur
Lemur (Linnaeus, 1758)
    L. catta (Linnaeus, 1758) Ring-tailed lemur
Eulemur (Simons and Rumpler, 1988)
    E. fulvus (E. Geoffroy, 1796) Brown lemurs
        E. f. fulvus (E. Geoffroy, 1796) Common
            brown lemur
        E. f. rufus (Audebert, 1800) Red-fronted
            brown lemur
        E. f. albifrons (E. Geoffroyi, 1796) White-
            fronted brown lemur
        E. f. sanfordi (Archbold, 1932) Sanford's
            brown lemur
        E. f. albocollaris (Rumpler, 1975) White-
            collared brown lemur
        E. f. collaris (E. Geoffroy, 1812) Collared
            brown lemur
    E. macaco (Linnaeus, 1766) Black lemur
        E. m. macaco (Linnaeus, 1766) Black lemur
        E. m. flavifrons (Gray, 1867) Sclater's black
            lemur

E. coronatus (Gray, 1842) Crowned lemur

E. rubriventer (I. Geoffroyi, 1850) Red-bellied lemur

E. mongoz (Linnaeus, 1766) Mongoose lemur

Varecia (Gray, 1863)

    V. variegata (Kerr, 1792) Ruffed lemurs

        V. v. variegata (Kerr, 1792) Black-and-white ruffed lemur

        V. v. rubra (E. Geoffroy, 1812) Red ruffed lemur

Family Indriidae (Burnett, 1828)

Avahi (Jourdan, 1834)

    A. laniger (Gmelin, 1788) Eastern woolly lemur

    A. occidentalis (Lorenz, 1898) Western woolly lemur

Propithecus (Bennett, 1832) Sifakas

    P. verreauxi (A. Grandidier, 1867)

        P. v. verreauxi (A. Grandidier, 1867) Verreaux's sifaka

        P. v. coquereli (Milne-Edwards, 1871) Coquerel's sifaka

        P. v. coronatus (Milne-Edwards, (1871) Crowned sifaka

        P. v. deckeni (Peters, 1870) Decken's sifaka

    P. diadema (Bennett, 1832)

        P. d. diadema (Bennett, 1832) Diademed sifaka

        P. d. candidus (A. Grandidier, 1871) Silky sifaka

        P. d. edwardsi (A. Grandidier, 1871) Milne-Edwards' sifaka

        P. d. perrieri (Lavauden, 1931) Perrier's sifaka

    P. tattersalli (Simons, 1988) Golden-crowned sifaka, Tattersall's sifaka

Indri (E. Geoffroy, 1796)

    I. indri (Gmelin, 1789) Indri, Babakoto

Family Daubentoniidae (Gray, 1870)

Daubentonia (Gray, 1870)

    D. madagascariensis (Gmclin, 1788) Aye-aye

FAMILY CHEIROGALEIDAE

This family includes five genera (*Microcebus, Mirza, Allocebus, Cheirogaleus* and *Phaner*) and a total of eight small nocturnal lemur species. These species range in body weight from the largest at about 600 gm to the smallest primate in the world, *Microcebus myoxinus*, in which adults weigh as little as 25 gm.

The genus *Microcebus* has a wide range in Madagascar and has been studied at only a handful of sites. More taxa may in fact await discovery, in addition to *M. myoxinus*, which has been "resurrected" as a species as a result of research carried out to the north of Morondava in southwest Madagascar.

All cheirogaleids move quadrupedally, and most have elongated bodies and short legs. Furthermore, all sleep during the day in small nests made from dead leaves or in holes in trees. At least one species of cheirogaleid can be found in most Malagasy forests, and often both a *Microcebus* and a *Cheirogaleus* species will be present. Some cheirogaleids undergo prolonged periods of seasonal torpor. Field identification should be fairly easy, since generic differences are substantial and congeneric species are usually geographically separated.

Microcebus: Mouse Lemurs

The genus *Microcebus* contains three known species of small nocturnal omnivores which are likely the most abundant and widespread of all Malagasy primates; one of these, *Microcebus myoxinus*, was first described in 1852 and then went unrecognized until 1993, when its distinctiveness was reconfirmed. Only a few Malagasy forests do not contain one of these species. They are the smallest living lemurs, and among the smallest primates. They have a gray to brown or rufous body coat and gray to off-white ventral pelage.

PHOTO BY RUSSELL A. MITTERMEIER

Fig. 6.1: Mouse lemur *(Microcebus murinus)* **in the forest at Beza-Mahafaly Special Reserve. Note the strong eye-shine.**

Key to illustrations on the following page (Fig. 6.2):
        a. *Microcebus* **sitting in fork of tree**
        b. *Microcebus* **climbing upside down on twigs**
        c. *Microcebus* **standing on horizontal branch**
        d. *Microcebus* **standing on twig**
        e. *Microcebus* **mating**

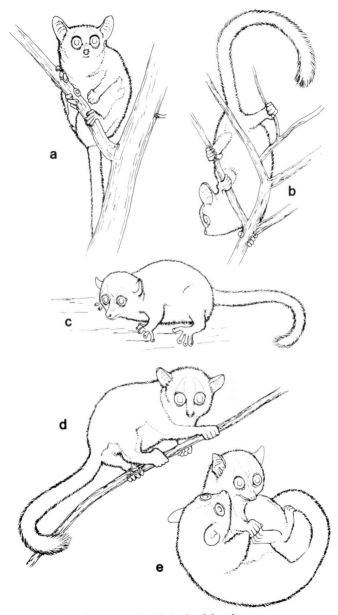

Fig. 6.2: *Microcebus* postural and behavioral drawings.

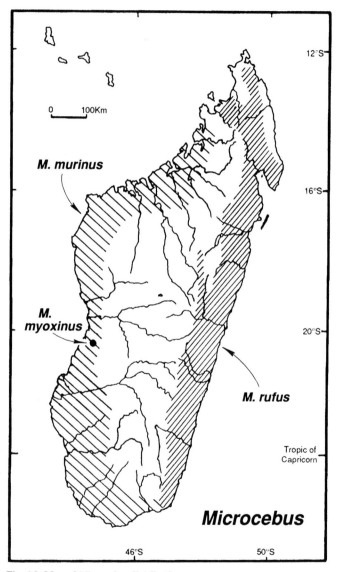

Fig. 6.3: Map of *Microcebus* distribution

Microcebus murinus   Color Plate 7
Gray Mouse Lemur   Page 324

French: Petit Microcèbe
German: Grauer Mausmaki, Maus Zwergmaki
Malagasy: Tsidy (north), Koitsiky, Titilivaha,
** Vakiandri (Morondava), Pondiky (Fort-Dauphin)**

Identification
    The gray mouse lemur has a body length of about 12.5 cm and
a tail length of about 13.5 cm, for a total length of about 24-27 cm.
Body weight varies from 50 to 90 gm seasonally. The dorsal
pelage is gray with dark hair bases and the underparts are lighter
off-white. Ears are long and fleshy in contrast to the shorter more
concealed ears of *Cheirogaleus* species and *Microcebus rufus*. In
addition, the species can be distinguished in the field from the fat-
tailed dwarf lemur, with which it is often sympatric, by its smaller
size and more active movement, and from Coquerel's dwarf
lemur (*Mirza coquereli*), which has longer ears and a considerably larger body. It is easily seen with a headlamp in all western
forests early in the night. Sightings may be rarer at the peak of the
dry season, when the animal is less active.

Geographic Range
    Microcebus murinus occurs throughout the dry deciduous
forests and spiny desert of the south and west from Fort-Dauphin
(= Tolagnaro) to at least the Sambirano River. It appears to be
replaced by *Microcebus rufus* in the Sambirano region.

Natural History
    The gray mouse lemur is reported to be more abundant in
secondary forest than in primary. In some places, it is even found
in gardens and in very degraded roadside brush and scrub habitat
(Martin, 1973; M. Pidgeon in Harcourt and Thornback, 1990),
and it also occurs in arid formations like Didiereaceae bush.
Population densities vary considerably, with 360 individuals/km^2
(Charles-Dominique and Hladik, 1971) in arid *Didierea* forest
and up to 1,300-3,600/km^2 in other western dry forests (Martin,
1972). Other estimates include those of Petter (1978) and Hladik
et al. (1980) who found 300-400/km^2 and 400/km^2, respectively,
in the Marosalaza Forest north of Morondava, and Ausilio and
Raveloarinoro (1993) who found 461-688/km^2 in the forests of

Tsimembo and 786/km^2 in the forests of Tsingy de Bemaraha.
Ganzhorn (1988), on the other hand, found much lower densities
at Ampijoroa in the Ankarafantsika Reserve, with 42 ± 19
individuals/km^2 there. Martin (1972) indicates that the species
occurs in "population nuclei," meaning that extrapolating from
small areas to much larger ones may be misleading. At some times
of the year the species can be difficult to find, especially in drier
periods.

The diet consists primarily of insects (mostly beetles), fruit,
flowers, and leaves (Martin, 1972). However, the gray mouse
lemur is also known to eat sap and gum (from *Euphorbia* and
Terminalia trees), secretions from homopteran larvae, and small
vertebrates such as frogs, geckos and chameleons (Martin, 1973;
Petter, 1978; Hladik, 1979; Barre *et al.*, 1988). As in the fat-tailed
dwarf lemur, fat is stored in the tail (though not to the same extent)
and periods of lethargy are common in the dry season. Significant
predators on *Microcebus* include the Madagascar long-eared owl,
Asio madagascariensis, and the common barn owl, *Tyto alba*
(Goodman *et al.*, 1993).

Although it is a solitary forager, the gray mouse lemur
congregates at daytime sleeping sites; composition of sleeping
groups changes seasonally. Sleeping sites are either tree holes
with leaf padding or spherical nests made of dead leaves and
concealed in heavy undergrowth. During the mating season
males are more commonly seen sleeping together with females
than at other times of the year when females and dependent
offspring sleep in groups of up to 15 (Martin, 1972). Home ranges
of females are grouped into core areas and one male's home range
can overlap those of several females. Females are considered to
be dominant over males, but this may not be a universal trait for
all populations during all seasons.

Mating is reported to take place in mid-September, with births
occurring in November after a gestation period of 59-62 days
(Martin, 1972). The infants, usually twins, are born in a leaf nest
or tree hole (Petter-Rousseaux, 1964, 1980). Offspring up to three
weeks of age are carried in their mother's mouth, but behave like
adults within two months (Petter-Rousseaux, 1964; Martin, 1972).
Females in captivity reach sexual maturity within a year but do
not appear to give birth until they are 18 months of age (Petter-
Rousseaux, 1964).

Conservation Status

The gray mouse lemur is one of the most widespread, abundant and adaptable lemur species and among the least threatened. Its small size, nocturnal habits and ability to persist and even thrive in altered habitats mean that it is likely to be with us for a long time to come. It is also found in all protected areas within its large western and southern range: the Andohahela, Ankarafantsika, Namoroka, Tsimanampetsotsa and Tsingy de Bemaraha Nature Reserves, the Analamera, Andranomena, Ankarana, Beza-Mahafaly and Cap Sainte Marie Special Reserves, and the Analabe and Berenty Private Reserves (Nicoll and Langrand, 1989; Harcourt and Thornback, 1990; Mittermeier *et al.*, 1992). However, levels of protection vary considerably in these different areas. Population figures are not available, but the species certainly numbers in the hundreds of thousands, if not millions.

Microcebus murinus breeds well in captivity, but is not as common in zoos as some of the larger, diurnal lemurs. Recent records suggest that there are more than 250 in captivity in over 50 zoos worldwide (Olney and Ellis, 1992; ISIS, 1993). The largest single colony is apparently the one at the Duke University Primate Center.

All things considered, the survival of this species is not cause for immediate concern, and it was given a *Low Priority* rating (3) in the IUCN/SSC Primate Specialist Group's *Lemurs of Madagascar: An Action Plan for their Conservation* (Mittermeier *et al.*, 1992). Using the latest IUCN Red List criteria, we place this species in the *Low Risk* category.

Where To See It

With a little patience, this species can be seen easily almost anywhere within its range. Listen for high-pitched squeaking vocalizations and look for tiny eyes shining back in the beam of your flashlight from the shrub layer up to the middle levels of the forest. However, do not expect the mouse lemur to sit in your beam for too long, as would be the case with the more lethargic *Lepilemur* or *Cheirogaleus*. Mouse lemurs are active and will move away from your beam, although you can usually follow them for short distances. Occasionally, with a little luck, it is possible to approach to within a few feet of this species and get a very good close look at it, and perhaps even a photograph using a flash. The mouse lemur, though common, is a very attractive little animal that no visitor to Madagascar's forests should miss.

Microcebus rufus
Brown or Rufous Mouse Lemur

Color Plate 7
Page 324

French: Microcèbe roux
German: Brauner Mausmaki
Malagasy: Tsidy, Tsitsidy, Tsitsihy (east, northeast)

Identification

This species is similar in size or slightly smaller than the gray mouse lemur, except that the tail is slightly longer (about 15 cm). Body weight varies from 45-80 gm (Petter *et al.*, 1977). Harcourt (1987) found an average weight of 50 gm during the southern winter at Ranomafana. Distinguishing characteristics are a brown to rufous dorsal coat color (hairs have a gray base) and smaller ears than the gray mouse lemur. Further, in the rufous mouse lemur, the nose is slightly less prominent and less sloping than in the gray mouse lemur. The species can be distinguished from the greater dwarf lemur (*Cheirogaleus major*), with which it is often sympatric, and by its much smaller size and more rapid movements.

Geographic Range

The rufous mouse lemur ranges throughout the eastern forests, including various stages of secondary growth, from Fort-Dauphin (= Tolagnaro) through the Tsaratanana Massif to the Sambirano. It occurs patchily north of Tsaratanana and seems to be absent from the more deciduous forest patches of the northern region. It is also found in a remnant patch of forest on the high plateau (Ambohitantely Special Reserve, Nicoll and Langrand, 1989).

Natural History

The rufous mouse lemur occurs at high densities throughout the eastern rain forest, including secondary forest formations, old plantations and even eucalyptus groves (though at greatly reduced densities in these introduced formations). In some sites, it is more abundant in secondary forest than in primary (Ganzhorn, 1987, 1988). Ganzhorn (1988) estimated a density of 110 ± 34 individuals/ km^2 in the Analamazaotra forest at Périnet (= Andasibe) and Petter and Petter-Rousseaux (1964) found 250-262 individuals/km^2 at Mahambo on the east coast.

M. rufus is omnivorous and feeds on fruit, flowers, insects, and very occasionally young leaves (Ganzhorn, 1988). It is usually seen feeding in shrubs and low trees, but may even range up to the tops of the tallest trees (Ganzhorn, 1988). Fat storage in the tail seems to be less important in this species than in the gray mouse lemur, probably because its rain forest food supply is less seasonal than that of the dry forests.

Social behavior is poorly known, but probably very similar to the gray mouse lemur. Both species often scent mark with urine and feces. Scent marking functions to delimit ranges and communicate with conspecifics (Tattersall, 1982). The species sleeps in tree holes and leaf nests during the day and has even been observed to use old bird nests (Martin, 1973; Pollock, 1979). No reports are available on how many animals sleep together during the day.

No data are available on mating period, gestation or litter size, although these are presumed to be similar to those of the gray mouse lemur.

Conservation Status

The brown mouse lemur, like its relative the gray mouse lemur, is one of the most widespread, abundant and adaptable lemurs in Madagascar, and is not presently threatened. Its small size, nocturnal habits, and ability to persist in altered habitats bode well for its survival. It is also known to occur within all the protected areas in its range: the Mantady, Montagne d'Ambre, Ranomafana and Verezanantsoro National Parks, the Andringitra, Andohahela, Betampona, Marojejy and Zahamena Nature Reserves, and the Ambatovaky, Ambohitantely, Analamazaotra, Anjanaharibe-Sud, Forêt d'Ambre, Lokobe, Manombo, Manongarivo and Nosy Mangabe Special Reserves (Pollock, 1984; Constable *et al.*, 1985; O'Connor *et al.*, 1986; Raxworthy and Rakotondraparany, 1988; Safford *et al.*, 1989; Nicoll and Langrand, 1989; Mittermeier *et al.*, 1992). However, levels of protection vary considerably in these different areas. Population figures are not available, but the species probably numbers in the hundreds of thousands if not millions.

Microcebus rufus apparently does well in captivity, although it has never been the focus of in-depth, conservation-oriented captive breeding efforts.

All things considered, the survival of this species is not cause for immediate concern, and it was given a *Low Priority* rating (3) in the IUCN/SSC Primate Specialist Group's *Lemurs of Mada-*

gascar: An Action Plan for their Conservation (Mittermeier *et al.*, 1992). Using the latest IUCN Red List criteria, we place this species in the *Low Risk* category.

Where To See It

As with the gray mouse lemur, this species is easy to see in the wild, and can be observed virtually anywhere within its eastern rain forest habitat. It may be slightly more difficult to locate than its western relative because of generally lower population densities and because of the denser vegetation of the rain forest region. However, it is unlikely to be missed by the patient observer.

The rufous mouse lemur can easily be observed in Périnet (= Andasibe), a few hundred meters from the Hotel de la Gare, along the main road and right around the Orchid Garden, as well as elsewhere in Périnet. It is also readily observable at Ranomafana, Mananara-Nord, Nosy Mangabe and other eastern rain forest stops on the Malagasy ecotourism circuit.

Microcebus myoxinus   **Color Plate 7**
Pygmy Mouse Lemur   **Page 324**

Identification

This species was first described over a century ago by Peters (1852), but afterwards was soon forgotten. In this century, the existence of a rufous mouse lemur living within the range of the gray mouse lemur (*Microcebus murinus*) was noted as far back as the 1960s by J.-J. Petter, who saw such animals in Ankarafantsika. In 1969, Petter and colleagues captured two rufous mouse lemurs in the private reserve of Analabe north of Morondava, and kept them in captivity for over a year (Petter *et al.*, 1971, 1977). R. D. Martin also examined these animals, and referred to them as *Microcebus murinus rufus* (Tattersall, 1982), but their taxonomic status was never clarified. In November 1985, Mittermeier photographed an individual of this species in Analabe, but did not realize what it was (this photo is shown in Plate 5a, p. 322).   In October 1992, J. Schmid and P. M. Kappeler captured a rufous-colored mouse lemur in the Kirindy forest north of Morondava, very close to Analabe where Petter first observed this animal in the 1960s, and finally described it in detail. In so doing, they realized that this animal was in fact the same described by Peters in 1852. The description that follows is based on a manuscript by Schmid and Kappeler and is reproduced here with their permission (P. M. Kappeler, pers. comm.).

The pygmy mouse lemur is much smaller and more gracile than either *M. murinus* and *M. rufus*. The fur is dense and short. The upper body is rufous-brown in color with an orange tinge, and the ventrum is creamy-white. A short dark median dorsal stripe is present, and a white stripe descends from the lower forehead to the tip of the muzzle. Its tail is more densely furred and longer, and its ears relatively shorter by comparison to the other two *Microcebus* species. This description is based upon a sample of 32 *M. myoxinus* (15 males, 17 females), which were compared with 52 *M. murinus* from the same location (Schmid and Kappeler, in press).

Available information, taken entirely from Schmid and Kappeler's work, indicates that *M. myoxinus* is the smallest of all living primates, with a mean weight of 30.6 g (range: 24.5-38 g), compared to a mean of 57.9 g (range: 39-84 g) for *M. murinus* from the same locality. The mean head-body-tail length is 198 mm (range: 178-219 mm) for *M. myoxinus* and 220.8 mm (range: 187-256 mm) for *M. murinus*. Comparable measurements for the eastern rain forest *M.rufus*, previously published, indicate that the eastern species is also larger than *M. myoxinus*. A mean weight of 50g (range: 41-70g) is given by Jenkins and Albrecht (1991) for *M. rufus* and a range of 45-80g is given by Harcourt (1987). Especially noteworthy is the much longer tail in *M. myoxinus*, both absolutely and relatively; it has a mean tail length of 136.2 mm compared to 115 mm for *M. rufus*.

An interesting behavioral difference, useful in field identification, is that this species tends to freeze when spotted, and is thus easily approachable, in contrast to *M. murinus*, which moves quickly away from the observer's flashlight beam.

This new data led Schmid and Kapeller to conclude that the pygmy mouse lemur is clearly not a subadult stage of *M. murinus* and that it is also distinct from eastern *M. rufus*, a decision with which we concur. We are therefore very pleased to add *M. myoxinus* to the species included in this book.

Although no common name exists for this species,we are suggesting "pygmy mouse lemur" in recognition that this primate is indeed the smallest of the small.

Geographic Range

M. myoxinus was "rediscovered" in the Kirindy Forest (20° 04' S, 44° 39' E), between the villages of Maronfandilia and Beroboka, some 60 km northeast of Morondava in a 10,000 ha forestry concession of the Centre de Formation Professionelle Forestière de Morondava (CFPR). It is also possible that it exists in Ankarafantsika (based on Petter's observations in the 1960's), and villagers report a second smaller mouse lemur in the Tsingy de Bemaraha Nature Reserve, which may be this animal as well. Indeed, *M. myoxinus* may occur over a large portion of the western dry deciduous forest, but much further research is needed before any further conclusions can be drawn.

Natural History

This new mouse lemur is nocturnal, occurs in western dry deciduous forest and is sympatric with *M. murinus*. Other than that, little is known of its ecology and behavior.

Conservation Status

Given the very limited information available on the pygmy mouse lemur, it is difficult to make a determination as to its conservation status at this time. Although we assume it will prove to be an adaptable species like its relatives, its very small known range leads us to assign it to the *Vulnerable?* category for the time being.

Where To See It

The only places where we know that this species can be seen are the Kirindy Forest and Analabe Private Reserve, north of Morondava.

Allocebus: Hairy-Eared Dwarf Lemur

The genus *Allocebus* contains a single species, *A. trichotis*, which was rediscovered in 1989 and is known only from a very restricted area of moist tropical forest in eastern Madagascar. First described as a species of *Cheirogaleus*, the nocturnal and little known hairy-eared dwarf lemur has subsequently been placed in its own monotypic genus (Petter-Rousseaux and Petter, 1967). Its closest affinities actually appear to be with *Microcebus rufus* (Schwartz and Tattersall, 1985), which it closely resembles in its small size and brownish-gray color.

The main external distinguishing character is the wavy hair on the ears, which gives rise to both its common and scientific names.

PHOTO BY BERNHARD MEIER

Fig. 6.4: Hairy-eared dwarf lemur (*Allocebus trichotis*)

Key to illustrations on the following page (Fig. 6.5):
- a. *Allocebus* climbing down twigs
- b. *Allocebus* standing quadrupedally on branch
- c. *Allocebus* standing bipedally
- d. *Allocebus* clinging upside-down on vertical branch
- e. *Allocebus* bridging between two supports
- f. *Allocebus* standing quadrupedally while monitoring its environment

Fig. 6.5: *Allocebus* postural and behavioral drawings (based on photographs by Bernhard Meier).

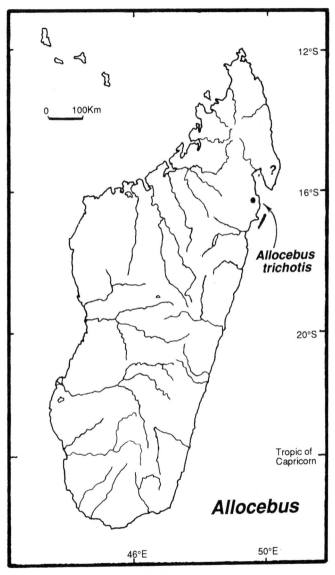

Fig. 6.6: Map of *Allocebus* distribution.

Allocebus trichotis   **Color Plate 7**
Hairy-Eared Dwarf Lemur   **Page 324**

French: Allocèbe
German: Büschelohrmaki
Malagasy: Tsidiala

Identification

A. trichotis is superficially very similar to mouse lemurs. It
has a body length of about 14 cm, a tail length of 16.8 cm, and a
body weight of about 80 g (Meier and Albignac, 1990). The most
obvious external character is the long wavy hair around the ears.
The dorsal body coat is rosy brownish-gray and the ventrum is
light gray. Distinguishing this small animal from *Microcebus
rufus* in the field is sure to be very difficult, unless one is very close
or actually has the animal in hand.

Geographic Range

The geographic range of *Allocebus* is one of the most poorly
known of all living lemurs. The only certain localities are in
lowland rain forest near Mananara, where an individual was
captured by Peyrieras in 1965 and others subsequently by Meier
and Albignac (1990). Observations were on both sides of the
Mananara River and additional localities will likely be found to
the north as well as some way inland. It is possible that the small
known range of this species is simply due to the paucity of
nocturnal surveys in the area and the difficulty of positive identification. Indeed, as we go to press, we have received reports of
possible sightings of *Allocebus* on the Masoala Peninsula as well
(P. Daniels, pers. comm.).

Natural History

Allocebus trichotis is a nocturnal species that has not yet been
studied in the wild. It is reported to jump frequently in a manner
similar to *Microcebus* (Meier and Albignac, 1989). No data is
available on its diet, but the tongue is long, which may suggest
some form of nectar-feeding. In captivity, it is reported to feed on
fruit, honey and locusts (Meier and Albignac, 1989). In May, this
species has a considerable fat deposit distributed all over its body,
not just stored in the tail as in *Cheirogaleus*. Local people do not
report seeing *Allocebus* between May and September, which
suggests that it may become torpid during that period (Meier and
Albignac, 1989). It has only been found in lowland rain forest

habitat. It sleeps in tree holes and always in large trees, though some were found at low heights by Meier and Albignac (1989). Local people report that usually two to three individuals are found in the same hole, but that as many as six may sometimes be found together.

Conservation Status

Until its rediscovery in 1989, the hairy-eared dwarf lemur was known from only five museum specimens, four of which were collected toward the end of the 19th century (Harcourt and Thornback, 1990). In 1965, Peyrieras captured the fifth specimen in the Andranomahitsy forest, near the village of Ambavala and 16 km from the town of Mananara on Madagascar's east coast (Meier and Albignac, 1989). Petter et al. (1977) failed to locate any *Allocebus* during their 1975 expedition to this forest, but Meier and Albignac were able to find it there early in 1989. While Tattersall (1982) suggests that *Allocebus* once occurred widely in Madagascar's eastern humid forests, Meier and Albignac (1989) believe that its current distribution is restricted and patchy. It is only known to occur in the Mananara-Nord Biosphere Reserve, outside the boundaries of the newly-created Verezanantsoro National Park (Mittermeier et al., 1992). No population figures are available, but a reasonable order of magnitude estimate would be 100-1,000.

Although protected somewhat by its small size and nocturnal habits, *Allocebus* is gravely threatened by the continued destruction of lowland rain forest throughout its restricted range and is not known to occur in any fully protected area. Therefore, it was given the *Highest Priority* rating (7) in the IUCN/SSC Primate Specialist Group's *Lemurs of Madagascar: An Action Plan for their Conservation* (Mittermeier et al., 1992). Using the latest IUCN Red List criteria, we place this species in the *Critically Endangered* category.

Where To See It

The forest southwest of Mananara is the only place where there is some chance of seeing this species in the wild. However, it is very difficult to obtain positive sightings and a search for this species is probably best left to the seasoned lemur watcher.

If you do happen to get a confirmed sighting, please report it immediately to the authors of this book.

Mirza: Coquerel's Dwarf Lemur

The genus *Mirza* contains a single species, *M. coquereli*, a
medium-sized, omnivorous, nocturnal lemur found in two major
areas of Madagascar's western dry deciduous forests. At approximately 300 gm, Coquerel's dwarf lemur is more than three times
the size of the *Microcebus* species, with which it was once lumped
together in the genus *Microcebus* (Petter *et al.*, 1977).   Tattersall
(1982) gives a justification for recognizing *Mirza coquereli* as a
distinct genus and separating it from *Microcebus* and other
cheirogaleids, citing both dental characters and behavior.

Coat color is rich brown or gray brown, and the ears are large
and very distinctive. The favored mode of locomotion is rapid
quadrupedal running, a feature in which it is much closer to the
small *Microcebus* and distinct from the slow-moving *Cheirogaleus.*

Key to illustrations on the following page (Fig. 6.7):
      a. *Mirza* resting on large branch
      b. *Mirza* preparing to leap
      c. *Mirza* in upside-down clinging posture
      d. Close-up of the face of *Mirza* (note the large ears)
      e. *Mirza* clinging sideways on vertical branch while
           monitoring its environment
      f. *Mirza* crouched on branch monitoring its environment
      g. *Mirza* in sitting posture

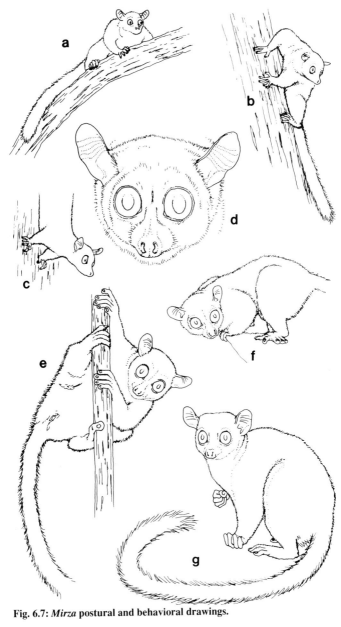

Fig. 6.7: *Mirza* postural and behavioral drawings.

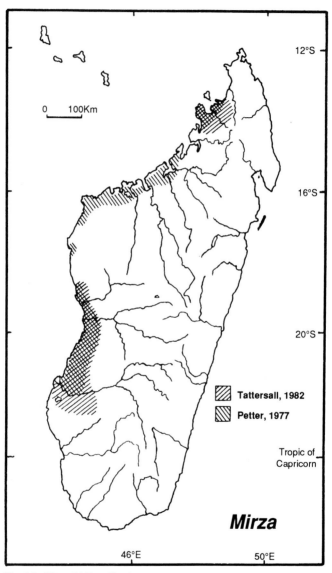

0   100Km

12°S

16°S

20°S

▨ Tattersall, 1982

▧ Petter, 1977

Tropic of
Capricorn

Mirza

46°E   50°E

Fig. 6.8: Map of *Mirza* distribution.

Mirza coquereli   Color Plate 7
Coquerel's Dwarf Lemur   Page 324

French: Microcèbe de Coquerel
Malagasy: Tsiba, Tilitilivaha, Siba (Morondava), Setohy, Fitily (north of Ambanja)

Identification

This animal is a medium-small nocturnal lemur with a long body and a long tail. Head and body length is 20 cm or more, and tail length is about 33 cm, for a total length of 50-55 cm. Body weight is about 300 g (Pagès, 1978), more than three times the *Microcebus* species. Hair is dark gray basally and the dorsal coat is rich brown or gray brown; rose or yellow shades are often found as well. Ventrally, the gray base is visible beneath rusty or yellow tips. The tail is thin and has long hair, giving it a slightly "bushy" appearance, and is dark towards the tip. Movement is rapid quadrupedal running, which easily distinguishes this species from the slower and more deliberate movement of similar-sized *Cheirogaleus* species. The large, evident ears also serve to distinguish *Mirza* from *Cheirogaleus*, which has concealed ears, and it can be distinguished from *Microcebus* species by its size. In areas like Analabe, north of Morondava, it is sympatric with *Phaner*, another active, medium-sized nocturnal species. However, it can be distinguished from *Phaner* by its larger ears and the absence of the forked pattern on the head.

Geographic Range

Coquerel's dwarf lemur has a discontinuous distribution in two major areas of the western dry deciduous forests. One is from Ankazoabo (just south of the Mangoky River) north to Antsalova and Belo-sur-Tsiribihina, and the other is further north in the Sambirano region (the Ampasindava Peninsula and the Ambanja area). Its occurrence between these two areas has been suggested by Petter *et al.* (1977) and it is likely that populations of *Mirza* still occur in this intermediate region. It has also been seen as far south as the north bank of the Onilahy River, about 40 km east of the coast (M. Pidgeon and M. Nicoll, in Harcourt and Thornback, 1990). The map in Fig. 6.8 shows its known distribution, differing somewhat in Petter *et al.* (1977) and Tattersall (1982), and the likely intermediate distribution suggested by Petter *et al.* (1977).

Natural History

Most information on the natural history of *M. coquereli* comes from studies in the dry, deciduous Marosalaza forest near Analabe, north of Morondava.   Population densities reported from this forested region range from 30 individuals/km^2 (Hladik *et al.*, 1980) to 50/km^2 (Petter *et al.*, 1971) but, in the latter study, reached as high as 210/km^2 in forests running along rivers.   In secondary forests near Ambanja, dominated by cashew nut trees (*Anacardium occidentale*), Andrianarivo (1981) recorded densities as high as 385/km^2, while Ausilio and Raveloarinoro(1993) recorded densities of 100/km^2 in the forests of Tsimembo.

Home ranges overlap extensively and all individuals studied seem to make heavier use of smaller core areas, which they defend aggressively (Pagès, 1978, 1980). Male ranges tend to overlap those of several females as well as those of other males. Males will interact positively (grooming, contact calling) with females when they make contact, and pairs travel together for short periods even during the dry season.

Coquerel's dwarf lemur is nocturnal and spends its day in a spherical nest, usually placed 2-10 m high in the fork of a large branch or among dense lianas, and   constructed of interlaced lianas, branches and leaves (Petter *et al.*, 1971; Pagès, 1980; Andrianarivo, 1981).   The occupancy of nests seems to vary. Pagès (1980) found only females and their offspring sharing nests, while Andrianarivo (1981) found nests with adult males, females and young, as well as bunches of nests clustered in "villages"about one hectare in size and inhabited by six to ten individuals. Animals leave the nest around dusk, at which time they may begin feeding or self-grooming, or continue resting. During the latter half of the night, they are more likely to be involved in social activities (Pagès, 1978, 1980).

M. coquereli feeds on a variety of foods including fruits, flowers, buds, gums, insects, insect secretions, spiders, frogs, chameleons and small birds (Pagès, 1980; Andrianarivo, 1981). Two of the most important food sources during the dry season (June-July) seems to be the secretions of cochineal and homopteran larvae (Pagès, 1980) and cashew fruits (Andrianarivo, 1981).

Mating takes place in the southern spring (October) and gestation lasts about three months (Petter-Rousseaux, 1980). Infants leave the nest after one month and are first carried in their mother's mouth. Eventually, they forage alone while maintaining vocal contact with the mother (Pagès, 1980).

Conservation Status

The status of *Mirza coquereli* is difficult to assess at this point in time. It seems adaptable and can survive, or even do well, in secondary forest. It occurs in fairly high densities in some parts of its range. It is also a small nocturnal animal that is less evident than its diurnal relatives. However, it is found in the western dry deciduous forest, which is becoming increasingly fragmented. Although there is no data on hunting of this species and it does not appear to be a special target of hunters, it is almost certainly taken for food along with *Cheirogaleus medius* and *Lepilemur* spp. in western Madagascar.

This species is found in the Tsingy de Bemaraha Nature Reserve, the Andranomena Special Reserve and the Analabe Private Reserve (Nicoll and Langrand, 1989; Harcourt and Thornback, 1990; Mittermeier *et al.*, 1992), which is a small list compared to more abundant nocturnal species like *Cheirogaleus* and *Microcebus*. There are no population figures available, but a reasonable order of magnitude estimate would be 10,000-100,000 (Mittermeier *et al.*, 1992). This species breeds well in captivity, although it is not widely kept. Of about 60 animals recently recorded from 13 institutions, more than a third were at the Duke University Primate Center (Olney and Ellis, 1992; ISIS, 1993).

Mirza coquereli was given a *High Priority* rating (5) in the IUCN/SSC Primate Specialist Group's *Lemurs of Madagascar: An Action Plan for their Conservation* (Mittermeier *et al.*, 1992). Using the latest IUCN Red List criteria, we place this species in the *Vulnerable* category.

Where To See It

Coquerel's dwarf lemur is easily seen in secondary forests near Ambanja in the northwest, especially those growing in abandoned cashew (*mahabibo*) orchards and can also be seen in the Analabe Private Reserve north of Morondava, where it is sympatric with four other nocturnal species (*Microcebus murinus, Cheirogaleus medius, Lepilemur ruficaudatus* and *Phaner furcifer*). Indeed, Analabe may be the best site in all of Madagascar for observing nocturnal lemurs.

Cheirogaleus: Dwarf Lemurs

The genus *Cheirogaleus* contains two known species, the greater dwarf lemur, *Cheirogaleus major*, and the fat-tailed dwarf lemur, *Cheirogaleus medius*. There is significant variation in pelage coloration in each species, and this variation remains poorly understood both from a geographic and a taxonomic perspective.

The dwarf lemurs are small nocturnal animals ranging in weight from 150-600 g. Body weight varies widely across seasons. Dwarf lemurs walk quadrupedally along branches at all levels of the forest and tend to jump less and move much more slowly than the closely related mouse lemurs. They are easily distinguishable from mouse lemurs in that both species of dwarf lemur have dark rings around the eyes and a muzzle-like pink nose, and are considerably larger. Furthermore, the anus is located a short distance along the tail, a feature that can be observed only at close range or if the animal is in hand. The two species of *Cheirogaleus* are notable for the seasonal storage of fat in the tail and for their seasonal torpor in the southern winter.

This genus is found throughout the island, with the two species generally being separated geographically between the eastern rain forest and the western dry forest. In the Sambirano and north of the Tsaratanana Massif, the two species occur in adjacent forests and possibly even in the same forests.

Key to illustrations on the following page (Fig. 6.9):
   a. *Cheirogaleus* standing quadrupedally
   b. *Cheirogaleus* standing on twigs
   c. *Cheirogaleus* clinging sideways to branch while
          monitoring its environment
   d. *Cheirogaleus* feeding
   e. *Cheirogaleus* clinging to branches while monitoring its
          environment

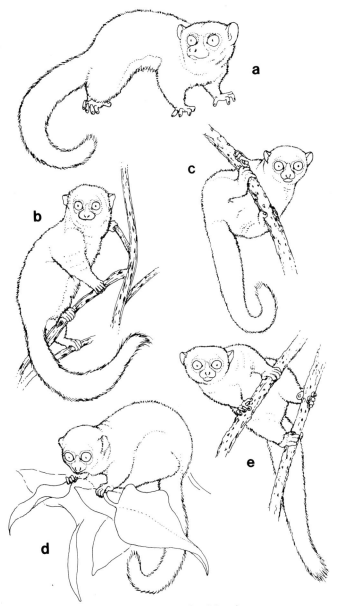

Fig. 6.9: *Cheirogaleus* postural and behavioral drawings.

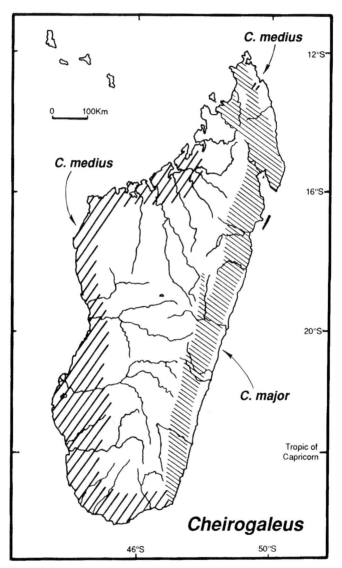

Fig. 6.10: Map of *Cheirogaleus* distribution.

Cheirogaleus major
Greater Dwarf Lemur

Plate 8
Page 325

French: Grand Cheirogale
German: Grosser Fettschwanzmaki
Malagasy: Tsitsihy, Tsidy, Hataka

Identification

This is the larger of the two dwarf lemurs and ranges in weight from 350-600 g. The head and body length is about 25 cm and tail length is slightly longer (about 27.5 cm), for a total length of 50-55 cm. Seasonal swelling of the tail is less notable than in the fat-tailed dwarf lemur. The dorsal pelage is dense and varies from gray-brown to reddish-brown, with the latter more common to the north. The underside is paler. There are dark rings around the eyes, and a light patch is thus highlighted between the eyes. The nose is fleshy and appears relatively larger than that of the fat-tailed dwarf lemur.

In the field, this species is most likely to be confused with *Lepilemur* or *Avahi*, which are similar in size and also usually freeze when first sighted. However, these two genera adopt a more vertical posture, and *Lepilemur* has large, readily visible ears compared to the smaller ears of *Cheirogaleus*. *Cheirogaleus* moves slowly and quadrupedally, whereas the other two genera are more likely to leap, especially *Avahi*. The greater dwarf lemur is easily distinguished from *Microcebus* by its larger size and slower movements, and it does not occur sympatrically with *Mirza*. Confusion with *Phaner* is also unlikely, since *Phaner* moves rapidly, vocalizes loudly and has the very distinctive forked pattern on its more elongate face.

Geographic Range

This species is found throughout the entire eastern rain forest, the Tsaratanana Massif and the Sambirano region, as well as on the Montagne d'Ambre and near Vohémar. It occurs at all altitudes, but in more seasonally dry areas (Montagne d'Ambre, Vohémar) it prefers moist forests found on larger hills. It is absent from forests that are primarily deciduous. All dwarf lemurs are least active during the southern winter (July to September), and are much more difficult to find at this time (Petter *et al.*, 1977).

Natural History

The greater dwarf lemur is a dietary generalist which has been seen to feed on fruit, flowers, young leaves, and insects. It accepts moderate levels of tannins and alkaloids in its diet (Ganzhorn, 1988), a trait shared with the widespread brown lemurs (*Eulemur fulvus* sspp.). It forages alone and sleeps in small groups during the day. The social behavior of the greater dwarf lemur is poorly understood. It is not known if this species hibernates like the fat-tailed dwarf lemur, but it is, in any case, less active during the southern winter.

Cheirogaleus major can be seen at high densities in some areas, with 75-110/km^2 being reported from Mahambo (Petter and Petter-Rousseaux, 1964) and 68 ± 38/km^2 in the Analamazao-tra forest at Périnet (= Andasibe) (Harcourt and Thornback, 1990).

The gestation period of *C. major* is 70 days and the infants are born in January during the Malagasy summer (Petter and Petter-Rousseaux, 1964). A litter of two to three offspring is usually produced (Petter *et al.*, 1977). Infants initially cannot cling to the mother and are carried in the mouth when necessary (Petter and Petter-Rousseaux, 1964). A month after birth the infants are able to follow the mother, and they start eating fruit at about 25 days. Lactation lasts about 15 months (Petter and Petter-Rousseaux, 1964).

Conservation Status

This species is one of the least endangered of the Malagasy lemurs. It has a large range, and its small size and nocturnal habits make it less evident to hunters than its larger diurnal relatives. Like all of the Malagasy lemurs, it is threatened by forest destruction since it cannot live outside the forest environment, but it can persist in secondary or degraded forest situations. It is hunted for food over much of its range, being caught in traps or located during the day by people poking sticks into sleeping holes (Petter *et al.*, 1977; E. Simons, pers. comm.).

The greater dwarf lemur occurs in a large number of protected areas: the Mantady, Montagne d'Ambre, Ranomafana and Verezanantsoro National Parks, the Andohahela, Betampona, Marojejy, Tsaratanana and Zahamena Nature Reserves, and the Ambatovaky, Anjanaharibe-Sud, Analamazaotra, Forêt d'Ambre, Manongarivo and Nosy Mangabe Special Reserves (Andriamampianina and Peyrieras, 1972; Constable *et al.*, 1985; O'Connor *et al.*, 1986; Raxworthy and Rakotondraparany, 1988; Nicoll and Langrand, 1989; Harcourt and Thornback, 1990; Mittermeier *et al.,* 1992). However, levels of protection vary considerably in these different areas. Population figures are not available, but a reasonable order of magnitude estimate would be >100,000 (Mittermeier *et al.,* 1992).

The species is considered difficult to breed in captivity, although it has bred on several occasions (Petter *et al.,* 1977). At the present time, Zoo Ivoloina in Madagascar has a pair and the Duke Primate Center a single individual (ISIS, 1993).

All things considered, the survival of this species is not cause for immediate concern, and it was given a *Low Priority* rating (3) in the IUCN/SSC Primate Specialist Group's *Lemurs of Madagascar: An Action Plan for their Conservation* (Mittermeier *et al.,* 1992). Using the latest IUCN Red List criteria, we place this species in the *Low Risk* category.

Where To See It

The greater dwarf lemur can be found in all the protected areas mentioned above and in many other forests as well. It can be seen easily in Périnet (=Andasibe) and in Ranomafana National Park, but only during the wet season. The main road from the Hotel de la Gare at Périnet is an especially good place to see this species in the wet season. Sightings during the dry season are difficult because of the animal's torpor. As with most other nocturnal species, the greater dwarf lemur is most easily found by using a flashlight or headlamp to locate eye shine. Most sightings are in the understory and lower to middle levels of the canopy, but the species also can be seen high up in the canopy as well.

Cheirogaleus medius   **Color Plate 8**
Fat-Tailed Dwarf Lemur   **Page 325**

French: Petit Cheirogale
German: Mittlerer Fettschwanzmaki
Malagasy: Matavirambo (northwest), Kely Be-ohy
**   (Morondava region), Tsidy, Tsidihy (far**
**   south)**

Identification

This species is smaller than the greater dwarf lemur, with a
head and body length of about 20 cm and a similar tail length, for
a total length of 40-50 cm. Its weight varies greatly seasonally,
ranging from an average of 142 g in November (beginning of the
rainy season) to 217 g in March when the rains end (Hladik *et al.*,
1980). Weights of up to 300 g have been reported in captivity.
The body pelage is gray with darker bases to hairs; the undersides
are lighter, and the throat varies from light brown to white. Unlike
the greater dwarf lemur, the lighter undersides can easily be seen
in side view between the front leg and belly.

The fat-tailed dwarf lemur has at times been divided into two
subspecies, *C. m. medius* and *C. m. samati*. However, Petter and
Petter (1971), Petter *et al.* (1977), and Tattersall (1982) consider
this to be unwarranted, and we follow their decision here.

In the field, this species is most likely to be confused with
Lepilemur or *Mirza,* and possibly *Microcebus*. It can be distinguished from *Lepilemur* by its distinctive lighter underparts, by
the form of its tail, and by body posture and movement, *Lepilemur*
being more likely to adopt a vertical posture and to leap, whereas
Cheirogaleus walks slowly and quadrupedally. *Mirza* has large
distinctive ears and moves rapidly and constantly. *Microcebus*
also has visible ears, moves more than *Cheirogaleus,* and is much
smaller. Confusion with *Phaner* is unlikely, since *Phaner* moves
constantly, vocalizes loudly and has the distinct forked pattern on
its more elongate face.

Geographic Range

C. medius is found throughout the west and south, westwards
from near Fort-Dauphin (= Tolagnaro) in the southeast, then
northwards to the Sambirano region. It is also found in the north
near Ambilobe (museum specimen), the Ankarana Special Re-

serve (Nicoll and Langrand, 1989), and Daraina (Vohémar), and may occur in other areas north of the Tsaratanana Massif.

Natural History

The fat-tailed dwarf lemur is found over a large area of the dry deciduous forests common in western and southern Madagascar, and can live in primary forest, older secondary forest and also gallery forest of the southern spiny desert. It has been counted at densities ranging from 20 to 400 individuals/km^2 (Hladik *et al.*, 1980), and has a range of up to 4 ha, sometimes with significant range overlap. This lemur is a solitary forager and has a diverse diet consisting primarily of fruit and flowers (nectar), but also including insects and small vertebrates (*e.g.*, the skin of a chameleon was found in one fecal sample) (Hladik, 1979; Hladik *et al.*, 1980).

The animal sleeps in tree holes during the day, with up to five individuals being found in one hole (Petter, 1978; Hladik, 1979; Hladik *et al.*, 1980). Fat is stored in the tail during the wet season and, from the beginning of the dry period (sometimes as early as March), this animal will hibernate for up to six months. It becomes active again just prior to the start of the wet season, usually around November.

Mating occurs in November, births in January, and juveniles remain active later in the dry season than do adults (Hladik *et al.*, 1980). The gestation period is 61-64 days, with litter size ranging from one to four, but twins are the most common (Foerg, 1982). Captive animals reach adult weight between 14 and 16 weeks of age and attain sexual maturity in one year (Foerg, 1982).

Conservation Status

C. medius is one of the least endangered of the Malagasy lemurs. It has a large geographic range and can occur in secondary forest at quite high densities. Furthermore, its small size, nocturnal habits and the fact that it goes into torpor for at least half the year make it much less evident than its diurnal and even some of its nocturnal relatives. Like all Malagasy lemurs, it is threatened by forest destruction and is captured for food over much of its range, either in traps or by being removed from its sleeping holes.

This species occurs in a number of protected areas: the Andohahela and Ankarafantsika Nature Reserves, the Andranomena, Ankarana and Beza-Mahafaly Special Reserves, and the Analabe and Berenty Private Reserves (Andriamampianina, 1981; O'Connor *et al.*, 1986, 1987; Nicoll and Langrand, 1989; Harcourt and Thornback, 1990; Hawkins *et al.*, 1990; Mittermeier *et al.*, 1992), although levels of protection vary considerably in these different areas. No population figures are available, but a reasonable order of magnitude estimate would be >100,000 (Mittermeier *et al.*, 1992).

This species breeds well in captivity. Over 160 individuals are currently held by at least two dozen zoos worldwide (Olney and Ellis, 1992; ISIS, 1993).

All things considered, the survival of the fat-tailed dwarf lemur is not cause for immediate concern and it was given a *Low Priority* rating (3) in the IUCN/SSC Primate Specialist Group's *Lemurs of Madagascar: An Action Plan for their Conservation* (Mittermeier *et al.*, 1992). Using the latest IUCN Red List criteria, we place this species in the *Low Risk* category.

Where To See It

The fat-tailed dwarf lemur can be seen in many places throughout its range, but usually only in the wet season. During the southern winter (June-September) this species hibernates. Particularly good sites for seeing the fat-tailed dwarf lemur include the Analabe Private Reserve, north of Morondava, and the dry forest near Daraina in the northwest, where high numbers exist. It also occurs in the Berenty Reserve west of Fort-Dauphin (= Tolagnaro), but it is more difficult to see there than at many other sites. As with other nocturnal species, it is best found using a flashlight or headlamp to locate its eye shine.

Phaner: Fork-Marked Lemurs

The genus *Phaner* contains one known species, *Phaner furcifer*, with four subspecies. From the time of its description by Blainville (as *Lemur furcifer*) in 1839 up until quite recently, the fork-marked lemur was considered to be a single monotypic species. However, it has long been known that *Phaner* is distributed in a series of isolated populations scattered around the periphery of Madagascar. In 1991, Groves and Tattersall pointed out that distinctions in coloration and internal anatomy exist between these populations, and that differentiation is warranted at least at the subspecific level. We provisionally recognize the taxonomic arrangement proposed by Groves and Tattersall (1991), and follow it below.

The upper parts of all subspecies are brown in color, the most striking feature being that from which the common name is derived, a dark line that runs along the center of the back, extending to the crown of the head where it forks, with a branch leading to each eye. The eyes are circled by rings of the same dark color, which may also extend some distance down the muzzle.

These are relatively large-bodied cheirogaleid lemurs with head-body lengths ranging from 22.7-28.5 cm and tail lengths from 28.5-37.0 cm for 12 specimens of two subspecies (*P. f. pallescens* and *P. f. electromontis*) (Tattersall, 1982). Body weight is 350-500 g (Petter *et al.*, 1977). They are also very vocal; indeed, their very loud, striking vocalizations readily indicate their presence and make them easy to identify. Most characteristic are various short, relatively high-pitched cries that are uttered in bursts. Locomotion is also highly characteristic. Fork-marked lemurs tend to run rapidly along horizontal tree branches, jumping from one to the next without pausing. When not moving their bodies, they will often bob their heads up and down and sideways, making for a very distinctive pattern of eye-shine in the observer's flashlight beam.

Distinct populations not yet named or properly characterized are found in Parcel 2 of the Andohahela Reserve (No. 11) in the far south (M. Pidgeon, in Harcourt and Thornback, 1990), and also in the region of Vohémar in the east, where the animal is easily seen near Daraina. *Phaner* is also possibly present on the Tsaratanana Massif, and to the north and east of Bombetoka Bay in the west.

PHOTO BY RUSSELL A. MITTERMEIER

Fig. 6.11: Fork-marked lemur (*Phaner furcifer pallescens*) from Analabe, southwestern Madagascar.

Key to illustrations on the following page (Fig. 6.12):
- **a.** *Phaner* clinging sideways to vertical branch
- **b.** *Phaner* in characteristic upside-down vertical clinging posture on tree trunk
- **c.** *Phaner* walking quadrupedally on branch
- **d.** *Phaner* eating gum on the trunk of *taly* tree
- **e.** *Phaner* clinging vertically to branch
- **f.** *Phaner* clinging sideways to branch
- **g.** *Phaner* clinging sideways to trunk of tree
- **h.** Close-up of *Phaner's* specialized lower dentition, the "tooth comb" used to gouge holes and feed upon tree exudates
- **i.** *Phaner* in upside-down vertical clinging posture feeding on tree exudates

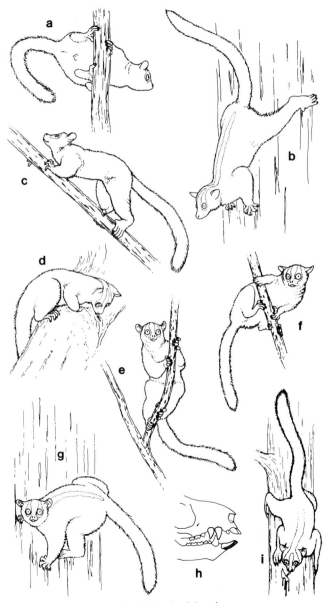

Fig. 6.12: *Phaner* postural and behavioral drawings.

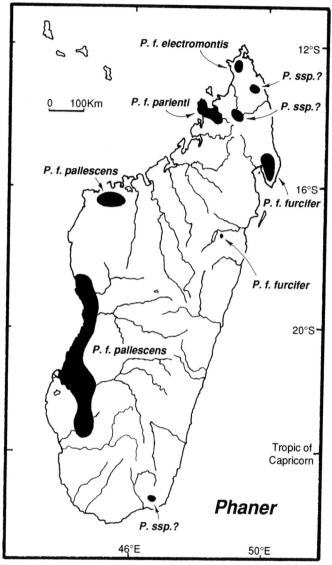

P. f. electromontis

P. ssp.?

P. ssp.?

P. f. parienti

0   100Km

P. f. pallescens

12°S

16°S

P. f. furcifer

P. f. furcifer

20°S

P. f. pallescens

Tropic of
Capricorn

Phaner

P. ssp.?

46°E   50°E

Fig. 6.13: **Map of** *Phaner* **distribution.**

Phaner furcifer furcifer   **Color Plate 9**
Eastern Fork-Marked Lemur   **Page 326**

French: Phaner Oriental, Lémurien à Fourche
          Oriental, Phaner à Fourche Oriental
German: Gabelstreifenmaki
Malagasy: Tanta, Tantaraolana

Identification
    This is the darkest brown in coloration of all *Phaner furcifer*
subspecies, and apparently relatively large-bodied. The fork
mark on the head is exceptionally well expressed and clear; the
dorsal stripe does not reach the base of the tail. Pelage is long and
dense. The best guide to identification of *Phaner* subspecies in
the field is locality.

Geographic Range
    This subspecies occurs on the Masoala Peninsula of northeast-
ern Madagascar, and possibly adjacent areas of the mainland.
Fork-marked lemurs have recently been reported from the Betampona and Zahamena Nature Reserves (Katz, 1990; Daniels, 1991),
and these sightings may represent *P. f. furcifer*, or perhaps a new
taxon.

Natural History
    P. f. furcifer is found in the rain forest of the Masoala
Peninsula, and remains unstudied.

Conservation Status
    This subspecies has a very restricted habitat, and could be in
trouble. Plans are underway to establish a protected area on the
Masoala Peninsula, which should give it some protection. How-
ever, at this point, it is not known to occur in any protected areas.
    This subspecies was given a *High Priority* rating (5) in the
IUCN/SSC Primate Specialist Group's *Lemurs of Madagascar:
An Action Plan for their Conservation* (Mittermeier *et al.*, 1992).
No population figures are available, but a reasonable order of
magnitude estimate would be 1,000-10,000. Using the latest
IUCN Red List criteria, we place this subspecies in the *Vulnerable*
category.

Where To See It
    This subspecies is most easily seen near Iaraka in the proposed
Masoala Reserve.

Phaner furcifer pallescens
Pale Fork-Marked Lemur

Color Plate 9
Page 326

**French: Phaner Occidental, Lémurien à Fourche
        Occidental
German: Gabelstreifenmaki
Malagasy: Tanta, Tantaraolana, Vakivoho**

Identification
Lightest in coloration of all *Phaner* (upper parts gray-fawn, with silvery tint), and possibly also the smallest, although available size data are inconclusive. Eleven specimens of this subspecies (four from Berobokay, five from Tabiky, two from Namoroka) ranged in head-body length from 22.7-28.5 cm, and in tail length from 28.5-37.0 cm (Tattersall, 1982). The fork and dorsal stripe are relatively poorly defined. As with all *Phaner*, the best guide to which subspecies is being observed is locality.

Geographic Range
Western Madagascar, in a narrow strip from just south of the Fiherenana River (Lambomakandro Forest) north to the Tsiribihina River. North of this, another isolate occurs in the area from the Namoroka Reserve to Soalala. This more northerly population is only provisionally referred to *P. f. pallescens* by Groves and Tattersall (1991), and may in fact be distinct.

Natural History
Phaner f. pallescens is the only fork-marked lemur subspecies to have been studied at all in the field, notably by Petter *et al.* (1975) in the dry deciduous Marosalaza forest near Morondava. Throughout much of the year, tree gum (especially from *Terminalia* trees) provides a substantial proportion of the diet, but insects, sap, buds, flowers and the exudates of insect colonies (particularly from the family Machaerotidae) are also consumed (Charles-Dominique and Petter, 1980). The dentition of *Phaner* includes a highly specialized dental comb consisting of an inclined row of lower incisor teeth, which is used to gouge holes in trees and stimulate the flow of gums and sap.

Ausilio and Raveloarinoro (1993) found population densities of 300-400/km^2 in the forests of Tsimembo. In the Marosalaza forest, *Phaner* spends the day sleeping in holes in large trees such as baobabs (*Adansonia* spp.) or sometimes in the abandoned nests of *Mirza coquereli* (Petter *et al.*, 1971, 1975). Certain males and females were found to sleep together during the day, to share ranges and to maintain vocal contact throughout most of the night (Charles-Dominique and Petter, 1980). In another case, a male with a range of 3.8 ha consorted with two females in adjacent and more or less exclusive ranges of about 4 ha each. Allogrooming was a regular activity between males, females and juveniles (Charles-Dominique and Petter, 1980).

Activity is greatest during the first hour following nightfall (the best time to see these highly vocal creatures), and much time spent at the edge of the range is devoted to vocalization between neighbors.

Mating occurs in June and a single infant is born in November or December. Young infants are kept in nests. When first taken from the tree hole by their mother, they are carried in her mouth, and then eventually ride upon her back (Petter *et al.*, 1971, 1975; Charles-Dominique and Petter, 1980).

Conservation Status

This subspecies has the largest range of the four subspecies, but even its range is quite limited and divided into two distinct portions of western dry deciduous forest, a habitat that is becoming increasingly reduced and fragmented. *P.f. pallescens* occurs in the Tsingy de Bemaraha Nature Reserve, the Andranomena Special Reserve, the Analabe Private Reserve (Nicoll and Langrand, 1989; Harcourt and Thornback, 1990; Mittermeier *et al.*, 1992) and the forests of Kirindy (a Swiss logging concession north of Morondava where hunting and logging are controlled). There are no population figures available, but a reasonable order of magnitude estimate would be 1,000-10,000 (Mittermeier *et al.*, 1992).

P. f. pallescens was given a *High Priority* rating (5) in the IUCN/SSC Primate Specialist Group's *Lemurs of Madagascar: An Action Plan for their Conservation* (Mittermeier *et al.*, 1992). Using the latest IUCN Red List criteria, we place this subspecies in the *Vulnerable* category.

Where To See It

The pale fork-marked lemur is most easily seen in the Analabe Private Reserve north of Morondava, where it is quite common. Although sympatric with four other nocturnal species in this reserve, it is easy to distinguish because of its loud vocalizations, rapid movements, and distinct fork-marked pattern. The bobbing of the head back and forth in the light of the flashlight is especially distinctive. Though not always evident, it is one of the best distinguishing behaviors for *Phaner*.

Phaner furcifer parienti   Color Plate 9
Pariente's Fork-Marked Lemur   Page 326

French: Phaner de Pariente, Lémurien à Fourche de Pariente
German: Gabelstreifenmaki
Malagasy: Tanta, Tantaraolana

Identification
This subspecies is intermediate in coloration between the paler *P. f. pallescens* to the south and the darker *P. f. electromontis* to the north. The head fork is well defined, and the dorsal stripe extends to rump. As with other *Phaner*, the best indication of which subspecies is being observed is locality.

Geographic Range
P. f. parienti occurs in the Sambirano region of northwest Madagascar south of Ambanja, including the Ampasindava Peninsula and extending south to the Andranomalaza River.

Natural History
P. f. parienti has not been studied in the wild.

Conservation Status
This subspecies is very restricted in range. It occurs in the Manongarivo and Tsaratanana Special Reserves (Raxworthy and Rakotodraparany, 1988; Nicoll and Langrand, 1989; Hawkins *et al.*, 1990). There are no population figures available, but a reasonable order of magnitude estimate would be 1,000-10,000.

P. f. parienti was given a *High Priority* rating (5) in the IUCN/SSC Primate Specialist Group's *Lemurs of Madagascar: An Action Plan for their Conservation* (Mittermeier *et al.*, 1992). Using the latest IUCN Red List criteria, we place this subspecies in the *Vulnerable* category.

Where To See It
Pariente's fork-marked lemur can most readily be seen in the forests of Beraty, west of Route National 6 about 45 km south of Ambanja. Anywhere that tall forest remains on the Ampasindava Peninsula is also a good bet.

Phaner furcifer electromontis   Color Plate 9
Amber Mountain Fork-Marked   **Page 326**
    Lemur

French: Phaner de la Montagne d'Ambre, Lémurien à
        Fourche de la Montagne d'Ambre
German: Gabelstreifenmaki
Malagasy: Tanta, Tantaraolana

Identification

The Amber Mountain fork-marked lemur is relatively large in body size, with measurements for one individual being head-body length 24.8 cm and tail length 36.5 cm. Its upper body parts are light in coloration, and the thick black dorsal stripe is well defined, extending back to the rump. As with all *Phaner*, the best indication of which subspecies is being observed is locality.

Geographic Range

This subspecies is found in the Montagne d'Ambre and its immediate vicinity in northern Madagascar, and probably in the forests surrounding Daraina.

Natural History

P. f. electromontis has not been studied in the wild.

Conservation Status

This subspecies has the smallest range of the four recognized forms of *Phaner* (although the population from the Andohahela Nature Reserve in the far south, if distinct, would have a much smaller one). Fortunately, most, if not all, of its range is within the Montagne d'Ambre complex of protected areas (Nicoll and Langrand, 1989; Harcourt and Thornback, 1990; Mittermeier *et al.*, 1992), specifically the Montagne d'Ambre National Park, and the Ankarana and Forêt d'Ambre Special Reserves, which are located in one of the better protected regions of Madagascar. There are no population figures available, but a reasonable order of magnitude estimate would be 1,000-10,000.

P. f. electromontis was given a *High Priority* rating (5) in the IUCN/SSC Primate Specialist Group's *Lemurs of Madagascar: An Action Plan for their Conservation* (Mittermeier *et al.*, 1992). Using the latest IUCN Red List criteria, we place this subspecies in the *Vulnerable* category.

Where To See It

This subspecies is best seen in the Forêt d'Ambre Special
Reserve within the Montagne d'Ambre complex. It is also seen
at the forestry station (Les Rousettes) and botanical garden of the
Montagne d'Ambre National Park.   Although native trees are
very tall and good viewing can be difficult, *P. f. electromontis* is
often seen in introduced tree species (*e.g.*, *Araucaria* spp. and
Eucalyptus spp.).

FAMILY MEGALADAPIDAE

Among the living lemurs, this family contains only the widely distributed, medium-sized, nocturnal genus *Lepilemur*. It is quite closely related to the very large extinct lemur genus *Megaladapis*, at least one of whose three species survived up to a thousand years ago, or perhaps even more recently. There are, however, sufficient differences between *Lepilemur* and *Megaladapis* for the two genera to be classified into separate subfamilies, the extant species falling into the subfamily Lepilemurinae.

The single nocturnal genus *Lepilemur* has a wide distribution within Madagascar that, among nocturnal lemurs, is rivalled only by the genera *Microcebus* and *Cheirogaleus*. Many local variants exist, and the diversity of species and subspecies within *Lepilemur* may eventually turn out to rival that of the more diurnal genus *Eulemur*.

Lepilemur: Sportive Lemurs, Weasel Lemurs

This is a genus of medium-sized lemurs, found in virtually all forested regions of Madagascar's periphery. Pelage coloration is less variable geographically than is typical among the polyspecific diurnal lemur genera. Petter and Petter-Rouseaux (1960) recognized a single species with five subspecies, but Petter *et al.* (1977) increased this to seven species, one with four subspecies. Tattersall (1982) provisionally recognized a single species with six subspecies, but now recognizes all or most of these as separate species. Jenkins (1987) recognized seven separate species, distinguishing *L. microdon* in the northern part of the eastern rain forest from *L. mustelinus* in the southern part, south of the Onibe River. In this guide, we follow Petter *et al.* (1977) and Jenkins (1987) in recognizing seven distinct species (but not the four subspecies listed in Petter *et al.* [1977]), with the proviso that this genus is long overdue for a taxonomic revision.

All species weigh less than 1 kg (with some *L. leucopus* weighing as little as 500 g) and range in head-body length from 25-28 cm and tail length from 24-28 cm, for a total length of 49-56 cm. They are vertical clingers and leapers, with elongated legs compared to trunk and arms. The face of *Lepilemur* is covered in short hair. The only likely confusion in the field is with *Avahi*.

However, most species are somewhat smaller than *Avahi* and have more prominent ears, and all lack the highly visible white patches on the back of the thighs which are so typical of *Avahi*. *Avahi* also has large owl-like eyes and a generally woollier appearance. At first glance, or in poor viewing conditions, *Lepilemur* may also be confused with *Cheirogaleus*, especially *Cheirogaleus major* in the eastern rain forest.

PHOTO BY RUSSELL A. MITTERMEIER

Fig. 6.14: White-footed sportive lemur (*Lepilemur leucopus*) in day-time sleeping hole at Berenty Reserve.

Key to illustrations on the following page (Fig. 6.15):
   a. *Lepilemur* in aggressive posture
   b. *Lepilemur* resting in daytime sleeping site in fork of
       tree
   c. *Lepilemur* peering out from daytime sleeping hole
   d. Mother and infant *Lepilemur* resting in vertical
       clinging posture
 e-f. *Lepilemur* leaping and twisting in mid-air from
       vertical clinging posture
   g. *Lepileumr* in resting posture
 h-k. Sequence of images showing *Lepilemur* landing on
       vertical trunk
   l. Side view of head

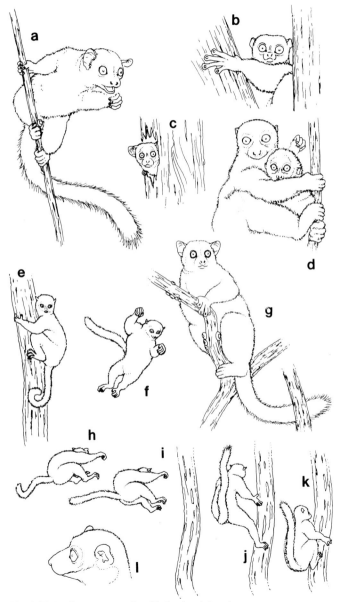

Fig. 6.15: *Lepilemur* postural and behavioral drawings.

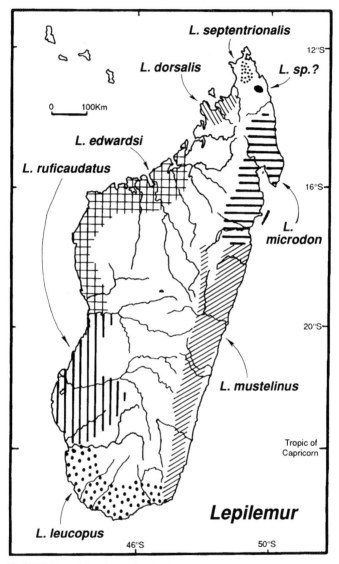

Fig. 6.16: Map of *Lepilemur* distribution.

Lepilemur mustelinus   **Color Plate 10**
Weasel Sportive Lemur   **Page 327**

Other English: Weasel Lemur
French: Lépilémur
German: Wieselmaki
**Malagasy: Trangalavaka, Kotrika, Fitiliky, Hataka,
          Varikosy**

Identification

This is a relatively large *Lepilemur*, probably weighing close
to 1 kg on average, although no exact weights or dimensions are
available. The fur is rather long and dense, variably chestnut
brown on the head and back, along which a darker median stripe
is often detectable. The tail color gets darker towards its tip. The
face is dark gray or brown, with lighter-colored cheeks and throat.
In the field, this species is most likely to be confused with the
similar-sized *Avahi laniger*, which also adopts a vertical clinging
posture, and to a lesser extent with *Cheirogaleus major*, which
usually moves quadrupedally. The concealed ears, white patches
on the thighs, generally woollier appearance, and large owl-like
eyes tend to distinguish *Avahi* from *Lepilemur*,whereas
Cheirogaleus major is smaller, has light-colored underparts, and
rarely uses the vertical clinging posture.

Geographic Range

L. mustelinus occurs in the southern part of the eastern humid
forests, from the Onibe River south to near Fort-Dauphin (=
Tolagnaro) (Petter and Petter-Rousseaux, 1979; Tattersall, 1982;
Jenkins, 1987). One early collecting record is as far north as
Vohémar, outside the rain forest belt, but there are no recent
reports of weasel lemurs there. To the north of the Onibe River,
Lepilemur populations are placed in the separate species, *L.
microdon*, by some authors, and we follow this arrangement here
(see the following section on *L. microdon*). However, individuals
from the southern and northern parts of this range are difficult or
impossible to discriminate on coloration and external features,
making more laboratory research necessary to clarify the relationship between these two animals.

Natural History

The weasel sportive lemur remains poorly studied. According to Ratsirarson and Rumpler (1988), it sleeps in tree holes 6-12 m above ground during the dry season, but uses nests of leaves and lianas in the wet season. Leaping is the principal mode of locomotion. Ganzhorn (1988) reports *L. mustelinus* to be mainly solitary and to eat leaves, fruit and flowers. The species has been found to accept high levels of alkaloids in the diet, which distinguishes it from the indriids, which accept high levels of tannins.

Conservation Status

L. mustelinus is affected by destruction of its eastern rain forest habitat and the fact that it is captured for food in many parts of its range. Usual capture techniques include the use of simple wooden traps and the extraction of animals from daytime sleeping sites.

The weasel sportive lemur is believed to occur in the Andohahela, Betampona and Zahamena Nature Reserves and the Mantady and Ranomafana National Parks (Nicoll and Langrand, 1989; Safford *et al.*, 1989; Harcourt and Thornback , 1990; Mittermeier *et al.*, 1992). There are no population figures available, but a reasonable order of magnitude estimate would be > 100,000.

This species is reported to be extremely difficult to keep in captivity (Petter *et al.*, 1977), and none are known to be in captivity at this time.

Based upon its high population estimate and probable occurrence in at least five protected areas, *L. mustelinus* was given a *Low Priority* rating (3) in the IUCN/SSC Primate Specialist Group's *Lemurs of Madagascar: An Action Plan for their Conservation* (Mittermeier *et al.*, 1992). Using the latest IUCN Red List criteria, we place this species in the *Low Risk* category.

Where To See It

These nocturnal lemurs are easy to see at Périnet (= Andasibe), but may be seen at other localities in the east as well. Look for their eyeshine at night in the middle to upper levels of the canopy. They can also be located during the day in sleeping sites, which are sometimes only a few meters above the ground. However, one can search for a long time without locating a daytime sleeping site. Use of experienced local guides is highly recommended, since they usually know of several regularly-used holes or vine tangles with good viewing conditions.

Lepilemur microdon   Plate 10
Small-Toothed Sportive Lemur   Page 327

Other English: Small-Toothed Weasel Lemur
French: Lépilémur au Petite Dents
Malagasy: Trangalavaka, Kotrika, Fitiliky, Hataka,
Varikosy

Identification

As originally described by Forsyth Major (1894), this species is very similar to *L. mustelinus,* which is found to its south. The only differences are that the fur of its forelimbs and shoulders is bright chestnut-colored, and it has a darkish dorsal stripe and markedly smaller molar teeth. Since *L. mustelinus* and *L. microdon,* if indeed distinct, are impossible to distinguish in the field, geographic location will be your only guide as to which species you have seen.

Geographic Range

Several recent authors have resuscitated the name *L. microdon* for this *Lepilemur* found in the eastern rain forests of Madagascar from the Onibe River north to the Tsaratanana/Andapa region (Petter *et al.,* 1977; Jenkins, 1987). As remarked earlier, *Lepilemur* taxonomy is in great need of revision, and the status of this species requires further analysis. However, until further research is conducted, we follow Petter *et al.* (1977) in recognizing this species as distinct from *L. mustelinus.*

Natural History

No studies have taken place within the geographic range of *L. microdon,* so its natural history remains unknown.

Conservation Status

The species occurs in at least the Marojejy and Tsaratanana Nature Reserves, and probably others as well. There are no population figures available, but a reasonable order of magnitude estimate would be > 100,000. There are none in captivity. *L. microdon* was given a *Low Priority* rating (3) in the IUCN/SSC Primate Specialist Group's *Lemurs of Madagascar: An Action Plan for their Conservation* (Mittermeier *et al.,* 1992). Using the latest IUCN Red List criteria, we place this species in the *Low Risk* category.

Lepilemur leucopus   **Color Plate 10**
White-Footed Sportive Lemur   **Page 327**

Other English: White-Footed Weasel Lemur
French: Lépilemur à Patte Blanche
German: Weissfuss-Wieselmaki
Malagasy: Songiky

Identification

This is a small *Lepilemur*, weighing on average 544 g (Russell, 1977), and with a head-body length of about 25 cm and a tail length of about 24 cm. The head and body are medium to light gray in color, but often with brownish fur around the head and shoulders. The tail is a very light brown. The whitish fur of the chest, stomach and inside of the limbs is often visible, especially around the base of the tail, even while the animal is clinging to a vertical support. The ears are rounded and relatively large.

In the field, this *Lepilemur* is most likely to be confused with *Cheirogaleus medius* and, to a much lesser extent, *Microcebus murinus*. It is best distinguished from *Cheirogaleus* by its vertical clinging body posture and its tendency to leap, whereas *Cheirogaeus* generally walks slowly and quadrupedally. *Cheirogaleus* also has largely hidden ears and lighter underparts. *Microcebus* is much smaller and more rapidly moving.

Geographic Range

The white-footed sportive lemur is found in the Didiereaceae and gallery forests of southern and southwestern Madagascar, from Fort-Dauphin (= Tolagnaro) at least as far west as the Linta River, and possibly to the Onilahy River (Petter *et al.*, 1977; Tattersall, 1982; Sussman and Richard, 1986).

Natural History

L. leucopus has been studied principally in gallery and Didiereaceae forests near Berenty (Charles-Dominique and Hladik, 1971; Hladik and Charles-Dominique, 1974; Russell, 1977, 1980); some of the results of the two main studies of this animal are in agreement, whereas others conflict. Both studies report densities of 200-350/km^2 in Didiereaceae forest and 450/km^2 in gallery forest. Small territories of approximately 0.2 ha are said to be defended by males and females alike, using vocalizations and displays rather than olfactory cues, but male territories overlap those of females.   Charles-Dominique and Hladik report that males and females sleep separately during the day, either in a tree hole or bundle of lianas, whereas Russell indicates that pairs often share and do not defend ranges, and sleep together as well.

The bulk of the white-footed sportive lemur's diet appears to consist of leaves (primarily of the Didiereaceae species, *Alluaudia procera* and *A. ascendens*), though flowers are also eaten during the dry season. Charles-Dominique and Hladik (1971, 1974) report the unusual behavior of caecotrophy, in which the relatively poor quality of this diet is compensated for by the reingestion of feces. While a relatively low level of activity was reported by Charles-Dominique and Hladik, Russell found that these lemurs were active for a relatively high 40% of waking time, and that their average nightly travel distances were 320-500 m, again high for lemurs of this size.

Mating occurs between May and July, and a single infant is born from September to November (Petter *et al.*, 1977).

Conservation Status
The principal threats to the survival of the white-footed sportive lemur are habitat destruction due to fire and overgrazing by livestock, and capture for food. It is found in the Andohahela and Tsimanampetsotsa Nature Reserves, the Beza-Mahafaly Special Reserve and the Berenty Private Reserve (Andriamampianina and Peyrieras, 1972; O'Connor et al., 1986; Sussman and Richard, 1986; Sussman *et al.*, 1987; Nicoll and Langrand, 1989; Harcourt and Thornback, 1990; Mittermeier *et al.*, 1992)). The degree of protection varies among these areas, the lemur populations probably being more secure in the smaller reserves at Berenty and Beza-Mahafaly. There are no population figures available, but a reasonable order of magnitude estimate would be >100,000 (Mittermeier *et al.*, 1992). There are none in captivity.

Based upon its presumed large population, occurrence in several protected areas and the fact that nocturnal lemurs are generally less threatened than diurnal ones, *L. leucopus* was given a *Low Priority* rating (3) in the IUCN/SSC Primate Specialist Group's *Lemurs of Madagascar: An Action Plan for their Conservation* (Mittermeier *et al.*, 1992). Using the latest IUCN Red List criteria, we place this species in the *Low Risk* category.

Where To See It

This species is most easily seen in the Berenty Private Reserve west of Fort-Dauphin (= Tolagnaro). It is common there and can be readily observed at night along the broad trails cutting through this small reserve. It is also relatively easy to see during the day, and local guides know the whereabouts of several regularly-used nest holes and other sleeping sites. Aside from Berenty, the animal can be seen in the dry portion of the Andohahela Nature Reserve, in the Beza-Mahafaly Special Reserve, and in many other parts of its range.

Lepilemur ruficaudatus   **Color Plate 10**
Red-Tailed Sportive Lemur   **Page 327**

Other English: Red-Tailed Weasel Lemur
French: Lépilémur à Queue Rousse
German: Rotschwanz-Wieselmaki
Malagasy: Boenga, Boengy (near Morondava)

Identification
    Lepilemur ruficaudatus is a relatively large *Lepilemur*, with a head and body length of about 28 cm, a tail length of 25-26 cm, and an average body weight of over 900 g. The pelage of the back and flanks is gray, washed with light brown, and the tail is reddish. Its face and throat are pale gray to pale brown, and its ears are quite prominent.
    This species can most easily be confused with *Cheirogaleus medius* or *Phaner*. It can be distinguished from *Cheirogaleus* by its vertical posture, its more distinctive ears, its somewhat larger size, and its tendency to leap rather than walk quadrupedally. *Phaner* is much more active and has the distinct forked pattern on its head.

Geographic Range
    The red-tailed sportive lemur is found in the dry forests of western Madagascar, apparently between the Onilahy and Tsiribihina Rivers, and extending southwards possibly as far as Ejeda (Petter and Petter-Rousseaux, 1979; Tattersall, 1982).

Natural History
    This species is poorly known, though apparently quite common in the dry deciduous forests of western Madagascar. Based upon their study in the Marosalaza forest, 50 km north of Morondava, Petter *et al.* (1971) estimated population densities of 180-350/km^2. In forests near the Mangoky River, Petter *et al.* (1975) estimated a density of 260/km^2.
    Hladik *et al.* (1980) describe *L. ruficaudatus* as a leaf-eater, though it also eats fruit (especially *Diospyros* spp.) in season. Mating occurs from May to July, and a single infant is born between September and November. The infant is initially transported in its mother's mouth, and "parked" on a branch or in a tree hole during foraging. Offspring cease to travel with their mothers at about one year of age (Petter-Rousseaux, 1964).

Conservation Status

The red-tailed sportive lemur is subject to habitat destruction as western forests are routinely burned to create pasture for livestock. In addition, the animal is captured for food throughout much of its range. *L. ruficaudatus* occurs in at least two protected areas, the Andranomena Special Reserve and the Analabe Private Reserve (Nicoll and Langrand, 1989). There are no population figures available, but a reasonable order of magnitude estimate would be > 100,000. Although this species has bred in captivity (Petter-Rousseaux, 1980), it is considered difficult to maintain. There are none reported in captivity at this time.

Based on its relatively large range and the high population estimate, the red-tailed sportive lemur was given a *Low Priority* rating (3) in the IUCN/SSC Primate Specialist Group's *Lemurs of Madagascar: An Action Plan for their Conservation* (Mittermeier *et al.*, 1992). Using the latest IUCN Red List criteria, we place this species in the *Low Risk* category.

Where To See It

This lemur is best seen in the private reserve at Analabe, north of Morondava, where it is sympatric with four other nocturnal genera (*Microcebus*, *Cheirogaleus*, *Mirza* and *Phaner*). All five can be seen during a brief wet season visit if one is willing to spend a lot of time in the forest at night.

Lepilemur edwardsi   **Color Plate 11**
Milne-Edwards' Sportive Lemur   **Page 328**

Other English: Milne-Edwards' Weasel Lemur
French: Lépilemur de Milne-Edwards
German: Edwards Wieselmaki
Malagasy: Repahaka, Boenga, Boengy

Indentification
    L. edwardsi is a little darker-colored than *L. ruficaudatus*.
The back and sides are dark to grayish brown, paler on the lower
back and darker on the upper back. Often there is a dark stripe
running along the center of the back. The face is a darkish gray
or brown, the tail a light brown. Body size appears to be identical
to that of *L. ruficaudatus*, with head-body and tail length each
being about 28 cm for a total length of 56 cm. This species may
be conspecific with *L. ruficaudatus*. However, pending further
investigation, we prefer to recognize two species.
    In the field, *L. edwardsi* is most likely to be confused with
Avahi occidentalis, which also adopts a vertical clinging posture.
It is best distinguished by its more prominent ears. *Avahi* also has
larger, distinctive owl-like eyes and a woollier appearance.

Geographic Range
    L. edwardsi is found in the dry deciduous forests of western
Madagascar to the north of the range of *L. ruficaudatus*, certainly
from Antsalova and possibly from the Tsiribihina River north to
the Bay of Mahajamba (Tattersall, 1982).

Natural History
    Milne-Edwards' sportive lemur has been studied in dry de-
ciduous forests in and around the Ankarafantsika Nature Reserve,
where it has been reported at densities of about 60 individuals/
km^2 (Ganzhorn, 1988). Home ranges appear to be about 1 ha, and
are defended by vigorous displays that include loud cries and
branch-shaking (Albignac, 1981a). Leaves appear to be the
mainstay of the diet, but fruit, flowers and fleshy seeds are also
eaten (Albignac, 1981a; Razanahoera-Rakotomalala, 1981;
Ganzhorn, 1988). Up to three individuals have been found
sleeping in the same spot during the day (Albignac, 1981a), but
they forage alone at night.

Conservation Status

This species is impacted by habitat destruction, primarily by fires set to create pasture for livestock, and it is also captured for food. It is found in the Ankarafantsika, Namoroka and Tsingy de Bemaraha Nature Reserves, and possibly several other protected areas within its range, but the degree of protection within these reserves varies significantly (Nicoll and Langrand, 1989; Harcourt and Thornback, 1990; Mittermeier *et al.*, 1992). There are no population figures available, but a reasonable order of magnitude estimate would be >100,000 (Mittermeier *et al.*, 1992). There are none in captivity.

Based on the presumed large population and its presence in a number of reserves, *L. edwardsi* was given a *Low Priority* rating (3) in the IUCN/SSC Primate Specialist Group's *Lemurs of Madagascar: An Action Plan for their Conservation* (Mittermeier *et al.*, 1992). Using the latest IUCN Red List criteria, we place this species in the *Low Risk* category.

Where To See It

This species is most easily seen at the Ampijoroa Station in the Ankarafantsika Nature Reserve, located right along the main road between Majunga (= Mahajanga) and Antananarivo. It is easily located at night by its eye-shine and vocalizations, and can also be found in tree forks and nest holes during the day, often quite close to the ground. The dry deciduous forest at Ampijoroa is much lower than in the eastern rain forest, and finding lemurs is generally much easier in such habitat.

Lepilemur dorsalis   Color Plate 11
Gray-Backed Sportive Lemur   Page 328

**Other English: Nosy Be Sportive Lemur; Nosy Be
                  Weasel Lemur
French: Lépilemur à Dos Gris
German: Nosy-Be-Wieselmaki
Malagasy: Apongy**

Identification

This is a small *Lepilemur*, with relatively short rounded ears
and a blunt-appearing dark gray to brown face. The back and sides
tend to a darkish brown, as do the tail and chest. No data on actual
size and weight are available.

This species might be confused with *Cheirogaleus medius* and
with *Avahi occidentalis*, but can be distinguished in the same way
as its relatives.

Geographic Range

L. dorsalis is found in the Sambirano region of northwest
Madagascar, centering on Ambanja and including the
Ampasindava Peninsula and the islands of Nosy Be and Nosy
Komba (Petter *et al.*, 1977; Tattersall, 1982).

Natural History

This lemur has been the subject of only brief field studies. It
inhabits humid forests that are subject to a short dry season, and
favors dense foliage for daytime sleeping. It feeds on leaves, fruit
and bark. Births occur from August through November, when a
single infant is born (Petter and Petter, 1971; D. Meyers, pers.
obs.).

Conservation Status

Lepilemur dorsalis suffers from habitat destruction due to
forest clearance for agriculture (principally coffee and rice) and
settlements, and it is also captured for food in some parts of its
range. It is known to occur in the Lokobe Nature Reserve on Nosy
Be and the Manongarivo Special Reserve (Quansah, 1988; Nicoll
and Langrand, 1989; Harcourt and Thornback, 1990; Mittermeier
et al., 1992). There are no population figures available, but a
reasonable order of magnitude estimate would be 10,000-100,000
(Mittermeier *et al.*, 1992). There are none in captivity.

Although *L. dorsalis* has a small range, it appears to be abundant within its range and occurs in several reserves, which is why it was given a *Low Priority* rating (3) in the IUCN/SSC Primate Specialist Group's *Lemurs of Madagscar: An Action Plan for their Conservation* (Mittermeier *et al.*, 1992). However, our reassessment has placed greater emphasis on the small range size, the disappearing habitat and the hunting pressure on this species. Therefore, using the latest IUCN Red List criteria, we place this species in the *Vulnerable* category.

Where To See It

This species is most easily seen in the Lokobe Nature Reserve on the island of Nosy Be. Several tours go to parts of this reserve, and local guides usually know of the whereabouts of daytime sleeping sites a few meters above the ground where the animal is quite easy to observe.

Lepilemur septentrionalis   **Color Plate 11**
Northern Sportive Lemur   **Page 328**

Other English: Northern Weasel Lemur
French: Lépilemur du Nord
German: Nördlicher Wieselmaki
Malagasy: Mahiabeala, Songiky

Identification

This is one of the smaller *Lepilemur* species, although no good measurements are available. Its ears are of only moderate prominence. The basic head and body color is a light gray-brown, perhaps a bit darker towards the tail, and often with a darker median stripe extending from the crown of the head along the spine. Brownish tinges are often present in the shoulder region. The tail is a pale brown, tending to get darker towards the tip.

This species might be confused in the field with *Phaner* or with *Cheirogaleus* if only a fleeting glimpse of the animal is obtained. However, it can be distinguished from *Cheirogaleus* by its vertical posture, the more evident ears and the darker underparts, and from *Phaner* by the absence of the forked pattern on the head. *Phaner* also moves rapidly and continuously, has a more elongate face, and the distinctive loud vocalizations.

Geographical Range

L. septentrionalis inhabits the deciduous forests of extreme northern Madagascar. In the west, its range extends from the Montagne d'Ambre southwards to the Mahavavy River near Ambilobe. In the east it extends southwards at least to the Manambato River, and probably to the Fanambana, north of Sambava (Ratsirarson and Rumpler, 1988).

Natural History

The northern sportive lemur is not well known. It is found mostly in very dry deciduous forests, but also occurs in the more humid forest formations of the Anakarana Massif (Hawkins *et al.*, 1990). Population densities have been variously estimated between 150 and 550 individuals/km^2 (Ratsirarson and Rumpler, 1988; Hawkins *et al.*, 1990), the higher counts being in more humid forest environments such as Ankarana. Meyers has estimated as low as 60 individuals/km^2 in the dry forest of Analamera. Ratsirarson and Rumpler (1988) report range sizes of about 1 ha, and indicate that adults rarely associate during the night's activity. Tree holes and leaf tangles are used as daytime resting places. As with other *Lepilemur*, leaves are believed to constitute the major part of the diet.

Conservation Status

L. septentrionalis suffers from forest destruction which is widespread in northern Madagascar, even within protected areas, and the animal is captured for food as well. It is found in the Montagne d'Ambre National Park and the Ankarana, Analamera and Forêt d'Ambre Special Reserves (Wilson *et al.*, 1988, 1989; Nicoll and Langrand, 1989; Harcourt and Thornback, 1990; Hawkins *et al.*, 1990; Mittermeier *et al.*, 1992). No population figures are available, but a reasonable order of magnitude estimate would be 10,000-100,000 (Mittermeier *et al.*, 1992). There are none in captivity.

Given its high population densities and its presence in a number of protected areas, the northern sportive lemur was given a *Low Priority* rating (3) in the the IUCN/SSC Primate Specialist Group's *Lemurs of Madagascar: An Action Plan for their Conservation* (Mittermeier *et al.*, 1992). However, given its small range and the fact that it is still hunted, we have reassessed its status. Using the latest IUCN Red List criteria, we place this species in the *Vulnerable* category.

Where To See It

This species is most readily seen in the Montagne d'Ambre complex of protected areas.

FAMILY LEMURIDAE

This family includes the best known and most widespread of the lemurs and consists of two subfamilies. The genera *Lemur*, *Eulemur* and *Varecia* are all considered "true" lemurs and are classified in the subfamily Lemurinae. The bamboo lemurs, *Hapalemur*, comprise the subfamily Hapalemurinae.

The Lemuridae range in weight from 700g-4.5 kg. With forelimbs slightly shorter than their hindlimbs, they move quadrupedally along branches and will leap across gaps in the forest. They are active diurnally, but all species except the ruffed lemur are also known to be active a certain amount of time during the night. The extent of this nocturnal activity remains poorly documented in most species. There is large variation in pelage coloration among this group from the bold black and white contrasts of the ruffed lemur through to the conservative grayish browns of bamboo lemurs. Practically all Malagasy forests contain at least one species from this family and most contain two or three.

Until recently, the genus *Lemur* was believed to include six species, with *Varecia* being closely related. However, recent studies (Simons and Rumpler, 1988; Groves and Eaglen, 1988) have suggested that *Lemur catta*, the name-bearer of the genus, may have closer affinities to the bamboo lemurs, *Hapalemur*. As a result, it is becoming popular to separate *Lemur catta* from the others, which are placed in the genus *Eulemur*. For the purposes of this guide, we have followed this new arrangement because it is becoming increasingly popular among lemur specialists. *

* One of us (Tattersall), however, is unhappy with this arrangement because relationships within the group are far from certain, as demonstrated by Tattersall and Schwartz (1991). In the view of Tattersall and Schwartz, it would be in the best interests of nomenclatural stability to return to the classification accepted in the mid-1970s, with *Varecia* and all species of *Eulemur* listed under the genus *Lemur*.

Hapalemur: Bamboo or Gentle Lemurs

All authorities agree in placing the bamboo lemurs in the family Lemuridae, although there is considerable uncertainty over their relationships to other genera within the family. The argument for separating *Lemur* from *Eulemur* is largely based on certain behavioral resemblances between *Hapalemur* and *Lemur catta*, but a phylogenetic relationship between the two is hard to demonstrate morphologically.

Three species of bamboo lemur are recognized, the gray bamboo lemur (*Hapalemur griseus*), with at least three subspecies (*griseus*, *occidentalis* and *alaotrensis*), the greater bamboo lemur (*H. simus*) and the golden bamboo lemur (*H. aureus*). A fourth subspecies of *H. griseus*, *H. g. "meriodionalis,"* is mentioned and actually named in the literature (Warter *et al.*, 1987), but not formally described, making it a *nomen nudum* until a formal description is published. It is not treated here, since insufficient information is available.

All *Hapalemur* species are medium to small-bodied, have moderately long hind limbs, prefer vertical resting postures, and leap readily between closely-spaced vertical supports. All have relatively blunt faces with short muzzles. Coloration is essentially gray, and activity is readily observed around dusk.

The genus is found throughout the east, in the north, in the Sambirano, and in parts of the west.

Key to illustrations on the following page (6.17):
- a. *Hapalemur griseus* in vertical clinging rest posture
- b. *Hapalemur griseus* resting braced between two trunks
- c. *Hapalemur griseus* sitting on horizontal branch
- d. *Hapalemur aureus* descending a branch
- e. *Hapalemur aureus* reaching up to feed on bamboo shoots
- f. *Hapalemur griseus* monitoring its environment from a vertical clinging posture
- g. *Hapalemur aureus* using a vertical clinging posture to feed on bamboo
- h. *Hapalemur griseus* with infant in crouched sitting posture
- i. *Hapalemur griseus* with infant in crouched sitting posture (the adult's mouth is open in threat)

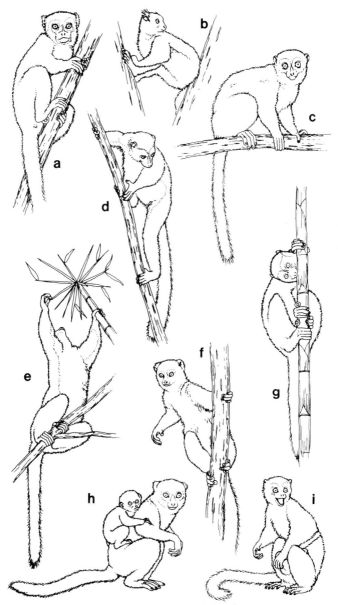

Fig. 6.17: *Hapalemur* postural and behavioral drawings.

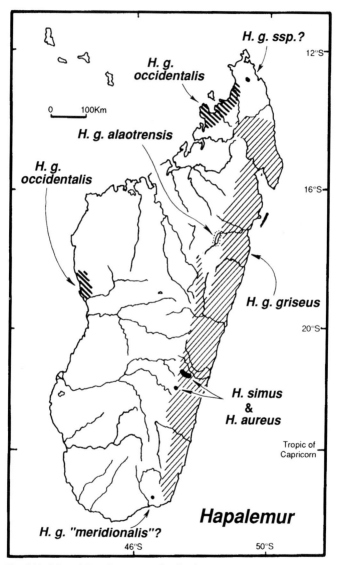

Fig. 6.18: Map of *Hapalemur* spp. distribution.

Hapalemur griseus griseus   Color Plate 12
Eastern Lesser Bamboo Lemur   Page 329

Other English: Gray Bamboo Lemur, Gray Gentle
**   Lemur**
French: Petit Hapalémur
German: Ostlicher Grauer Halbmaki
Malagasy: Bokombolo, Kotrika

Identification

Hapalemur griseus griseus and its western relative, *H. g. occidentalis*, are the smallest of the bamboo lemurs, ranging from 700 g to over 1 kg. Head and body length is around 28 cm and tail length is about 37 cm, for an overall length of 60-70 cm. The body color is gray, with a rufous head and often rufous patches on the dorsal coat and shoulders. The face is lighter. This subspecies does not have a pale area around the eyes and the muzzle is shorter than in the western gray lemur (*H. g. occidentalis*). In the southern part of its range, deep rusts and browns are found overlaying the gray of the body coat and the rust patch on the head can be quite noticeable. To the north, these rust-colored areas are more olivaceous. The southern form (*H. g. "meridionalis"*) discussed by Warter *et al.* (1987) is apparently darker in color.

This subspecies is usually easy to identify because it is the smallest of the diurnal lemurs and has a shorter muzzle than members of the genus *Eulemur* (the only other sympatric diurnal lemurs with which it might be confused). It also is usually associated with bamboo. Distinguishing it from its two relatives (*H. aureus* and *H. simus*), with which it is sympatric in the Ranomafana and Kianjavato area, can be more difficult if only a fleeting view of the animal is obtained in the field. However, with a good clear sighting, *H. griseus griseus* can easily be distinguished from *H. aureus* by its smaller size and lack of a golden-colored face, and from *H. simus* by its lack of ear tufts and much smaller size.

Geographic Range

H. g. griseus is found throughout all remaining eastern forests from the Tsaratanana Massif in the north to Fort-Dauphin (= Tolagnaro) in the south (Tattersall, 1982), wherever bamboo is present. This relatively continuous distribution is broken only around Lac Alaotra where the Alaotran bamboo lemur is found. Details of the micro-distribution of the two subspecies in this area are lacking.

Natural History

The eastern lesser bamboo lemur occurs in various types of eastern forest, but is found at highest densities near stands of bamboo and bamboo vines (Petter and Peyrieras, 1970a). Its diet is mostly bamboo, primarily new shoots and leaf bases, to which it gains access by pulling new leaves from the end of a branch, biting the soft base, and discarding the tough leaf blade. Other food items include fig leaves, grass stems, young leaves, and small fruit (Wright, 1986). Group size varies between two and six, and groups not uncommonly contain more than two adult females (Petter and Peyrieras, 1970a; Pollock,1986; Wright, 1986). Reports of home range size vary from 6-10 ha at Périnet (= Andasibe) (Wright, 1986) to as much as 15 ha at Ranomafana (Wright, 1989). Population density has been estimated at 47-62/ km^2 at Périnet (= Andasibe) (Pollock, 1979), but lower densities are found in other primary forests.

This subspecies has been reported to be crepuscular in activity (Petter and Peyrieras, 1975), but was primarily diurnal in Wright's (1986) study. This flexibility is similar to that found in *Eulemur* species.

Births seem to occur from October through January (Pollock, 1986), and gestation length is about 140 days (Petter and Peyrieras, 1970a). Infants are carried on the mother's back soon after birth and may be "parked" for short periods of time (Wright, pers. comm.). Males have been seen to carry infants in captivity (Petter and Peyrieras, 1975).

Conservation Status

The eastern lesser bamboo lemur is reported to occur in the Mantady, Ranomafana and Verezanantsoro National Parks, the Andohahela, Marojejy and Zahamena Nature Reserves, and the Ambatovaky, Analamazaotra, Anjanaharibé-Sud, Manombo, and Tsaratanana Special Reserves, and possibly Manongarivo as well (Nicoll and Langrand, 1989; Harcourt and Thornback, 1990; Mittermeier *et al.*, 1992). There are no population figures available, but a reasonable order of magnitude estimate would be >100,000 (Mittermeier *et al.*, 1992). There may be as many as 50 *H. g. griseus* in captivity in five institutions worldwide, including Madagascar's Parc Tsimbazaza and Zoo Ivoloina (Olney and Ellis, 1992; ISIS, 1993).

Hapalemur g. griseus was given a *Low Priority* rating (3) in the IUCN/SSC Primate Specialist Group's *Lemurs of Madagas-*

car: An Action Plan for their Conservation (Mittermeier *et al.*, 1992). Using the latest IUCN Red List criteria, we place this subspecies in the *Low Risk* category.

Where To See It

The two best places to see the eastern lesser bamboo lemur on the tourist circuit are Périnet (= Andasibe) and Ranomafana National Park. In these areas and elsewhere, it is most likely to be observed at dusk in stands of common bamboo. In Périnet, one group is often seen in bamboo right next to the warden's house and at the start of one of the trails going up the hill to the most-visited indri group.

Hapalemur griseus occidentalis   **Color Plate 12**
Western Lesser Bamboo Lemur   **Page 329**

Other English: Western Gentle Lemur, Western Bamboo Lemur
French: Hapalémur Occidental
German: Westlicher Grauer Halbmaki
Malagasy: Bekola, Kofi, Ankomba Valiha, Bokombolo

Identification

The western lesser bamboo lemur is more uniformly gray-brown in coat color and slightly smaller than its eastern cousins. Head and body length is about 28 cm and tail length about 38 cm, for a total range of 55-66 cm, but no body weights have been recorded. The face is generally paler than in other *Hapalemur*.

As with its eastern relative, this subspecies is unlikely to be confused with other diurnal sympatric species, it being considerably smaller than *Eulemur* and usually associated with bamboo.

Geographic Range

The western lesser bamboo lemur is found in several isolated regions of forest in the west of Madagascar. These include forests of the Lake Bemamba region, between Maintirano and Belo-sur-Tsiribihina, as well as the entire Sambirano region from south of Maromandia north through Beramanja (Tattersall, 1982). Collection records suggest that populations also exist between these two areas, but this has not been verified. A population that appears to represent *H. g. occidentalis* has recently been reported from the Ankarana Massif in northwest Madagascar (Hawkins *et al.*, 1990), but its taxonomic status remains to be clarified.

Natural History

H. g. occidentalis appears to inhabit forest that contains bamboo or bamboo vines (Petter and Peyrieras, 1970a; Tattersall, 1982). Based on a study conducted in the Manongarivo Special Reserve, group size appears to be small (one to four individuals) and the animal is principally active by day (Raxworthy and Rakotondraparany, 1988). Otherwise, very little is known about this subspecies.

Conservation Status

The western lesser bamboo lemur is threatened by regular

burning of its habitat to provide pasture for livestock. Although it has a scattered distribution, it is reported to occur in the Tsingy de Bemaraha Nature Reserve and the Ankarana (?) and Manongarivo Special Reserves (Raxworthy and Rakotondraparany, 1988; Nicoll and Langrand, 1989; Harcourt and Thornback, 1990; Hawkins *et al.*, 1990; Mittermeier *et al.*, 1992). There are no population figures available, but a reasonable order of magnitude estimate would be at the low end of 10,000-100,000 (Mittermeier *et al.*, 1992). A single individual of this subspecies is reported in captivity at France's Mulhouse Zoo (ISIS, 1993).

The western lesser bamboo lemur's distribution is scattered and its status uncertain in the few protected areas in which it is reported to occur. Therefore, it was given a *Priority* rating (4) in the IUCN/SSC Primate Specialist Group's *Lemurs of Madagascar: An Action Plan for their Conservation* (Mittermeier *et al.*, 1992). Using the latest IUCN Red List criteria, we place this subspecies in the *Vulnerable* category.

Where To See It
This lemur is not easily seen, but the best opportunities are around Lac Bemamba and in the Manongarivo Special Reserve, where one might have to spend several days in the forest to ensure success.

Hapalemur griseus alaotrensis   **Color Plate 12**
Lac Alaotra Bamboo Lemur   **Page 329**

Other English: Alaotran Gentle lemur
French: Hapalémur du Lac Alaotra
German: Alaotra Halbmaki
Malagasy: Bandro

Identification
The Lac Alaotra bamboo lemur is larger than *H. g. griseus* and apparently weighs over 1 kg, although no exact weights for wild animals are known. Head-body length is about 40 cm and tail length is about the same, for a total of roughly 80 cm (Tattersall, 1982). The head is rounder and the body coat is darker than that of the gray bamboo lemur. It is not likely to be confused with other lemurs in the field, since it is the only lemur living in the reed beds of Lac Alaotra (and indeed the only primate restricted to this kind of habitat).

Geographic Range
H. g. alaotrensis is currently known only from the reed beds of Lac Alaotra, the largest lake in Madagascar. Pollock (1986) suggests that much of the lake area (800 km^2) is suitable habitat for this animal, but it has not been reported from forests surrounding this lake. However, recent information indicates that it is now extinct in the southern part of the lake (A. T. C. Feistner, pers. comm.). Also, apparently it used to occur 60 km north of Lac Alaotra, at a site called Andolamena, but it went extinct there as a result of two dams built in 1955 and 1958 (M. Pidgeon, pers. comm.).

Natural History
The only in-depth study of this animal has been conducted very recently by T. Muschler and A. T. C. Feistner, in 1992 and 1993. This research indicates that the *bandro* lives in groups of 3-5 individuals with a maximum of 7 (although associations of 30-40 were reported by Petter and Peyrieras, 1975, at the end of the wet season). Groups contain a single adult male, and may be territorial. A single infant is usually born in January or February of each year, and the young are carried on their mother's back from the moment of birth (Petter and Peyrieras, 1975).

The diet of the *bandro* apparently consists of the leaves and shoots of the reed *Phragmites communis* (Graminae) and other plants growing in the lake (Petter and Peyrieras, 1975; Pollock, 1986). The typical mode of locomotion is vertical clinging and leaping. Although the ability to swim is not known in any other lemur, it has been suggested that the *bandro* is capable of swimming (Petter and Peyrieras, 1975).

Conservation Status

The *bandro* is threatened by a number of factors, which have been investigated by T. Muschler and A. T. C. Feistner in their recent study. Lac Alaotra is the largest rice-growing area in Madagascar; much of the lake margin has already been converted, and more continues to be, and irrigation projects are also changing the nature of the lake. Routine cutting of papyrus and reeds for construction of mats, fish traps, screens, barriers and fencing also presents a problem, though a lesser one (Pollock, 1986).

In addition to these threats, the bandro is under heavier hunting pressure than most other lemurs, a factor that has long been recognized (Petter and Peyrieras, 1970a; Jolly *et al.*, 1984), but has only recently been investigated in detail. The recent study by T. Muschler and A. T. C. Feistner indicated that this lemur is hunted for food and as a pet. In the wet season from December to April, many are captured as pets, and the animals are also caught as pets or for food in the dry season, when the reed beds are burned by local people (Petter and Peyrieras, 1970a).

In the survey by Muschler and Feistner, 25% of people interviewed either had *H. g. alaotrensis* as pets or had had them in the recent past. In one village, eight *H.g. alaotrensis* were being kept as pets in one 10-day period, and of 31 villages surveyed, only three had had no *H. g. alaotrensis* in the past 10 months. Furthermore, the animals survive only about two months in captivity, so there is a considerable turnover.

A variety of hunting methods are employed to capture this lemur. Direct pursuit by dogs is the most common, but they may also be captured by using a harpoon, a snare, a stick to knock them out or into the water, and by burning their reed bed habitat, causing them to flee into the hands of waiting hunters. Some villages have a *fady* (taboo) against eating the *bandro*, but others do not.

Given its small population, estimated by Mutschler and Feistner (pers. comm.) at 6,000-15,000, its very restricted habitat, and the fact that it does not occur in any protected area, led us to give it the Highest Priority rating in the IUCN/SSC Primate Specialist Group's *Lemurs of Madagascar: An Action Plan for their Conser-*

vation (Mittermeier *et al.*, 1992). Using the latest IUCN Red List criteria (and taking into account that the only other known population of this animal is already extinct), we place *H. g. alaotrensis* in the *Critically Endangered* category.

Efforts to delineate and set aside a protected area for *H. g. alaotrensis* should be considered one of the two or three highest lemur conservation priorities. This very interesting animal occupies a niche unique not just among the lemurs but among all primates making it of considerable scientific importance. A substantial expansion of the captive colony, which as of 1994 consisted of eight animals at the Jersey Wildlife Preservation Trust and one at the Duke University Primate Center, should also be a priority.

Where To See It
The only way to see this elusive lemur is to travel by pirogue through the reed beds of Lac Alaotra, but finding them can be quite difficult and is best left to the seasoned lemur watcher.

The best starting points are Andreba on the eastern side of the lake, or Andilano Atsinio on the western side. In Andreba, ask for a local fisherman named Richard, who regularly works with field biologists. Both Andreba and Andilano Atsinio can be reached from Ambatondrazaka, the main town on the lake's south side, located some 40 minutes by plane or 6-7 hours by car from Antananarivo.

PHOTO BY THOMAS MUTSCHLER

Fig. 6.19: The Lac Alaotra bamboo lemur, *Hapalemur griseus alaotrensis*, in its natural habitat.

Hapalemur aureus
Golden Bamboo Lemur

Color Plate 13
Page 330

French: Hapalémur Doré
German: Goldener Bambuslemur
Malagasy: Bokombolomena, Varibolomena

Identification

This recently discovered species is intermediate in size between the other two species of bamboo lemur, *H. griseus* and *H. simus*. Head and body length is about 34 cm, tail length is about 41 cm (for an overall length of 70-80 cm), and the body weight averages 1.6 kg (Glander *et al.*, 1992). Coat color is reddish-brown, and darker on the shoulders, back, and top of the head. The nose is pink, the face is dark and surrounded by gold-colored hair on the cheeks, the side of the face and around the eyes. The ears do not have tufts as in the greater bamboo lemur, but rather are covered with light hair which does not extend much beyond the tip of the ear.

Hapalemur aureus can be distinguished from its two sympatric relatives in several ways. The golden coloration, especially on the face, distinguishes it from both *H. g. griseus* and *H. simus*, and it is larger than the former and smaller than the latter. The lack of ear tufts also differentiates it from *H. simus*.

Geographic Range

Hapalemur aureus was discovered in 1986 and described in 1987. It is known from the forests of Ranomafana National Park in southeastern Madagascar, where it is sympatric with *H. g. griseus* and *H. simus* (Meier and Rumpler, 1987). A recent survey (1993) extended its distribution south to the Andringitra Nature Reserve as well (E. Sterling, pers. comm.).

Natural History

Most information concerning the natural history of the golden bamboo lemur comes from studies by Patricia Wright (Wright *et al.*, 1987) and Bernhard Meier (Meier and Rumpler, 1987). Group size ranges from 2-6 and is often 3 or 4. The main study group's home range was about 80 ha and the average daily path length was under 400 m in the winter (Wright *et al.*, 1987). The diet of *H. aureus* consists mostly of new shoots (as opposed to the pith, which is eaten by *H. simus*) of the giant bamboo

(*Cephalostachium viguieri*), but also includes bamboo creeper and bamboo grass (Meier and Rumpler, 1987; Meier *et al.*, 1987). Glander *et al.* (1989) have found astonishingly high levels of cyanide in the shoots of giant bamboo, as well as in the blood and feces of the golden bamboo lemur. The levels of this toxin would kill most other mammals. This adaptation may allow for reduced feeding competition and hence for sympatry among the three species of bamboo lemurs, since the other two species avoid this food (Wright, 1989).

Activity is highest at dawn and dusk and nocturnal activity is common. Births are in November and December.

Conservation Status
Approximately 1,000 golden bamboo lemurs are estimated to occur in Ranomafana National Park (Mittermeier *et al.*, 1992), but this population continues to be threatened by slash-and-burn agriculture around the park's borders (Meier and Rumpler, 1987). There are no population estimates available for the Andringitra Nature Reserve. Two animals were captured in 1987 and brought to Madagascar's Parc Tsimbazaza, where the first infant was born in captivity. This unique captive colony now numbers five animals.

Given the critically small population of this species and the fact that it occurs only in two protected areas that are still under threat from human encroachment, the golden bamboo lemur was given the *Highest Priority* rating (6) in the IUCN/SSC Primate Specialist Group's *Lemurs of Madagascar: An Action Plan for their Conservation* (Mittermeier *et al.*, 1992). Using the latest IUCN Red List criteria, we place this species in the *Critically Endangered* category.

Where To See It
The golden bamboo lemur can be seen in Ranomafana National Park around the research station at Talatakely, but a visit of at least two or three days is recommended. Use of local guides to find the animals is essential.

Hapalemur simus   **Color Plate 13**
Greater Bamboo Lemur   **Page 330**

Other English: Broad-Nosed Bamboo Lemur, Broad-Nosed Gentle Lemur
French: Grand Hapalémur
German: Grober Halbmaki
Malagasy: Varibolo

Identification

This is by far the largest species of the genus *Hapalemur*, with the weight of one adult male reported at 2.4 kg (Meier *et al.*, 1987). The greater bamboo lemur looks very similar in coat color and coloration pattern to the gray bamboo lemur, but generally is darker. It is sympatric with both *Hapalemur griseus* and *Hapalemur aureus* and can be confused with both in the wild, unless one gets a very clear look at the animal. It is much larger and darker than *H. griseus* and somewhat larger than *H. aureus*, and can be distinguished by the prominent white ear tufts and blunter, broader face. *H. simus* also lacks the golden facial hairs distinctive of *H. aureus*.

The white ear tufts and the blunt muzzle also help to distinguish the greater bamboo lemur from sympatric *Eulemur fulvus rufus*, with which it is similar in size.

Geographic Range

The greater bamboo lemur has been studied and surveyed in the humid forests of the Ranomafana region, from Kianjavato in the east through Vohiparara in the west, extending some 50 km from north to south (Meier and Rumpler, 1987; Wright *et al.*, 1987). However, reports exist of its occurrence near Vondrozo and Maroantsetra (Tattersall, 1982), and it apparently occurs in the Andringitra Nature Reserve as well (E. Sterling, pers. comm.). In former times, *H. simus* was widespread in Madagascar. Subfossil remains have been found at Ampasambazimba in the Itasy Basin, in the Grotte d'Andrafiabé on the Ankarana Massif and in the Grottes d'Anjohibé near Majunga (= Mahajanga) (Godfrey and Vuillaume-Randriamanantena, 1986; Wilson *et al.*, 1988). Further survey work might still locate additional populations outside the currently very restricted range.

Natural History

The diet of the greater bamboo lemur is primarily bamboo (up to 98%), and includes the soft pith found inside large bamboo stalks. Food sources also include flowers of the traveler's palm (*Ravenala madagascariensis*), fruits of *Artocarpus integrifolius*, *Ficus* spp. and *Dypsis* spp., and leaves of *Pennisteum clandestinum* (Meier and Rumpler, 1987). In eating giant bamboo, *H. simus* strips the outside of the live stalk and tears apart the bamboo pole to get to the pith, an impressive accomplishment for a small animal. This system of foraging leaves dramatic evidence of the lemur's presence. The greater bamboo lemur has been observed in agricultural plantations within the eastern rain forest where giant bamboo (*Cephalostachium vigueri*) is prominent.

Group size ranges from 4 to 12, and animals are active primarily during the night. Further studies of this species' ecology and behavior are urgently needed.

Conservation Status

The greater bamboo lemur is threatened by slash-and-burn agriculture and the cutting of bamboo. These factors, in addition to hunting with slingshots (Meier, 1987), appear to have resulted in the extirpation of this species in the forests around Kianjavato and still threaten it in other forests of this region (Meier and Rumpler, 1987). *Hapalemur simus* is now protected only in Ranomafana National Park, where the population is estimated to be 1,000 (Wright, 1988; Mittermeier *et al.*, 1992). Several individuals have been brought into captivity in France and in Madagascar, but there has been no coordinated captive breeding program to date (Olney and Ellis, 1992; ISIS, 1993).

Based upon its critically small population, its occurrence in only one (and possibly two) protected areas, and the severe threats to any small populations still found in unprotected forests, the greater bamboo lemur was given the *Highest Priority* rating (6) in the IUCN/SSC Primate Specialist Group's *Lemurs of Madagascar: An Action Plan for their Conservation* (Mittermeier *et al.*, 1992). Using the latest IUCN Red List criteria, we place this species in the *Critically Endangered* category.

Where To See It

The best location for seeing this species is in the forest at the Agricultural Station of Kianjavato, but permission is difficult for visitors to obtain. Ranomafana National Park is the only real alternative, and has the advantage of being the only known area where all three *Hapalemur* species are sympatric. Finding all three is possible, but requires perseverance and time as all are secretive. However, it is well worth the effort because both *H. aureus* and *H. simus* are among the rarest and most endangered of all primates.

PHOTO BY RUSSELL A. MITTERMEIER

Fig. 6.20: Greater bamboo lemur (*Hapalemur simus*), one of the most endangered Malagasy lemurs.

Lemur: Ring-tailed Lemur

Until 1988, the genus *Lemur* included *Lemur catta* plus the five species now allocated to *Eulemur*. However, noting that *L. catta* appeared to show some affinities to *Hapalemur,* Simons and Rumpler (1988) and Groves and Eaglen (1988) proposed separating *Eulemur* as a distinct genus. This is not accepted by all authorities; Tattersall and Schwartz (1991), for example, reviewed the evidence and concluded that available data were inadequate to determine relationships within Lemuridae and did not justify major changes in nomenclature. They suggested a return to the pre-1970s nomenclature in which all seven species listed below under *Lemur*, *Eulemur* and *Varecia* were lumped together in the single genus *Lemur*. However, use of *Eulemur* and *Varecia* has gained wide acceptance, and we believe that it is more useful to recognize the distinctiveness of these different animals. We therefore follow Simons and Rumpler (1988) and Groves and Eaglen (1988) in recognizing *Lemur*, *Eulemur* and *Varecia* as distinct genera.

Key to illustrations on the following page (Fig. 6.21):
   a. *Lemur catta* feeding on tamarind fruit
  b, d, e. *Lemur catta* in mid-leap
   c. *Lemur catta* male anointing tail with scent from the
     antebrachial gland on the palmar surface of
     the wrist
   f. *Lemur catta* climbing in tree

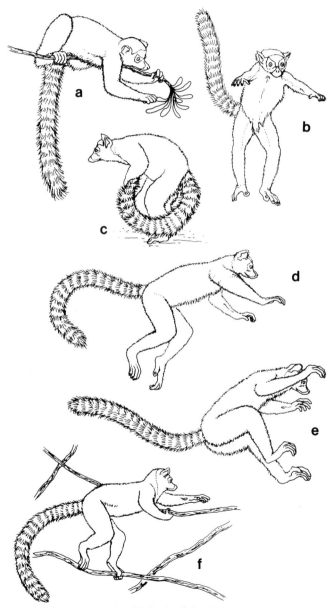

Fig. 6.21: *Lemur* postural and behavioral drawings.

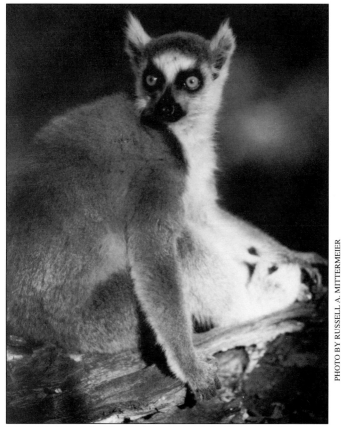

PHOTO BY RUSSELL A. MITTERMEIER

Fig. 6.22: Ring-tailed lemur (*Lemur catta*), in the Berenty Reserve. This species is the most terrestrial of the living lemurs.

Key to illustrations on the following page (Fig. 6.23):

      a. *Lemur catta* examining scent on branch at group range boundary

      b. *Lemur catta* resting with infant on back

      c. *Lemur catta* in seated "sun-worshipping" posture

      d. *Lemur catta* descending vertical tree trunk

      e. *Lemur catta* scent marking a tree using perianal glands

      f. *Lemur catta* with infant walking quadrupedally on the ground

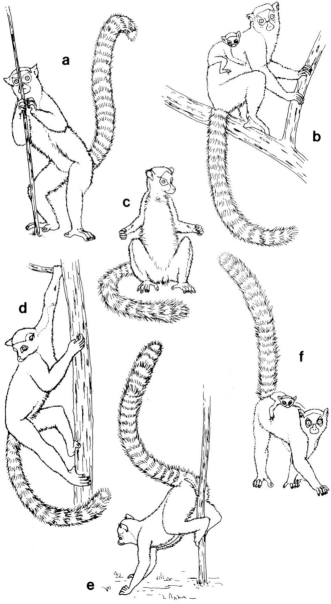

Fig. 6.23: *Lemur* postural and behavioral drawings

PHOTO BY RUSSELL A. MITTERMEIER

Fig. 6.24: Ring-tailed lemur (*Lemur catta*).

Key to illustrations on the following page (Fig. 6.25):

       a. *Lemur catta* running quadrupedally
       b. *Lemur catta* standing bipedally
       c. *Lemur catta* infant suckling
       d. *Lemur catta* with tail in characteristic "stink fight"
          position
       e. Close-up of face of *Lemur catta*
       f. *Lemur catta* sitting on the ground
       g. *Lemur catta* group moving on the ground (note the
          characteristic tail postures)

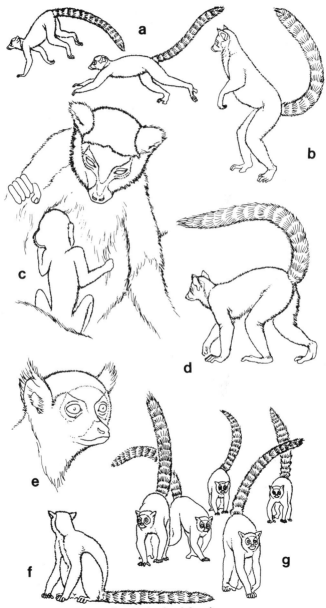

Fig. 6.25: *Lemur* postural and behavioral drawings.

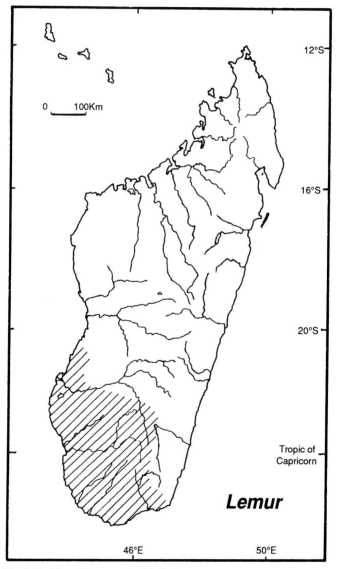

Fig. 6.26: Map of *Lemur catta* distribution.

Lemur catta   **Color Plate 12**
Ring-Tailed Lemur   **Page 329**

French: Maki, Maki Mococo, Maque
German: Katta
Malagasy: Maki, Hira

Identification

This is the only surviving semi-terrestrial diurnal lemur in Madagascar. Its head and body length are about 42.5 cm and the tail length about 60 cm, for a total length of about 100+ cm. Adult body weight varies from 3 to 3.5 kg. The back is gray to rosy brown, limbs and haunches are gray, and the crown and neck are dark gray. The underside is white. The face is white except for dark triangular eye patches and a black nose. Ears are angular with white hair on top. The tail, which gives this lemur its common name, is ringed with alternating black and white bands. Both sexes possess dark "antebrachial" glands near the wrists; in males they are overlaid with a horny spur.

This species is the best known of all Malagasy lemurs and is immediately identified by its strikingly banded tail. It cannot be confused with other lemurs within its range or with any other Malagasy lemur.

Geographical Range

The ring-tailed lemur is limited to south and southwestern Madagascar, from Fort-Dauphin (= Tolagnaro) west and extending as far north as Morandava on the west coast. One additional population occurs near the mountains of Andringitra on the southeastern plateau.

Natural History

The ring-tailed lemur is the most intensively studied of all lemur taxa. It inhabits many forest types throughout its range, including dry scrub and Didiereaceae forest, as well as deciduous and gallery forests. Densities are higher in undisturbed gallery forests than in drier habitats.

The diet consists of fruit, leaves, flowers, herbs, other plant parts including bark, and sap from close to three dozen different plant species; the kily tree (*Tamarindus indica*) is especially favored (Jolly, 1966; Sussman, 1974, 1977; O'Connor, 1987). The proportion of fruit versus leaves varies according to forest type. Ring-tailed lemurs feed in all forest strata and spend more time on the ground than any other lemur (Sussman, 1974, 1977).

Group size ranges from 3 to over 20 individuals and averages about 18, with multiple adult males and females. Females remain in their natal groups and are dominant over males (Jolly, 1966; Sussman, 1977); males transfer between groups. Home range sizes vary from 6 ha to as large as 23 ha (Budnitz and Dainis, 1975; Sussman, 1977). Day ranges may vary considerably, but were recorded by Sussman (1977) to be 900-1000 m.

Females first give birth at three years of age (Sussman, 1989), and most of them subsequently produce offspring annually. Mating begins in mid-April (Jolly, 1966; Budnitz and Dainis, 1975) and most young are born in August and September, after a gestation period of 134-138 days (Van Horn and Eaton, 1979). Within two weeks after birth, after initially clinging to its mother's underside, the infant can be seen riding on her back. Infant mortality is high; at the Beza Mahafaly Reserve about half of all infants die in their first year and only 40% reach maturity (Sussman, 1991). *Lemur catta* alarm calls distinguish between terrestrial and avian predators, indicating that predation may be a factor in infant mortality.

Conservation Status

Although generally considered a common species because it is so often seen in captivity and is readily observed in the wild, indications are that *L. catta* may be more threatened than originally believed (Sussman and Richard, 1986). It has a strong preference for gallery forests along rivers and for *Euphorbia* bush, but these habitats are disappearing rapidly within the region because of fires, overgrazing by livestock, and cutting of trees for charcoal production. Satellite imagery analysis by Green and Sussman (1991), for instance, indicates that gallery forests are disappearing in southern Madagascar. If it in fact requires gallery forest for its survival, rather than just preferring this habitat, it could be in serious trouble; however, this remains to be determined. Furthermore, *L. catta* is hunted for food in certain areas and frequently kept as a pet (O'Connor, 1987).

Fortunately, *Lemur catta* occurs in all protected areas within its range, including Isalo National Park, the Andohahela, Andringitra and Tsimanampetsotsa Nature Reserves, the Beza-Mahafaly Special Reserve and the Berenty Private Reserve (Nicoll and Langrand, 1989), but levels of protection vary considerably in these areas. Population figures are not available, but a reasonable order of magnitude estimate would be 10,000-100,000 (Mittermeier *et al.*, 1992).

The ring-tailed lemur breeds very well in captivity; close to 1,000 are registered with ISIS by approximately 140 zoos worldwide, and this is undoubtedly an underestimate (ISIS, 1993).

This species was given a *High Priority* rating (5) in the IUCN/ SSC Primate Specialist Group's *Lemurs of Madagascar: An Action Plan for their Conservation* (Mittermeier *et al.*, 1992) largely because of its taxonomic distinctiveness as a monotypic genus. Using the latest IUCN Red List criteria, we have to place this species in the *Vulnerable* category. However, further survey work, especially on the relationship of this species to gallery forest, may result in a change in the threat category.

Where To See It

This species can be seen in all the protected areas within its range, but it is most easily observed at close range in the Berenty Private Reserve, about 1 1/2 hours by car to the west of Fort-Dauphin (= Tolagnaro). This reserve is the first stop on most tours to Madagascar and is a must for the first time visitor. Habituated groups of *L. catta* and *Propithecus v. verreauxi* can be seen within minutes of arriving at the reserve.

In Berenty, *L. catta* is seen mainly in gallery forests dominated by *kily* or tamarind trees (*Tamarindus indica*). To see it in Didiereaceae scrub, one can travel three to four hours on dirt roads from Berenty to Hazafotsy at the edge of the Andohahela Nature Reserve, an outstanding experience that takes the visitor through an interesting portion of southern spiny desert inhabited by scattered villages of Antandroy, the traditional people of the region.

Another good site for *L. catta* is the Beza-Mahafaly Special Reserve, about five to six hours east of Tuléar (= Toliary). A much less visited reserve, this area has a more natural aspect and is quite attractive, but takes longer to reach than Berenty.

L. catta can also be easily observed in Isalo National Park, where troops can be seen, walking and climbing among the rocky cliffs, rather like baboons in southern Africa.

Eulemur: True Lemurs

The genus *Eulemur* includes five species: the brown lemurs (*E. fulvus*), with six subspecies; the black lemurs (*E. macaco*), with two subspecies; the crowned lemur (*E. coronatus*); the red-bellied lemur (*E. rubriventer*); and the mongoose lemur (*E. mongoz*). Not all agree that the five species in this genus deserve distinction from *Lemur catta*, although we follow this taxonomy here because it is starting to receive wider use (but see footnote on p. 143). The validity of these five species seems quite well established, but taxonomic questions do exist at the level of subspecies.

Most recent authors have recognized seven subspecies of *E. fulvus* (*fulvus, rufus, albifrons, albocollaris, collaris, sanfordi* and *mayottensis*). However, we believe that the populations on the Comores (*E. f. "mayottensis"*) are really nothing more than introduced *E. f. fulvus*, and therefore not worthy of recognition as a distinct taxon. This reduces the number of *fulvus* taxa covered in this book to six.

Traits shared by the species of *Eulemur* include: medium size (body weights from 2 to 3 kg), sexual dichromatism (except for *E. f. fulvus*), quadrupedal locomotion, and significant ´nocturnal activity. Males often scent mark with the anogenital region, the hands and the head. Females mark with urine and the anogenital region, and often elicit over-marking in males. In most species, the males mark the females as well.

The genus *Eulemur* is found in almost all forested areas of Madagascar except the extreme south.

Key to illustrations on the following page (Fig. 6.27):
  a. *Eulemur f. fulvus* female and infant standing quadrupedally
  b. *Eulemur mongoz* female and infant sitting on branch
  c. *Eulemur f. albifrons* male walking quadrupedally on branch
  d. *Eulemur f. fulvus* female standing and feeding
  e. *Eulemur f. fulvus* female in sitting posture
  f. *Eulemur rubriventer* male in vertical clinging resting posture

Fig. 6.27: *Eulemur* postural and behavioral drawings.

PHOTO BY RUSSELL A. MITTERMEIER

Fig. 6.28: Female red-fronted brown lemur (*Eulemur fulvus rufus*) in the Analabe Private Reserve, north of Morondava.

Key to illustrations on the following page (Fig. 6.29):

- a. *Eulemur f. rufus* female climbing horizontally
- b. *Eulemur f. albifrons* female sitting in a tree fork
- c. *Eulemur m. macaco* male and female standing quadrupedally on a rock and monitoring their environment
- d. *Eulemur mongoz* male sitting in a tree fork
- e. *Eulemur f. fulvus* female grooming
- f. *Eulemur m. macaco* female standing on a branch and monitoring its environment
- g. *Eulemur m. macaco* male sitting on forked branches
- h. *Eulemur f. sanfordi* male resting with tail over shoulder
- i. *Eulemur f. albifrons* male sitting on branch

Fig. 6.29: *Eulemur* postural and behavioral drawings.

PHOTO BY RUSSELL A. MITTERMEIER

Fig. 6.30: Female crowned lemur (*Eulemur coronatus*).

Key to illustrations on the following page (Fig. 6.31):

    a. *Eulemur f. fulvus* female leaping with baby clinging to its waist

    b. *Eulemur m. macaco* male standing bipedally to monitor its environment

    c. *Eulemur f. fulvus* female standing quadrupedally

    d. *Eulemur f. albifrons* female standing quadrupedally and feeding

    e. *Eulemur f. rufus* female with infant climbing on vertical trunk

Fig. 6.31: *Eulemur* postural and behavioral drawings.

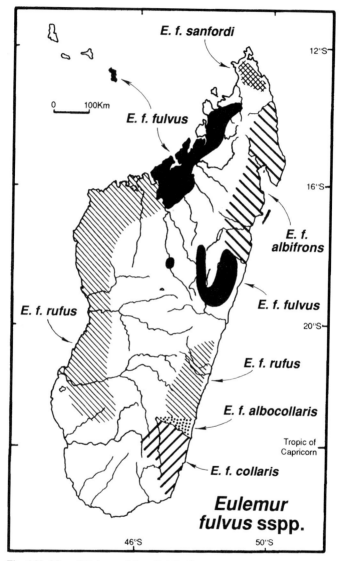

Fig. 6.32: Map of *Eulemur fulvus* distribution.

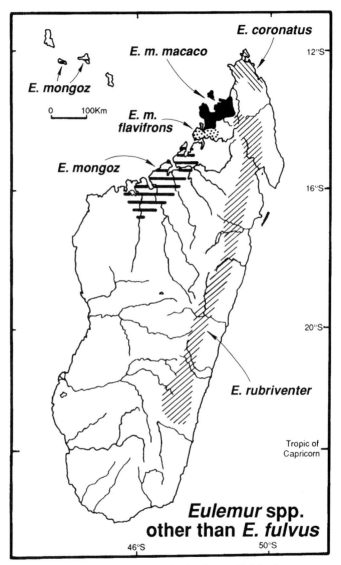

Fig. 6.33: Map of *Eulemur* spp. distribution (except *E. fulvus*).

Eulemur fulvus fulvus   Color Plate 14, 17
Common Brown Lemur   Page 331, 334

French: Lémur Brun
German: Brauner Maki
Malagasy: Varika, Varikosy (east coast),
            Dredrika (northwest)
Comores: Komba

Identification

Eulemur f. fulvus is a medium-sized lemur with a body length
up to 50 cm and the tail slightly longer, for an overall length >100
cm.   Body weight is around 2.6 kg. The most notable character
is the absence of obvious sexual dichromatism in this subspecies.
Both sexes are brown to gray-brown dorsally, and have light
beards and dark faces. There is high variation in the degree of light
patches above each eye on the forehead.   Northern populations
and the Mayotte population both have large patches; to the south
and southeast only slight patches can be discerned. At several
locations in the east, this subspecies is found relatively near the
white-fronted lemur and may be intergrading.   The common
brown lemur has a range that is adjacent to the geographic ranges
of three other subspecies.   Intermediates can be expected in the
wild (and should be reported to the authors of this book since they
are of considerable scientific interest).

In the field, *E. f. fulvus* is most likely to be confused with *E.
mongoz* in the west and *E. rubriventer* in the east, especially if
only a fleeting glimpse of the animals is obtained. However, if a
clear sighting is made, this lemur can easily be distinguished by
coloration and facial patterns, and by the absence of sexual
dimorphism (both *E. mongoz* and *E. rubriventer* exhibiting distinct sexual dimorphism).

Geographic Distribution

This subspecies is found in western Madagascar north of the
Betsiboka River, where it lives on the high plateau in scattered
forest fragments; in the east it occurs to the north of the Mangoro
River; and it is also found on the island of Mayotte in the
Comores (where it was presumably introduced by man).   The
western populations can be divided into a southern population
known primarily from the area of Ankarafantsika and a northern
population from the Manongarivo Reserve (Andranomalaza River)

up to the Mahavavy River south of Ambilobe. This northwestern population is extremely similar in coloration to the Mayotte population and may be found throughout the moister forests of the Sambirano region, and likely on the slopes of the Tsaratanana Massif. The eastern population is more problematic. It is found generally northeast of Antananarivo, but includes populations well into the suggested range of the white-fronted lemur. Some level of intergradation exists, but details are lacking.

Natural History

The common brown lemur has been studied at Périnet (= Andasibe) (Ganzhorn, 1988) and Ampijoroa (Harrington, 1975), and on the island of Mayotte (Tattersall, 1977a). Group size varies from 3-12 on the mainland, but from 2-29 on Mayotte. Home ranges vary from seven hectares in the west to likely over 20 ha in the east, with population densities of 0.4-0.6 individuals/ ha. High densities of 10 individuals/ha were observed on Mayotte and group composition was fluid. Larger groups formed and divided into smaller groups throughout the day.

The diet consists of fruit at varying stages of ripeness, young leaves, and flowers. On Mayotte, Tattersall (1982) described high seasonal variation in the diet such that fruit, leaves, or flowers could predominate in any one month. This seasonal variability reflects the degree of flexibility in the diet of brown lemurs in general. Ganzhorn (1988) examined the lemur community at Périnet (= Andasibe) and found that *E. f. fulvus* accepts significant levels of both tannins and alkaloids in its diet. This tolerance of plant chemical defenses, together with high rates of fiber digestion, helps to explain the wide-spread geographic distribution of the species. This dietary flexibility has also been suggested as a factor mitigating within-group feeding competition and thus reducing the need for female dominance (Pereira *et al.,* 1989).

Conservation Status

Forest destruction is the principal threat to the survival of the common brown lemur, as it is to *E. fulvus* as a species, but hunting is also a factor. This subspecies is found in the Mantady National Park, the Ankarafantsika Nature Reserve and the Ambatovaky, Ambohitantely, Analamazaotra, Bora, Manongarivo and Tsaratanana Special Reserves, and possibly in one or more protected areas where the subspecies of brown lemur present has not been identified (Nicoll and Langrand, 1989; Harcourt and Thornback, 1990; Mittermeier *et al.*, 1992). There are no population figures available, but a reasonable order of magnitude estimate of *E. f. fulvus* numbers in Madagascar would be >100,000 (Mittermeier *et al.*, 1992). On Mayotte, a population estimate of about 50,000 in 1975 (Tattersall 1977b) had been reduced to less than half as of the last survey (Tattersall, 1991). About 140 common brown lemurs are reported to be in captivity in approximately 40 zoos worldwide (ISIS, 1993).

Given its presumably large population, widespread distribution and presence in at least eight protected areas, *Eulemur f. fulvus* was given a *Low Priority* rating (2) in the IUCN/SSC Primate Specialist Group's *Lemurs of Madagascar: An Action Plan for their Conservation* (Mittermeier *et al.*, 1992). Using the most recent IUCN Red List criteria, we place this subspecies in the *Low Risk* category.

Where To See It

The eastern population of *E. f. fulvus* is most easily seen at Périnet (=Andasibe), where it is one of the most common lemurs. In the west, it is best seen at the Ampijoroa station in the Ankarafantsika Nature Reserve. On Mayotte, it is commonly seen at dusk in large mango trees in secondary forest patches, especially at La Convalescence and Le Bénara, a few kilometers along the main road from Mamoudzou to Sada.

Eulemur fulvus rufus   **Color Plates 14,17**
Red-Fronted Brown Lemur   **Pages 331, 334**

Other English: Rufous Brown Lemur
French: Lémur à Front Roux
German: Rotstirnmaki
Malagasy: Varika, Varikamavo (east)

Identification

Eulemur fulvus rufus is a medium-sized lemur with a body
length over 40 cm, a tail length of 55 cm (for an overall length of
between 90-100 cm), and weight around 2.7 kg. In coat color,
males are gray to gray-brown and females are rufous to brown.
Both sexes have pale patches over the eyes as in *E. f. fulvus*; in
the western population these are large and continue down around
the eyes, ending in light cheeks in the females. *E. f. rufus* males
have thick cream-colored hair surrounding the head, more rufous
on the crown. The eastern males have more notable eye patches.
Eastern females tend to be more rufous to rust in coat color. A
short russet beard is found in females.

In the western part of its range, this subspecies is unlikely to
be confused with any other sympatric lemur, since it is the only
representative of the genus *Eulemur* in this region. In the east, it
might be confused with sympatric *E. rubriventer*, especially if
only a fleeting glimpse of the animal is obtained. Refer to the
color plates for distinguishing features between these two similar-
sized, sexually dimorphic taxa.

Geographic Range

The red-fronted brown lemur is found in western and eastern
Madagascar (Petter *et al.*, 1977; Tattersall, 1982). In the west, it
is known from the Betsiboka River south to the Fiherenana River
near Tuléar (=Toliary), but also has been sighted south of the river
in the forests of Lambomakandro. In the east, the limits of its
distribution are poorly defined, but it appears to occur from the
Mangoro River south to the Andringitra Massif. The southern
limit of its range is apparently the Manampatrana River, which
separates *E. f. rufus* from *E. f. albocollaris*. There also is a small
introduced population of red-fronted lemurs at the Berenty Private Reserve in southern Madagascar (O'Connor, 1987).

Natural History

   E. f. rufus has been studied in the west in the deciduous forests of Antserananomby and Tongobato (Sussman, 1974, 1975, 1977) and in the east at Ranomafana (Meyers, 1988; Overdorff, 1991). A comparison of these studies reveals the degree of variability in the behavioral ecology of the subspecies and the species as a whole. In the west, population density is reported to be extremely high (reaching 10 individuals/ha), with day ranges between 125 and 150 m, and home ranges between 0.75 and 1.0 ha. In the east, population density is much lower and home ranges are as large as 100 ha. Group size ranges from 4 to 17 (average size of 9 individuals) in the west, and from 6 to 18 (average size of 8 individuals) in the east (0.25 individuals/ha); day ranges vary from 457 m to 1,471 m. Dominance hierarchies are unknown in either population and rates of aggression are low.

   The diet of the western population is primarily leaves, pods, stems, flowers, bark and sap of the *kily* tree (*Tamarindus indica*). In the east, Overdorff (1991) found higher dietary diversity and a predominance of fruit, unlike in the west. Other food items include insects, bird nests, and dirt (in the east).

   Reproduction is seasonal. Mating occurs in June, births in September and October, and weaning occurs by January (Sussman, 1977).

Conservation Status

   The primary threat to this subspecies is habitat destruction. In the western forests this is due largely to burning to clear land for pasture; in the east the cause is slash-and-burn agriculture and cutting of forest for fuelwood and construction. The red-fronted lemur is found in the Isalo and Ranomafana National Parks, the Namoroka and Tsingy de Bemaraha Nature Reserves, the Andranomena, Kalambatritra and Pic d'Ivohibe Special Reserves, and the Analabe and Berenty Private Reserves, and it may possibly occur in one or more protected areas where the subspecies of brown lemur has not been identified (Sussman, 1977; O'Connor, 1987; Meyers, 1988; Nicoll and Langrand, 1989; Harcourt and Thornback, 1990; Mittermeier *et al.*, 1992). There are no population figures available, but a reasonable order of magnitude estimate would be >100,000 (Mittermeier *et al.*, 1992). Approximately 100 *E. f. rufus* are held in 22 zoos worldwide, including Zoo Ivoloina in Madagascar (Olney and Ellis, 1992; ISIS, 1993).

   Given its presumably large wild population and occurrence in a number of protected areas, the red-fronted brown lemur was given a *Low Priority* rating (2) in the IUCN/SSC Primate Specialist Group's *Lemurs of Madagascar: An Action Plan for their Conservation* (Mittermeier *et al.*, 1992). Using the latest IUCN Red List criteria, we place this subspecies in the *Low Risk* category.

Where To See It

An excellent place to see the red-fronted brown lemur in the east is at the Ranomafana National Park. In the west, the private reserve of Analabe, north of Morondava, is the best possibility. An introduced group is also easily seen in the Berenty Private Reserve in the far south, coexisting with the native *Lemur catta* and *Propithecus v. verreauxi* populations.

Eulemur fulvus albifrons
White-Fronted Brown Lemur

Color Plates 15,17
Pages 332, 334

French: Lémur à Front Blanc
German: Weisskopfmaki
Malagasy: Varika

Identification

Eulemur fulvus albifrons is a medium-sized lemur with a head and body length of 40 cm, a tail over 50 cm, and a body weight of about 2.3 kg. The defining characters are more or less restricted to the heads of males. They include thick white or cream head hair covering the ears and continuous with a thick white beard, contrasting black face and snout, and a slight dark line down the center of the head. The body coat of males is dark brown with a light brown ventrum. Due to the large geographic range, high variation exists in these characters. Females are less variable. They possess gray heads and the face is sharply outlined as a result of longer hair surrounding the short face hair. The gray of the face continues posteriorly to near the shoulders where it gradually grades into the brown of the back and haunches. In both sexes, the tail is a darker color than the dorsal coat.

The male is easily distinguished from other subspecies by its distinctive white face, but females of different subspecies are sometimes difficult to distinguish from one another.

In the field, *E. f. albifrons* could only be confused with *E. rubriventer* or *Varecia variegata rubra* (on the Masoala Peninsula). However, this is highly unlikely, since the white face of the male *albifrons* should serve to distinguish this animal from other sympatric Lemuridae. It is also smaller than *Varecia* and lacks the very distinctive raucous vocalizations.

Geographic Range

This subspecies is found throughout most of the remaining northeastern rain forest. In the northern part of its range, the white-fronted brown lemur occurs from the Bemarivo River near Sambava, south to near Tamatave (= Toamasina) where it may grade into *E. f. fulvus*. Potentially, the white-fronted lemur may be found as far west as Tsaratanana and it occurs at least as far south as the Betampona Nature Reserve.

Natural History

Very little is known of this subspecies, except that it generally occurs at medium to low densities.

Conservation Status

Destruction of Madagascar's eastern rain forests, primarily for slash-and-burn agriculture, is the principal threat to the survival of *E. f. albifrons*, but it is also hunted for food in many parts of its range. This subspecies is described as common in the Zahamena Nature Reserve, occurs in the Betampona and Marojejy Nature Reserves and in the Nosy Mangabe Special Reserve, and may possibly occur in one or more protected areas where the subspecies of brown lemur has not been identified (Pollock, 1984; Constable *et al.*, 1985; Raxworthy, 1986; Nicoll and Langrand, 1989; Harcourt and Thornback, 1990; Mittermeier *et al.*, 1992). There are no population figures available, but a reasonable order of magnitude estimate for *E. f. albifrons* would be >100,000 (Mittermeier *et al.*, 1992). More than 200 white-fronted lemurs are reported in captivity in more than 40 zoos worldwide, including a colony at Zoo Ivoloina in Madagascar (Olney and Ellis, 1992; ISIS, 1993).

Given its presumably large wild population, occurrence in several protected areas, and a relatively successful captive breeding effort, the white-fronted brown lemur was given a *Low Priority* rating (2) in the IUCN/SSC Primate Specialist Group's *Lemurs of Madagascar: An Action Plan for their Conservation* (Mittermeier *et al.*, 1992). Using the latest IUCN Red List criteria, we place this subspecies in the *Low Risk* category.

Where To See It

This subspecies can be seen in most forests in its range, but is difficult to observe for any length of time if it is locally hunted. The easiest place to see the animal is on the island of Nosy Mangabe, near Maroantsetra in the Bay of Antongil in northeastern Madagascar.

Eulemur fulvus sanfordi   **Color Plates 15, 18**
Sanford's Brown Lemur   **Pages 332, 335**

French: Lémur de Sanford
German: Sanfordmaki
Malagasy: Ankomba, Beharavoaka

Identification

The head and body length of this subspecies is just under 40 cm, the tail length is over 50 cm, for an overall length of 90-100 cm. The body weight is approximately 2.3 kg. The most notable character of this subspecies are the lavish ear tufts of the males, which are off-white, cream, or slightly rufous. The ear tufts are complemented by thick beards of similar color, giving the appearance of a ragged mane from the top of the ears down to around the face. The nose, the top of the snout, and the area between the eyes are black. The head is dominated by a dark "T" that connects the eyes and nose, surrounded by light forehead and cheeks which are delineated from the ear tufts and beard by shorter hair. The top of the head is cream to brown and always lighter than the brown body color. The ventrum is light brown; the tail is brown. Females are brown on the back, flanks and tail, with a lighter ventrum, and a gray face. The gray continues over the head onto the shoulders and to the upper part of the back. Light patches are often found over the eyes. It is difficult to distinguish female Sanford's brown lemurs from female white-fronted brown lemurs.

E. f. sanfordi is sympatric with *E. coronatus* throughout its range, but can be easily distinguished from this animal. *E. coronatus* has the V-shaped orange pattern on the head in both sexes, and lacks the distinctive white ear tufts and beard of male *E. f. sanfordi*.

Geographic Range

Sanford's brown lemur has a very restricted range in northern Madagascar. It occurs from the Ampasindava peninsula, west of Diego-Suarez (= Antsiranana), south to the Mahavavy River in the west and to the Manambato River in the east (Petter *et al.*, 1977; Petter and Petter-Rousseaux, 1979; Meyers and Ratsirarson, 1989). Populations of *Eulemur fulvus* occur south of the Manambato river and appear to be intermediate (especially concerning the ear tufts) between Sanford's brown lemur and the white-fronted brown lemur, which occurs further to the south.

Higher densities are found on the slopes of the Montagne d'Ambre and in other primarily evergreen forests than in the drier forest patches in the region, including the Analamera Special Reserve. These lemurs are absent from the driest forests such as those on the Cap d'Ambre north of Antsiranana and further to the southeast near Daraina.

Natural History

Sanford's brown lemur has been studied in the Ankarana Special Reserve and the Montagne d'Ambre National Park . In Ankarana, it appears to favor secondary forest and is active at night as well as during the day (Wilson *et al.*, 1988, 1989; Fowler *et al.*, 1989). Group sizes appear to be larger, up to 15 individuals, in Ankarana (Wilson *et al.*, 1989); in Montagne d'Ambre, they range from 3 to 9 individuals (B. Freed, pers. comm.). Home range sizes as large as 14.4 ha have been reported from Montagne d'Ambre (Arbelot-Tracqui, 1983), and there is considerable home range overlap. Although agonistic interactions were observed between groups, these were not territorial in the traditional sense.

The diet consists primarily of fruit of varying degrees of ripeness, but includes other plant items according to their seasonal availability (buds, young leaves, flowers, etc.) as well as invertebrates (centipedes, millipedes, and spiders).

Matings occur in late May and gestation is about 120 days, births occurring in late September and early October (Arbelot-Tracqui, 1983; Wilson *et al.*, 1989; B. Freed, pers. comm.).

Conservation Status

The primary threat to the survival of Sanford's brown lemur is habitat destruction, although it does appear to survive in degraded habitats. It is found in the Montagne d'Ambre National Park and in the Analamera and Ankarana Special Reserves, but the level of protection varies among these reserves (Nicoll and Langrand, 1989; Harcourt and Thornback, 1990; Mittermeier *et al.*, 1992). Nicoll and Langrand (1989) report widespread and increasing poaching at Montagne d'Ambre, as well as the threat of brush fires on the park's periphery. Hawkins *et al.* (1990) also report hunting in Analamera. Although hunting does not appear to be a problem in the Ankarana Special Reserve, tree felling is increasing within that reserve.

There are no population figures available, but a reasonable

order of magnitude estimate would be 10,000 - 100,000 (Mittermeier *et al.*, 1992).   The only captive breeding groups   of
Sanford's brown lemur are at the Duke University Primate Center
(USA)   and the Banham Zoo (UK), which together hold 17
animals (ISIS, 1993).

This subspecies' very restricted range, the continuing threats
to wild populations, and minimal captive breeding efforts are
offset to some degree by the fact that it is found in three protected
areas, which is why it was given a *Low Priority* rating (3) in the
IUCN/SSC Primate Specialist Group's *Lemurs of Madagascar:
An Action Plan for their Conservation* (Mittermeier *et al.*, 1992).
However, a reassessment of its status has placed more weight on
the various threats to its survival. Therefore, using the latest IUCN
Red List criteria, we place *E. f. sanfordi* in the *Vulnerable*
category.

Where To See It

Both the Montagne d'Ambre National Park and the Ankarana
Special Reserve are good places to see Sanford's brown lemur. It
can often be seen right at the headquarters of the Montagne
d'Ambre National Park, in the forest at the edge of the clearing.
In Ankarana, it is most easily seen in the Canyon Forestière.

Eulemur fulvus albocollaris   Color Plates 16, 18
White-Collared Brown Lemur   Pages 333, 335

French: Maki à Fraise, Lémur à Collier Blanc
Malagasy: Varika

Identification

The taxonomic status of this subspecies remains uncertain. It was separated from the collared lemur (*E. f. collaris*) due to the discovery of chromosome numbers unique among brown lemurs (2N=48, Rumpler, 1975), and some researchers believe that both *albocollaris* and *collaris* are so distinctive morphologically that both warrant recognition as separate species (Y. Rumpler, pers. comm.). However, others believe that the morphological similarities between *albocollaris* and *collaris* are so strong that full taxonomic separation may prove inappropriate (Hamilton *et al.*, 1980). Pending the results of ongoing research, we continue to use the widely accepted arrangement in which both *albocollaris* and *collaris* are considered subspecies of *E. fulvus*.

Coloration of the white-collared lemur is extremely similar to that of the collared lemur, except that male *E. f. albocollaris* have white beards compared to cream to rufous beards in *collaris*. Female white-collared lemurs are more rufous in body coat, similar to female *E. f. rufus*.

Geographic Range

The white-collared lemur has the most restricted range of any *E. fulvus* subspecies. Its known distribution includes the thin strip of eastern forest south of the Manampatrana River down to the Mananara River (Tattersall, 1982). An isolated population occurs in the Manombo Special Reserve near Farafangana.

Natural History

This subspecies has not been studied in the wild, but is known to inhabit eastern rain forest.

Conservation Status

The white-collared lemur has a small range and, like other eastern rain forest lemurs, is threatened by habitat destruction. The only protected area in which it occurs, the Manombo Special Reserve, requires better management and protection (Nicoll and Langrand, 1989). There are no population figures available, but a reasonable order of magnitude estimate would be 1,000-10,000 (Mittermeier *et al.*, 1992). The only individuals known to be in captivity are part of a small breeding group in Strasbourg, France.

Given the very restricted range of this subspecies, its presumed small population, and the fact that it is known to occur in only one protected area, it was given a *Priority* rating (4) in the IUCN/SSC Primate Specialist Group's *Lemurs of Madagascar: An Action Plan for their Conservation* (Mittermeier *et al.*, 1992). Using the latest IUCN Red List criteria, and the recommendations of experts most familiar with this subspecies (P. Wright, pers. comm.; N. Rowe, pers. comm.), we place this subspecies in the *Endangered* category.

Where To See It

The best place to see the white-collared lemur is the strip of forest just west of the town of Vondrozo, west of Farafangana. As with many of the other poorly known lemurs, we recommend an expedition to see this subspecies only for the more seasoned lemur watcher on a second or third trip to Madagascar.

Eulemur fulvus collaris   Color Plates 16, 18
Collared Brown Lemur   Pages 333, 335

French: Lémur à Collier Roux
German: Halsbandmaki
Malagasy: Varika

Identification

The collared brown lemur is similar in length to other *E. fulvus* subspecies and weighs about 2.5 kg. Males are brownish-gray with a dark stripe down the back, a dark tail and tail tip and a lighter ventrum. The muzzle, forehead, and head are black, and light patches are noticeable over the eyes (but variable). Males also possess a thick, elongated cream- to rufous-colored beard. Female collared lemurs have a rufous to brown coat and a gray face. They also have a reddish beard which is significantly shorter than that of males. Female *E. fulvus collaris* are virtually indistinguishable from female *E. f. albocollaris,* except that the latter have coats which are brighter rufous in color. Male *E. f. collaris* can be distinguished from *E. f. albocollaris* by the cream to rufous beard, the beard in *albocollaris* being white.

Of note for this subspecies is the existence of polymorphism in chromosome numbers, which include 2N = 50, 51, and 52 (Buettner-Janusch and Hamilton, 1979).

Geographic Range

The collared brown lemur is found in southeastern Madagascar and ranges from the Mananara River near Vangaindrano, south to Fort-Dauphin (= Tolagnaro), but the extent of its northern and western limits is not well established (Petter *et al.*, 1977; Petter and Petter-Rousseaux, 1979; Tattersall, 1982; Harcourt and Thornback, 1990). No populations are known from the plateau west of the eastern escarpment; the southern limit to its range is abrupt, as rain forest changes to the arid Didiereaceae-dominated bush just west of Fort-Dauphin (= Tolagnaro).

Natural History

The ecology and behavior of this subspecies remain to be studied.

Conservation Status

The primary threat to the survival of *E. f. collaris* is habitat destruction, but it is also reported to be widely hunted for food and trapped occasionally for the local pet trade. The only protected area in which it is known to occur naturally is Parcel 1 of the Andohahela Special Reserve, but a few collared brown lemurs also have been introduced to the Berenty and St. Luce Private Reserves (Jolly *et al.*, 1982; O'Connor *et al.*, 1986; Nicoll and Langrand, 1989; Harcourt and Thornback, 1990; Mittermeier *et al.*, 1992). There are no population figures available, but a reasonable order of magnitude estimate would be at the lower end of 10,000-100,000 (Mittermeier *et al.*, 1992). Approximately 40 *E.f. collaris* are in captivity in six U.S. and European institutions, the largest colony being at the Duke University Primate Center (Olney and Ellis, 1992; ISIS, 1993).

Due to its presumed population size, the collared brown lemur was given a *Low Priority* rating (3) in the IUCN/SSC Primate Specialist Group's *Lemurs of Madagascar: An Action Plan for their Conservation* (Mittermeier *et al.*, 1992). However, given the fact that it is found in only one protected area and is apparently under pressure even there, we have reassessed its status. Using the latest IUCN Red List criteria, we place this subspecies in the *Vulnerable* category.

Where To See It

The collared lemur is most easily seen in the very small St. Luce Private Reserve north of Fort-Dauphin (= Tolagnaro) along the coast. As with Berenty and Analabe, this area is owned by M. Jean de Heaulme, and arrangements to visit this reserve can be made through him in Fort-Dauphin. Another possibility is the rain forest portion (Parcel 1) of the Andohahela Nature Reserve, especially along the road to the Col de Maningotra, a pass through the mountains in the rain forest portion of the reserve. This area is a couple of hours by four-wheel drive vehicle from Fort-Dauphin (= Tolagnaro) and again arrangements to visit this area can be made through M. de Heaulme.

Eulemur macaco macaco
Black Lemur

Color Plates 19, 21
Pages 336, 338

French: Lémur Macaco
German: Mohrenmaki
Malagasy: Ankomba, Komba

Identification

Black lemurs are of medium size with a body length about 41 cm and a tail length of 55 cm, for an overall length of between 90 100 cm. Body weight is around 2.4 kg. Ears are lavishly tufted with long hair originating on and around the ear. The tuft is black in males and white in females. Both sexes have rust to brown eyes. Males are uniformly black. Females have a dark dorsal coat which lightens to a deep rust or brown on the sides of the back and then off-white ventrally. The extremities and often the tail are dark. The face is dark, and rufous beards are found in some individuals; the top of the head is black, gray, or sometimes white.

Eulemur macaco is usually the only *Eulemur* in its range (although there is some sympatry with *E. f. fulvus*). In any case, its striking sexual dimorphism makes it very difficult to confuse with any other species.

Geographic Range

This subspecies is found only in the northwest, primarily in the Sambirano region (Fig. 6.34). The northern limit is the Mahavavy River and the southern limit for pure *E. m. macaco* is the Sambirano River. South of the Sambirano, the degree of subspecies intergradation is still under investigation (Rabarivola *et al.*, 1991). The western part of the range includes the Ampasindava Peninsula, the islands of Nosy Be and Nosy Komba, and the dry forests along the coast northeast of Ambanja, including the peninsula leading to Nosy Faly. The eastern limit is probably high on the Tsaratanana Massif. Black lemurs are found sympatrically with *E. f. fulvus* in the Galoka and Manongarivo Mountains (Tattersall, 1976b; Meyers *et al.*, 1989). *E. m. macaco* has also been introduced onto the tiny island of Nosy Tanikely near Nosy Komba (R. A. Mittermeier, pers. obs.).

Natural History

Black lemurs have been reported from undisturbed forest, secondary forest, timber plantations and in disturbed forests intermingled with crops such as coffee and cashew trees (Andrews, 1989). Relatively little is known of black lemur ecology or social behavior. These primates are generally similar to *Eulemur fulvus* in group size and composition, averaging between 7- 10 and with a range of 2-15 (Petter, 1962; Andrews, 1989). However, groups in some populations have sex ratios biased towards males. Groups maintain separate ranges during the day but may aggregate during the night. On the islands of Nosy Be and Nosy Komba, Petter (1962) recorded peak activity during early morning and late afternoon, while Birkel (1987) reported groups feeding well into the night.

Black lemurs feed on ripe fruit, leaves, flowers, and occasionally insects (Petter, 1962; Petter and Petter, 1971; Petter *et al.*, 1977). They pass seeds rapidly, and may be an important seed dispersal agent in the Sambirano.

Females give birth to a single young, usually between September and November (Petter and Petter, 1971).

Conservation Status

Eulemur macaco macaco is found in the Lokobe Nature Reserve on the island of Nosy Be, and in the Tsaratanana Nature Reserve on the mainland (Raxworthy and Rakotondraparany, 1988; Nicoll and Langrand, 1989; Harcourt and Thornback, 1990; Mittermeier *et al.*, 1992), but forests within and outside these reserves have been or are being destroyed or have already been, largely for slash-and-burn agriculture. A population on the island of Nosy Komba, near Nosy Be, is a major tourist attraction and is protected, although the habitat on this island is badly degraded. In addition, black lemurs are poached from the Lokobe Nature Reserve and are sometimes killed when they raid crops. There are no population figures available, but a reasonable order of magnitude estimate would be 10,000-100,000 (Mittermeier *et al.*, 1992). The black lemur breeds fairly well in captivity, there being approximately 275 in over 50 institutions worldwide (Olney and Ellis, 1992; ISIS, 1993).

Given the fact that *Eulemur m. macaco* is found in several protected areas and is believed to number in the tens of thousands, it was given a *Low Priority* rating (3) in the IUCN/SSC Primate Specialist Group's *Lemurs of Madagascar: An Action Plan for*

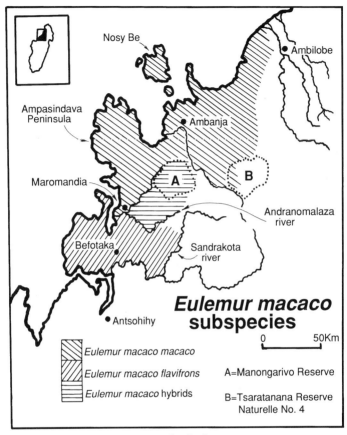

Nosy Be

Ambilobe

Ampasindava
Peninsula

Ambanja

Maromandia

A

B

Andranomalaza
river

Befotaka

Sandrakota
river

Eulemur macaco

Antsohihy

subspecies

0   50Km

Eulemur macaco macaco

Eulemur macaco flavifrons   A=Manongarivo Reserve

Eulemur macaco hybrids   B=Tsaratanana Reserve
                                Naturelle No. 4

Fig. 6.34: Map of *Eulemur macaco* distribution.

their Conservation (Mittermeier *et al.*, 1992). However, given its small range and the fragmented nature of its habitat, we have elevated its status. Using the latest IUCN Red List criteria, we place this subspecies in the *Vulnerable* category.

Where To See It

The best place to see the black lemur is on the island of Nosy Komba, located a short distance from Nosy Be by boat. On this largely degraded island, several groups of black lemurs come to a feeding site where tourists can give them bananas sold by local villagers. The animals are very habituated and will sit on the visitor, provided he or she has sufficient bananas and remains calm and collected. To see the animals in better habitat, one can visit the Lokobe Nature Reserve, right next to Nosy Be's capital of Hellville and the only intact forest remaining on the island. Several enterprising villagers run tours to the edge of the reserve, which include an outrigger canoe ride, a walk in the forest (where *Lepilemur dorsalis* can also be seen), and a picnic. Both Nosy Komba and Lokobe are now on the regular tourist circuit and are a must for first-time visitors to Madagascar. The small introduced population on Nosy Tanikely near Nosy Komba is also easily observed; coral reefs surrounding this island are a popular snorkeling destination on the tourist circuit as well.

Eulemur macaco flavifrons   **Color Plates 19, 21**
Sclater's Black Lemur   **Pages 336, 338**

Other English: Blue-Eyed Black Lemur
French: Lémur Flavifrons
German: Sclater's Mohrenmaki
Malagasy: Ankomba, Ankomba Joby (black males),
                Ankomba Mena (red females)

Identification

Sclater's black lemur is similar in size and weight to the black lemur. The distinguishing characters are non-tufted ears and gray to blue eyes. General body hair is shorter and softer in appearance. Males have a noticeable tuft of hair rising up from the forehead and tapering off towards the back of the head, where hair length is uniform over the rest of the body. Females are lighter than female *E. m. macaco* and have rufous to tan (and sometimes gray) coats dorsally and on the tail, a light off-white ventrum, a reddish beard, and dark extremities. Female faces are light around the eyes, but darker on the top of the muzzle leading to the black nose.

This subspecies is the only representative of the genus *Eulemur* within its range, and impossible to confuse with any of the smaller sympatric lemur species.

Geographic Range

This subspecies occurs south of the Sambirano in northwest Madagascar (Fig. 6.35). Pure populations are found south of the Andranomalaza River near Moromandia and south to the Sandrakota River near Befotaka. The eastern limit is poorly known, but may be the Sandrakota River as well. Western populations inhabit small mixed forest and coffee plantations throughout most of this region. The largest known populations are just south of the Andranomalaza River and northwest of Befotaka. Hybrids, very similar in appearance except for possessing light brown eyes, are found in moist forests at the southern limit of the Manongarivo Special Reserve (Meyers *et al.*, 1989).

Natural History

The ecology and behavior of Sclater's black lemur has not been studied. Its habitat is dry western forest and coffee and citrus plantations with adjacent dry forest patches.   Sex ratio appears biased towards males, both in the wild and in captivity.

Conservation Status

Eulemur macaco flavifrons is not presently found in any protected area, although *E. m. macaco* and *E. m. flavifrons* hybrids occur in the Manongarivo Special Reserve. It is threatened by hunting, trapping and forest destruction. There are no population figures available, but a reasonable order of magnitude estimate would be 100-1,000 (Mittermeier *et al.*, 1992). Efforts to breed this subspecies in captivity are now underway, with four institutions in the U.S. and Europe currently holding more than 30 animals (ISIS, 1993).

Sclater's black lemur was given the *Highest Priority* rating (6) in the IUCN/SSC Primate Specialist Group's *Lemurs of Madagascar: An Action Plan for their Conservation* (Mittermeier *et al.*, 1992). Using the latest IUCN Red List criteria, we place this subspecies in the *Critically Endangered* category.

Where To See It

Sclater's black lemur is best seen in the vicinity of the small town of Marovato Sud, 9 km south of Moromandia.

Eulemur coronatus   **Color Plates 20, 22**
Crowned Lemur   **Pages 337, 339**

French: Lémur Couronné
German: Kronenmaki
Malagasy: Ankomba, Gidro

Identification

The crowned lemur is smaller than most other species of the genus *Eulemur*, with a head and body length of about 34 cm, a tail length of about 45 cm (for a total length of 75-85 cm), and a body weight of around 2 kg. The species is notably sexually dichromatic. Females have short gray body hair and are lighter on the ventrum. The face is gray and the cheeks and throat are pale. Male body coat is dark gray-brown dorsally, the tail is dark, the face gray and the nose black. The limbs are paler than the back. Both sexes have an orange V-shaped pattern pointing forward on the head. In males, a black patch fills the V and covers part of the head, while often the orange crown color circles around the face to connect with the red beard. It can easily be distinguished from *E. f. sanfordi*, the only other sympatric member of the genus *Eulemur*, by the presence of the V-shaped crown and by the absence of white ear tufts and beard that are so characteristic of male *E. f. sanfordi*.

Geographic Range

The crowned lemur is found from the extreme north, on the Cap d'Ambre peninsula, southwest to Ambilobe and probably some distance down the Mahavavy River. To the east, its limit is some point just north of Sambava, possibly the Bemarivo River (Tattersall, 1982). Throughout this range, the crowned lemur exists in practically all forests. It is found at high densities in many dry forests, and tends to occur at lower densities in the moister forests of the region.

Natural History

This species has been studied in the dry forests of Ankarana (Wilson *et al.*, 1989; Hawkins *et al.*, 1990) and Sakalava (Arbelot-Tracqui, 1983) and in the humid forests on Mt. d'Ambre (Arbelot-Tracqui, 1983; B. Freed, pers. comm.). Densities range from about 50 animals/km^2 in humid forest to more than 100/km^2 in dry forest, which is the preferred habitat. It is reported to travel in all levels of the forest, seeming to prefer the canopy level, and is likely to be found in lianas, thick cover and terminal branches. It also readily descends to the ground to eat fallen fruit, lick earth (Arbelot-Tracqui, 1983; Wilson *et al.*, 1989) or travel (Petter *et al.*, 1977). Group size doesn't appear to differ significantly between the two habitat types, the average size being five or six and the maximum about 15 individuals (B. Freed, pers. comm.). Large groups often split into foraging subgroups of one to four. Such subgroups often use vocalizations to maintain contact with or to locate other subgroups when separation distances are large. Interactions between groups are rare, but aggressive interactions are reported between crowned lemur and Sanford's lemur groups.

Although primarily diurnal, *E. coronatus* also is active at night, at which time it has been observed to travel and feed. Its diet consists largely of fruit, both in dry and moist forests, but also includes young leaves, flowers, pollen and occasionally insects (B. Freed, pers. comm.). The crowned lemur generally feeds lower in the forest than Sanford's lemur, which may help avoid aggressive interactions.

In Ankarana and Montagne d'Ambre, mating occurs in late May and June, and births take place from mid-September through October. In captivity, a gestation length of 125 days has been established, and twin and singleton births appear to be equally common (Kappeler, 1987).

Conservation Status

The crowned lemur occurs in Montagne d'Ambre National Park, and the Analamera, Ankarana and Forêt d'Ambre Special Reserves. However, the level of protection varies from one area to the next (Nicoll and Langrand, 1989; Harcourt and Thornback, 1990; Mittermeier *et al.*, 1992). Poaching is widespread and increasing in Montagne d'Ambre National Park, which is also threatened by brush fires and illegal logging on its periphery (Nicoll and Langrand, 1989). The Analamera Special Reserve is unguarded and unmanaged (Hawkins *et al.*, 1990). While hunting is not a problem at Ankarana, logging threatens a significant portion of lemur habitat (Wilson *et al.*, 1988).

There are no population figures available, but a reasonable order of magnitude estimate would be 10,000-100,000 based on known densities and recent estimates of forest cover within this species' range. There are approximately 40 *E. coronatus* in captivity in eight institutions (Olney and Ellis, 1992).

Based upon an earlier (lower) population estimate, the crowned lemur was given a *Priority* rating (4) in the IUCN/SSC Primate Specialist Group's *Lemurs of Madagascar: An Action Plan for their Conservation* (Mittermeier *et al.*, 1992). Using the latest IUCN Red List criteria, we place this species in the *Vulnerable* category.

Where To See It
The best place to see the crowned lemur is in the Ankarana Special Reserve, but it is also easily seen in Montagne d'Ambre National Park, even in the vicinity of park headquarters (although it is not as easy to see there as Sanford's lemur).

Eulemur rubriventer   Color Plates 20, 22
Red-Bellied Lemur   Pages 337, 339

French: Lémur à Ventre Rouge
German: Rotbauchlemur
Malagasy: Tongona, Soamiera, Barimaso

Identification

The red-bellied lemur is a medium-sized species with a body
length of just under 40 cm, a tail length just under 50 cm, for a total
length of roughly 90 cm; body weight is about 2 kg (Glander *et
al.*, 1992). The body pelage is thick and long; the upper parts are
a rich dark chestnut brown and the tail is black. In males, the chest
and underparts are reddish brown, while in females the ventrum
is pale or white. The face is dark and a patch of naked skin below
each eye shows a pale teardrop pattern in males, but is much less
noticeable in females. There is variation in this general pattern,
and it may be geographically distributed, meaning that subspecies
may exist. However, much more information is needed before
any taxonomic decisions can be made.

This species could be confused with *Eulemur fulvus* subspecies in the wild, especially if one only gets a fleeting glimpse of
a retreating group. However, if the animals are seen clearly,
distinguishing them should be easy. Refer to the color plates for
differences between this species and the sympatric *E. fulvus* sspp.
(*albifrons, fulvus, rufus, albocollaris*).

Geographic Range

E. rubriventer occurs at low densities throughout most of the
forested eastern escarpment from the Tsaratanana Massif in the
north through at least the southern end of the Andringitra Massif
(Petter and Petter, 1971; Tattersall, 1982; Jolly *et al.*, 1984). It
appears to be restricted to middle to high altitude rain forests. The
largest known population is in Ranomafana National Park.

Natural History

The only studies of the red-bellied lemur have been conducted
in the forests of Ranomafana National Park (Meier, 1987; Dague
and Petter, 1988; Overdorff, 1988, 1991). It lives mostly in small
family groups ranging from two to five individuals. Groups travel
and feed as single units throughout this range, led primarily by
females, and the only evidence of territorial behavior is from the

most recent study by Overdorff (1991).

Red-bellied lemurs are active during the night as well as the day, although variations in activity patterns appear to be seasonal and related to the availability of preferred food sources. Dague and Petter (1988) identified 30 and Meier (1988) 67 different plant species which provide this species with fruit, flowers and leaves. Fruits were the most important part of the diet and included the introduced Chinese guava (*Psidium cattleyanum*). Overdorff (1991) was the first to report invertebrates (millipedes) as a part of the dict.

Young are born in September and October, and they ride as often on the male as on the female for the first five weeks. After this time, females often reject the infants, while males carry them up to the age of 100 days. On average, one infant per year is born in each group, and infant mortality is about 50 percent.

Conservation Status

The red-bellied lemur suffers primarily from destruction of Madagascar's eastern rain forests. It is found in the Mantady and Ranomafana National Parks, the Andringitra, Marojejy and Zahamena Nature Reserves, and the Ambatovaky, Analamazaotra and Tsaratanana Special Reserves (Nicoll and Langrand, 1989; Harcourt and Thornback, 1990; Mittermeier *et al.*, 1992). There are no population figures available, but a reasonable order of magnitude estimate would be 10,000-100,000 (Mittermeier *et al.*, 1992). There are about 30 *E. rubriventer* in captivity in five institutions worldwide, including Madagascar's Parc Tsimbazaza and Zoo Ivoloina (ISIS, 1993).

The red-bellied lemur was assigned a *Low Priority* rating (3) in the IUCN/SSC Primate Specialist Group's *Lemurs of Madagascar: An Action Plan for their Conservation* (Mittermeier *et al.*, 1992). Using the latest IUCN Red List criteria, we place this species in the *Vulnerable* category.

Where To See It

The best place to see this species is in the Ranomafana National Park, where it is common. It also occurs in Périnet (=Andasibe), but is quite difficult to observe there.

Eulemur mongoz   **Color Plates 22, 23**
Mongoose Lemur   **Pages 339, 340**

French: Lémur mongoz
Malagasy: Dredrika, Gidro
German: Mongozmaki
Comores: Komba

Identification

Eulemur mongoz is a medium-sized, sexually dichromatic species with body length up to 35 cm and tail length up to 48 cm, for a total length of 75-83 cm. Body weight is about 2 kg. Females have gray heads, forelimbs, and shoulders, blending into brown on the back, flanks, rump and hind limbs. The face is dark gray, the cheeks and beard are white and slightly bushy. The abdomen is white to light brown. Males are gray-brown and darker than females, and have brown on the shoulders and extremities. The most noticeable sexual difference is the rufous cheek and beard of the males. Males have an off-white to light brown ventrum. In both sexes, the snout may be lighter on the sides.

In the field, this species can be confused with *E. f. fulvus*, especially if a clear view of the animals is not possible. However, if they are seen at close range, they can be easily distinguished by the lack of sexual dichromatism in *E. f. fulvus*.

Geographic Range

The mongoose lemur is found in the northwestern part of Madagascar, and is one of only two lemurs also found outside of Madagascar, with populations occurring in the Comores on the islands of Moheli and Anjouan, where they were almost certainly introduced by man. On the mainland, it is found on both sides of the Betsiboka River basin in the west, and occurs to the southwest of the Mahavavy River, near Ambato-Boéni, and north through the Ankarafantsika Nature Reserve to around Antsohihy. Exact limits of distribution are poorly known as forests in this region are highly fragmented.

Natural History

The mongoose lemur has been studied at Ampijoroa (Tattersall and Sussman, 1975; Sussman and Tattersall, 1976), and on the islands of Mohéli and Anjouan (Tattersall, 1976a, 1977b, 1977c, 1983). In western Madagascar it is found in dry deciduous forests, while on the islands of the Comores it also occurs in more humid forests. Mongoose lemurs studied at Ampijoroa were found to be nocturnal (Tattersall and Sussman, 1975), crepuscular (Albignac, 1981) and diurnal (Petter, 1962; Harrington, 1975, 1978). Harrington (1978) and Andriatsarafara (1988) also report a shift from diurnal to nocturnal activity sometime about June, which coincides with the onset of the dry season. Tattersall (1976a, 1977c) suggests that similar variation in the activity patterns of mongoose lemurs in the Comores is influenced by climatic factors.

On the mainland, groups of *Eulemur mongoz* tend to be small, three to four individuals, and usually contain an adult male, an adult female and their immature offspring (Tattersall and Sussman, 1975). Larger groups were found on Mohéli, suggesting that the typical small group sizes and pair bonding are influenced by seasonal and habitat-related environmental factors.

Home ranges are small and overlap significantly. Intergroup encounters are reported to be rare, but are the cause of great agitation, vocalizations and scent marking. Harrington (1978), reports that mongoose lemur groups frequently traveled and intermingled with groups of *Eulemur f. fulvus*.

The diet of mongoose lemurs includes flowers (especially nectar), fruit and leaves. The flowers of the kapok tree (*Ceiba pentandra*) were a favored food item at Ampijoroa (Tattersall and Sussman, 1975). This species may be an important pollinator.

The birth season appears to be around mid-October on Anjouan and in Madagascar (Tattersall, 1976a), and it seems that females can give birth every year (Schmidt, 1986).

Conservation Status

Eulemur mongoz is found in only one protected area in Madagascar, the Ankarafantsika Nature Reserve, which is under heavy pressure due to forest clearance for pasture, charcoal production and cropland (Nicoll and Langrand, 1989). Primary habitat in the Comores is disappearing rapidly. Although this species is protected by law and by local customs in the Comores, there is little enforcement, and the influx of Malagasy has led to increased hunting of these lemurs for food (Tattersall, 1977b, 1983). In addition, children commonly capture infants for pets by killing the mothers. There are no population figures available available, but a reasonable order of magnitude estimate would be 1,000-10,000 (Mittermeier *et al.*, 1992).

There are apparently fewer than 100 mongoose lemurs in captivity in at least 35 institutions worldwide, and the breeding record remains poor (Olney and Ellis, 1992; ISIS, 1993.

Eulemur mongoz was given a *Priority* (4) rating in the IUCN/ SSC Primate Specialist Group's *Lemurs of Madagascar: An Action Plan for their Conservation* (Mittermeier *et al.*, 1992). Using the latest IUCN Red List criteria, we place this species in the *Vulnerable* category.

Where To See It

The mongoose lemur is most easily seen at the Ampijoroa station in the Ankarafantsika Nature Reserve. This station is located right along the main highway from Majunga (= Mahajanga) to Antananarivo, about a two hour drive from Majunga.

Varecia: **Ruffed Lemurs**

Varecia was formerly included within the genus *Lemur*, but is now considered a distinct genus. A single species, *variegata*, is generally recognized with two distinct subspecies, the black-and-white ruffed lemur (*Varecia variegata variegata*) and the red ruffed lemur (*Varecia vareigata rubra*). It is evident that this dichotomy is an oversimplification which discounts the range of variation in pelage pattern and color that exists within this species. Many variants of the black-and white ruffed lemur occur, tending to vary from more white on the body in the south to generally darker forms just north of Maroantsetra. Other forms may be present, including intermediates between the two recognized subspecies. Unfortunately, distributional information is lacking, much ruffed lemur habitat has disappeared, and genetic studies have not yet been conducted, making it difficult to determine relationships among the different forms. Therefore, for the purposes of this book, we continue to recognize only one subspecies each of the red and black-and-white forms, but illustrate the numerous variants described in the literature in Plates 25-27.

Ruffed lemurs are the largest of the living quadrupedal lemurs and are clearly recognizable by their striking coloration and the luxuriance of their pelage, especially around the face. Identification is further aided by their characteristically long faces and their raucous loud call, in which all group members usually join. They are difficult to confuse with other sympatric species.

Ruffed lemurs are found in the rain forests of eastern Madagascar from the Mananara River south of Farafangana to the Masoala Peninsula.

Key to illustrations on the following page (Fig. 6.35):
- a. *Varecia* standing quadrupedally on a rock
- b. *Varecia* female grooming young using the tooth comb
- c. *Varecia* employing hind limb suspensory posture to monitor its environment
- d. *Varecia* using hind limb suspensory posture for feeding
- e. *Varecia* resting in the fork of a tree
- f. *Varecia* standing quadrupedally on a branch
- g. *Varecia* in a seated resting posture
- h. *Varecia* leaping from one tree branch to another

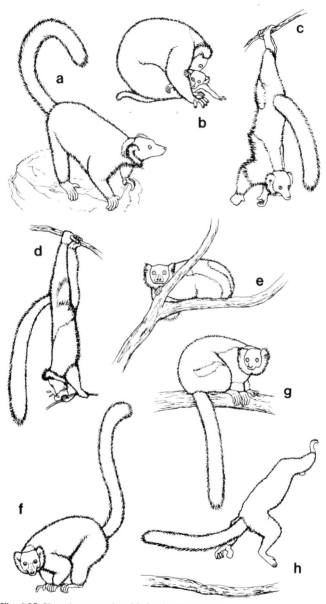

Fig. 6.35: *Varecia* postural and behavioral drawings.

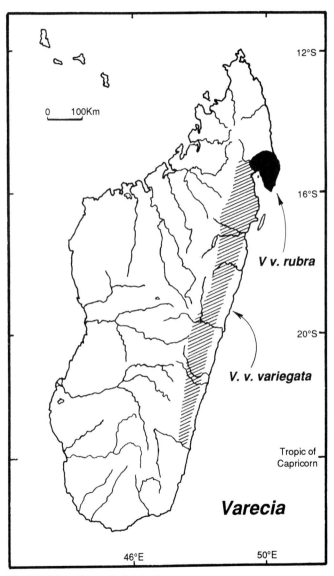

Fig. 6.36: Map of *Varecia* distribution.

Varecia variegata variegata   Color Plates 24-27
Black-and-White Ruffed Lemur   Pages 341-344

French: Lémur Vari
German: Schwarzweisser Vari
Malagasy: Vari, Varikandana, Varikandra

Identification

The black- and-white ruffed lemur has a head and body length
of about 55 cm and tail length about 60 cm, for a total length of
110-120 cm. Body weight ranges from 3.5 to 4.5 kg. Significant
variation in coat color exists, but almost always the hair is black
on the ventrum, tail, extremities, inner aspect of limbs, forehead
and the circumorbital area, and on top of the head. The ears are
lavishly tufted ("ruffed") with long thick white hair. Many forms
have been described (see Petter *et al.,* 1977; Tattersall, 1982) and,
though no taxonomic conclusions are drawn here, a number of
variants are illustrated in Plates 25-27 (modified from Ceska *et
al.*, 1992). Towards the south, the dorsal coat is mostly white,
with black often restricted to the shoulders and flanks. Towards
the north, black dominates the dorsal pelage, but a white band
across the back, and white forearms and flanks are common.
Several "subspecies" have been named within the black-and-
white ruffed lemur group (*e.g.*, *variegata, subcincta, editorum*),
but their validity remains uncertain. For a more detailed discussion, see Tattersall (1992). Further research on the taxonomy of
the ruffed lemurs has been identified as a high conservation
priority (Mittermeier *et al.*, 1992).

Varecia variegata variegata occurs sympatrically with several *Eulemur fulvus* subspecies and with *Eulemur rubriventer*, but
it is easily distinguished from them by its striking black and white
coloration, its larger size, its raucous vocalizations, and the
distinctive ear tufts.

Geographic Range

Varecia variegata variegata inhabits lowland to mid-altitude
(1200 m) eastern rain forests from the Mananara River south of
Farafangana north to the Antainambalana River (just north of
Maroantsetra). Throughout this large range, the population
distribution is very patchy, especially for an eastern forest lemur.
Ruffed lemurs tend to be rare at higher altitudes (over 1200 m) and
are found at low densities at just over 1100 m in Ranomafana
National Park.

Natural History

One long-term study of *Varecia variegata variegata* has been carried out to date, on the island of Nosy Mangabe (Morland, 1990, 1991). The black-and-white ruffed lemur is the most frugivorous of the living lemurs, but also feeds on nectar, seeds and leaves according to the season (White, 1989). In general, ruffed lemurs are most active in early morning and in late afternoon/evening.

Group size and density appear to vary considerably. Petter *et al.* (1977), Pollock (1979) and Jolly *et al.* (1984) report group sizes between two and five individuals, while Morland (1990,1991) reports much larger groups of 8-16 individuals and densities of 20-30 animals/km^2 on Nosy Mangabe. All group members use a common home range, and aggression is seen between groups. Females form the core of the group and defend its territory. The weakest social bonds appear to be between males. Grouping patterns change seasonally; females aggregate in larger numbers during the wet summer and are more dispersed during the drier winter.

The mating season begins in May on Nosy Mangabe (Morland, 1990, 1991), and most matings are observed in June and July. Twins are usually born in September and October. Studies in captivity record larger litter sizes and have determined a gestation period of 90-102 days (Hick, 1976; Bogart *et al.*, 1977; Boskoff, 1977). Unlike most other lemurs, infant ruffed lemurs are at first left in nests rather than carried by their mothers (Petter *et al.*, 1977; Klopfer and Dugard, 1976; Jolly *et al.*, 1984). Later, they are carried in the mother's mouth, but in captivity begin to follow the mother around by about three weeks of age, and are fully mobile at about seven weeks (Klopfer and Boskoff, 1979).

Conservation Status

The black-and-white ruffed lemur is severely threatened by continued destruction of Madagascar's lowland eastern rain forests and also because it is heavily hunted and trapped for food throughout its range (Constable *et al.*, 1985; Lindsay and Simons, 1986; Nicoll and Langrand, 1989; M. Rakotomalala, pers. comm.).

Varecia variegata variegata is found in a number of protected areas: the Mantady, Ranomafana and Verezanantsoro National Parks, the Andringitra, Betampona and Zahamena Nature Reserves, and the Ambatovaky, Analamazaotra and Nosy Mangabe Special Reserves (Pollock, 1984; Nicoll and Langrand, 1989;

Harcourt and Thornback, 1990; Morland, 1990, 1991; Mittermeier *et al.*, 1992). However, levels of protection within these
areas vary considerably. There are no population figures available, but a reasonable order of magnitude estimate would be
1,000-10,000 (Mittermeier *et al.*, 1992).

The black-and-white ruffed lemur breeds very well in captivity. There are more than 400 animals in over 100 institutions
worldwide (Olney and Ellis, 1992; ISIS, 1993). The Duke
University Primate Center maintains the largest colony. Two
pairs of captive-born ruffed lemurs were recently returned to
Madagascar from this institution and the San Antonio and San
Diego Zoos (Katz, 1991).

Based on its low estimated population numbers and the fact
that it is a popular target for hunters,*Varecia variegata variegata*
was given a *High Priority* rating (5) in the IUCN/SSC Primate
Specialist Group's *Lemurs of Madagascar: An Action Plan for
their Conservation* (Mittermeier *et al.,* 1992). Using the latest
IUCN Red List criteria, we place this subspecies in the *Endangered* category. If further research indicates that one or more of
the named "subspecies" of the black-and-white ruffed lemur (*e. g.,
variegata, subcincta, editorum*) are valid, some of these would
possibly enter the *Critically Endangered* category.

Where To See It
The black-and-white ruffed lemur is most readily seen on the
island of Nosy Mangabe off Maroantsetra in northeastern Madagascar, the one site in which it has been studied. This island can
be reached by small boat from Maroantsetra, and hotels and
bungalows are available in the town. Facilities are minimal on
Nosy Mangabe, so advance preparation must be made, and
permission obtained for overnight stays.

Varecia variegata variegata can also be seen in Ranomafana
National Park, about an hour-and-a-half walk from the Talatakely
research site, and near Kianjavato at Ambatovavy, on the road to
Manankara. The latter is a sacred site, so permission should be
sought before entering. Elsewhere, the black-and-white ruffed
lemur is much more difficult to see, although a stay of several
days in one of the other protected areas in which it occurs may well
yield results.

Varecia variegata rubra   **Color Plates 24, 28**
Red Ruffed Lemur   **Pages 341, 345**

French: Lémur Vari Rouge
German: Roter Vari
Malagasy: Varimena, Varignena

Identification

The red ruffed lemur is similar in size to *Varecia variegata variegata*. Its head and body length is about 53 cm, the tail length about 60 cm, for a total length of about 110-120 cm. Body weight is just under 4 kg. Most of the dorsal body coat is deep rusty red. There is a white patch on the neck and small patches of white may appear on the heels, digits and muzzle. The ventrum, extremities, tail, inside of limbs, forehead, and crown (excluding ears) are black. Variation in these characters may exist, and should be noted and reported when observed in the field.

As with the black-and-white ruffed lemur, the red ruffed lemur is difficult to confuse with any other lemur. It occurs sympatrically with *Eulemur fulvus albifrons*, but is larger, has the distinctive raucous vocalization and the characteristic ear tufts. Also *E. f. albifrons* males have a striking white face, which immediately distinguishes them from *V. variegata rubra*.

Geographic Range

This subspecies is restricted to the forests of the Masoala Peninsula near Maroantsetra in northeastern Madagascar (Petter *et al.*, 1977; Petter and Petter-Rousseaux, 1979; Tattersall, 1977a, 1982). The northern and western limits of its range remain unverified; red ruffed lemurs have been seen just east of the Antainambalana River, which divides this subspecies from the black-and-white ruffed lemur (Petter *et al.,* 1977; Tattersall, 1982; D. Meyers, pers. obs.). Simons and Lindsay (1987) report that it now occurs at low densities or is locally extinct in heavily disturbed parts of its range.

Natural History

Little is known of this subspecies as it has only recently been studied in the wild, but its ecology and social behavior appear to be similar to the black-and-white ruffed lemur.

Conservation Status

Unfortunately, the only protected area in the range of the red ruffed lemur, the former Masoala Nature Reserve, was degazetted in 1964 to permit logging. Deforestation of this region continues, and hunting and trapping of red ruffed lemurs for food is common throughout this animal's small range (Tattersall, 1977a; Constable *et al.*, 1985; Simons and Lindsay, 1987). There are no population figures available, but a reasonable order of magnitude estimate would be 1,000-10,000 (Mittermeier *et al.*, 1992). Efforts are underway to reestablish a protected area on the Masoala Peninsula, but they are far from complete.

Varecia variegata rubra has bred with some success in captivity. About 300 animals are held by more than 70 institutions worldwide (Olney and Ellis, 1992; ISIS, 1993).

The *Highest Priority* rating (6) was given to the red ruffed lemur in the IUCN/SSC Primate Specialist Group's *Lemurs of Madagascar: An Action Plan for their Conservation* (Mittermeier *et al.*, 1992). Using the latest IUCN Red List criteria, we place this subspecies in the *Critically Endangered* category.

Where To See It

The only place to see the red ruffed lemur is on the Masoala Peninsula, where it is still relatively easy to find in areas that are not badly degraded. Coastal areas directly across from the island of Nosy Mangabe are a good starting point, since trails used by local people usually lead into the interior of the peninsula where the lemurs are most likely to be seen.

FAMILY INDRIIDAE

This family contains the three genera *Indri*, *Propithecus* and *Avahi*. The first two are large-bodied (3-7+ kg) and diurnal, the last is much smaller (about 1 kg) and nocturnal. All three are typical, thigh-powered vertical clingers and leapers, preferring postures in which the trunk of the body is held vertically, and making spectacular leaps of up to 10 m between vertical supports. In peripheral branches of the trees, suspensory postures are common. All indriids have greatly elongated legs compared to their arms and trunks, and are physically highly distinctive. The only real possibility of confusing any indriid with a member of another lemur family is at night, when *Avahi* might be mistaken for *Lepilemur* or possibly *Cheirogaleus*.

Avahi: Woolly Lemurs

Regarded until recently as a monospecific genus with two subspecies, *Avahi laniger laniger* and *A. l. occidentalis*, this genus has been divided into two distinct species, *A. laniger* and *A. occidentalis*, as a result of recent work by Rumpler *et al.*

The genus *Avahi* contains the only nocturnal lemurs of the family Indriidae which, because of their large eyes, appear relatively short-faced and round-headed. Nonetheless, they are typical indriid-type, thigh-powered vertical clingers and leapers, with long hind limbs compared to the trunk and forelimbs. *Avahi* body size is medium to small, with individuals generally weighing in the neighborhood of 1 kg or less. At about 32 cm, the length of the tail is slightly greater than that of the head plus body, which averages 28 cm, for an overall length of 55-65 cm.

At a distance, at night, *Avahi* is often difficult to distinguish from species of the larger-eared *Lepilemur*, but at reasonably close range both kinds of woolly lemurs can be identified by the white patches on the backs of the thighs. These patches are usually highly visible when the animals are in their favored vertical body posture. At first glance, *Avahi* may also be confused in the field with *Cheirogaleus*, especially *C. major* in the eastern rain forest. However, *Cheirogaleus* does not use a vertical posture (unless in the act of climbing up a vertical support), has contrastingly light underparts, and a much different tail.

PHOTO BY CHRIS RAXWORTHY

Fig. 6.37: Eastern avahi *(Avahi laniger)* in the Zahamena Reserve.

Key to illustrations on the following page (Fig. 6.38):

    a. A group of *Avahi* huddled together in the characteristic
       sleeping posture

    b. *Avahi* infant "parked" on a branch by its mother

    c. *Avahi* in a supported sitting posture

    d. *Avahi* in a sitting posture

    e. *Avahi* mother and infant resting in the fork of a tree

    f. *Avahi* in the vertical clinging posture, showing the partly
       wound-up tail of an animal that has recently been
       disturbed

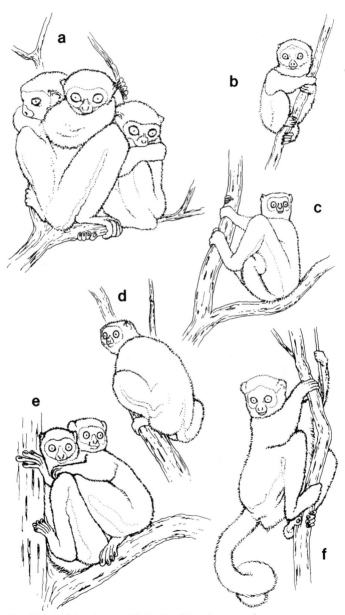

Fig. 6.38: *Avahi* postural and behavioral drawings.

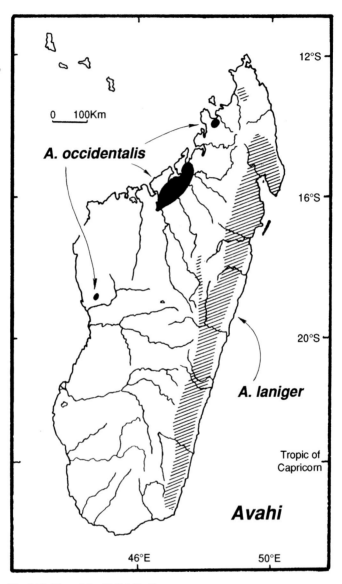

Fig. 6.39: Map of *Avahi* distribution.

Avahi laniger   **Color Plate 23**
Eastern Woolly Lemur   **Page 340**

Other English: Eastern Avahi
French: Avahi Laineux Oriental
German: Ostlicher Wollmaki, Breitschnauzen-
**   halbmaki**
Malagasy: Fotsifé, Ampongy, Avahy, Fotsifaka

Identification

The eastern woolly lemur is slightly larger than the western species, and darker colored. It has dense short fur, tightly curled on the back. The back is gray-brown to reddish, becoming paler towards the tail, which is a rusty red. The chest and belly are gray. The face is brownish, with a lighter band or distinct patches above the eyes, and lighter fur on the cheeks and throat. The ears are small, and largely hidden in the fur. In a sample of four animals of each sex, females weighed on average 1316 g, males 1033 g (Glander *et al.*, 1992).

Avahi laniger is most likely to be confused with eastern rain forest *Lepilemur*, which also adopt a clinging posture, and, to a lesser extent, *Cheirogaleus*. It can be distinguished from *Lepilemur* by its somewhat larger size, the concealed ears and the generally woollier appearance. *Cheirogaleus major* does not employ the vertical clinging posture, is considerably smaller, and has distinctive white underparts, and does not leap long distances like *Avahi*.

Geographic Range

Avahi laniger is found in the eastern rain forest from Fort-Dauphin (= Tolagnaro) near Madagascar's southern tip north to the Andapa region near Sambava (Petter *et al.*, 1977; Tattersall, 1982). It has also been reported recently from the Ankarana Massif to the south and west of Anivorano Nord (Fowler *et al.*, 1989; Hawkins *et al.*, 1990). It is uncertain which species of *Avahi* was seen in this area, but this sighting raises the question of its possible occurrence on the Tsaratanana Massif. This poorly surveyed area links the northeastern region with the Sambirano, and woolly lemurs have not yet been reported there.

Natural History

There have been no long-term studies of eastern woolly lemurs to date. However, research at Analamazaotra Special

Reserve (Charles-Dominique and Hladik, 1971; Ganzhorn, 1988) provides estimates of very high densities (72-100 individuals/ km²) and suggests a social organization based on monogamous pairs and their offspring (Pollock, 1975; Petter and Charles-Dominique, 1979). Groups of up to five have been reported, and home ranges of 1-2 ha are aggressively defended (Albignac, 1981b; Razanahoera-Rakotomalala, 1985; Ganzhorn *et al.*, 1985; Harcourt, 1988).

Although *Avahi* eats flowers and fruits to a small extent, its diet consists primarily of leaves, which provide an unusually low level of nutrition for a primate of such small size, but which may also explain its low level of activity at night. Daytime sleeping sites are usually in clumps of dense foliage where group members huddle together, and can be very low to the ground (Albignac, 1981b).

Single births take place in August and September (Ganzhorn *et al.*, 1985). Infants ride initially on the mother's ventrum, but transfer to her back after an undetermined period.

Conservation Status
   The eastern woolly lemur suffers from destruction of its habitat for timber and slash-and-burn agriculture. Being nocturnal, it is less subject to hunting than some of its diurnal relatives. However, like many other medium-sized lemurs in the eastern rain forests, it too is eaten by some people, occasionally being captured in its daytime sleeping sites. *A. laniger* occurs in the Mantady and Ranomafana National Parks, the Andohahela, Andringitra, Betampona, Marojejy and Zahamena Nature Reserves, and the Ambatovaky, Ambohitantely, Analamazaotra, Anjanaharibe-Sud and Manombo Special Reserves (Nicoll and Langrand, 1989; Harcourt and Thornback, 1990; Mittermeier *et al.*, 1992). There are no population estimates available, but a reasonable order of magnitude estimate would be >100,000. None are currently held in captivity.

   The eastern woolly lemur has a widespread distribution throughout the eastern forests, occurs in at least 12 protected areas and is afforded some security due to its nocturnal habits. Although it received a *Priority* rating (4) in the IUCN/SSC Primate Specialist Group's *Lemurs of Madagascar: An Action Plan for their Conservation* (Mittermeier *et al.*, 1992) because of taxonomic uniqueness, using the latest IUCN Red List criteria, we place this species in the *Low Risk* category.

Where To See It

The two best places to see the eastern woolly lemur on the regular tourist circuit are at Périnet (=Andasibe) and the Ranomafana National Park. As mentioned under *Indri*, the station at Périnet is easy to reach from Antananarivo, and Ranomafana is a day-long drive and requires at least 2-3 days at the site for a worthwhile visit. *Avahi laniger* can also be seen in other eastern forest protected areas within its range, but densities vary and much patience is required. *Avahi* can also be seen in daytime sleeping sites, especially if local guides know of a particular one and can lead you to it.

Avahi occidentalis   **Color Plate 23**
Western Woolly Lemur   **Page 340**

Other English: Western Avahi
French: Avahi Occidental
German: Westlicher Wollmaki
Malagasy: Fotsifé, Tsarafangitra

Identification
    The western woolly lemur is generally lighter in coloration
than its eastern relative (especially in individuals from the
Ankarafantsika region), and body size is somewhat smaller (four
individuals weighed an average of 859 g [Bauchot and Stephan,
1966]). The dense, tightly curled fur of the back is a light to
medium gray, sometimes flecked with brown or olive, and becomes paler towards the rear.   The tail is usually gray but
sometimes can be reddish. The face, throat and cheeks are pale in
color, not brown as in *Avahi laniger*.
    As with the eastern species, *Avahi occidentalis* is most likely
to be confused in the field with *Lepilemur* and, to a lesser extent,
Cheirogaleus medius.   However, it can be distinguished in the
same ways as *A. laniger,* with *Cheirogaleus medius* being even
less likely than *C. major* to be taken for *Avahi* because of its
smaller size.

Geographic Range
    Avahi occidentalis occurs to the north and east of the
Betsiboka River, from the Ankarafantsika Reserve north to the
Bay of Narinda (Petter *et al.*, 1977; Tattersall, 1977, 1982), and
also in the Manongarivo Special Reserve just south of Ambanja
in the Sambirano region (Raxworthy and Rakotondraparany,
1988).   Another isolate has been reported in the Tsingy de
Bemaraha Reserve north of Ankavandra (Mutschler and
Thalmann, 1990), and this population, like that from the Sambirano area, appears to be darker than the Ankarafantsika animals.

Natural History
    The western woolly lemur is poorly known. Albignac (1981b)
reports that, in the dry deciduous forests of Anakarafantsika,
groups consist of an adult pair and immature offspring (to a
maximum of five individuals) living in territories of 3 to 4 ha.
These ranges are less vigorously (and vocally) defended than

those of the eastern woolly lemur, with more overlap between neighboring groups. Ganzhorn (1988) very roughly estimated population density in the dry deciduous forest of Ankarafantsika at 67 individuals/km^2. Young leaves and buds seem to be the preferred food items, and at least 20 species of plants are included in this lemur's diet (Albignac, 1981b; Razanahoera-Rakotamalala, 1981). Feeding takes place more at the beginning and at the end of the night, and individuals are not very active in between, rarely traveling more than 200 m.

Conservation Status

The western woolly lemur is threatened by forest destruction due to burning to create pasture for livestock, and by some hunting. It is found in the Ankarafantsika and Tsingy de Bemaraha Nature Reserves, the Manongarivo Special Reserve, and possibly the Ankarana Special Reserve (Raxworthy and Rakotodraparany, 1988; Fowler et al., 1989; Nicoll and Langrand, 1989; Harcourt and Thornback, 1990; Mutschler and Thalmann, 1990; Mittermeier et al., 1992). There are no population figures available, but a reasonable order of magnitude estimate would be at the low end of 10,000-100,000 (Mittermeier et al., 1992). There are no western woolly lemurs reported in captivity at this time.

Avahi occidentalis was given a *Priority* rating (4) in the IUCN/SSC Primate Specialist Group's *Lemurs of Madagascar: An Action Plan for their Conservation* (Mittermeier et al., 1992). Using the latest IUCN Red List criteria, we place it in the *Vulnerable* category.

Where To See It

Avahi occidentalis is easily seen at the Ampijoroa Forest Station in the Ankarafantsika Nature Reserve, where it is abundant. It is easier to locate in the lower, less dense western dry deciduous forest than is its relative in the eastern rain forest. The other areas in which it occurs are less accessible and off the regular tourist circuit.

Propithecus: Sifakas, Simponas

All *Propithecus* are relatively large-bodied, and diurnal. They are short-faced, and have extremely long legs relative to the trunk and the arms, preferring vertical postures that often involve clinging to vertical tree trunks. Much of their locomotion consists of leaping between such vertical supports, propelled by the power of the long hind limbs. However, in terminal tree branches a wide variety of suspensory postures is adopted, particularly in the search for food. On the ground they bound along in an upright position on their hind limbs.

Three species of *Propithecus* are currently recognized. Two, *P. verreauxi* and *P. diadema,* are widely distributed and differentiated into several subspecies. *P. verreauxi* is a relatively small-bodied species (under 4 kg on average) readily identified by its raucous "si-fak!" call. The third species, *P. tattersalli*, is monotypic and has a very restricted distribution in northern Madagascar.

We provisionally recognize four subspecies of *P. verreauxi* and also discuss a form, *P. v. "majori"*, that is almost certainly just a color variant of *P. v. verreauxi*. The status of two of the the subspecies discussed here, *P. v. coronatus* and *P. v. deckeni*, is still under investigation, with some authors believing that *coronatus* and *deckeni* are synonymous (Tattersall, 1982, 1986), and others continuing to believe that subspecific distinction may be warranted. Pending further study, we continue to recognize these two taxa as distinct.

All *P. diadema* subspecies are of relatively large body size (average body weight about 5-7+ kg), with the tail shorter than the head-body length. Four subspecies of *P. diadema* are currently recognized from the humid forests of eastern and northern Madagascar, though there is some debate over whether *P. d. holomelas* should be regarded as separate from *P. d. edwardsi* . For the purposes of this field guide, we follow Tattersall (1982, 1986) in considering *holomelas* synonymous with *edwardsi*, but further investigation of the area from which *holomelas* was first described is certainly warranted.

Key to illustrations on the following page (Fig. 6.40):
>   **a. *Propithecus verreauxi verreauxi* jumping from a tree to the
>   ground**
>   **b - g. *Propithecus verreauxi verreauxi* using the characteristic
>   bipedal hopping locomotion across the ground**

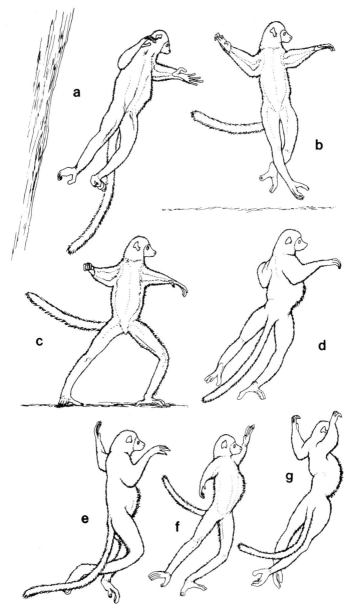

Fig. 6.40: *Propithecus* postural and behavioral drawings.

PHOTO BY RUSSELL A. MITTERMEIER

Fig. 6.41: Coquerel's sifaka *(Propithecus verreauxi coquereli)* from the Ampijoroa Station in Ankarafantsika Nature Reserve.

Key to illustrations on the following page (Fig. 6.42):
   a. *Propithecus verreauxi verreauxi* in a suspensory feeding
      posture
   b. *Propithecus verreauxi verreauxi* feeding
   c. *Propithecus verreauxi coquereli* leaping
   d. *Propithecus verreauxi coquereli* sitting in a tree fork
   e. *Propithecus verreauxi verreauxi* in suspensory posture

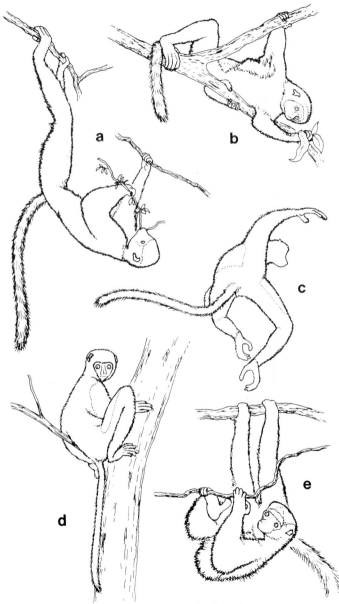

Fig. 6.42: *Propithecus* postural and behavioral drawings.

PHOTO BY DAVID HARING

Fig. 6.43: The golden-crowned or Tattersall's sifaka *(Propithecus tattersalli).*

Key to illustrations on the following page (Fig. 6.44):
   a. *Propithecus verreauxi coquereli* in the characteristic "chair" sitting posture
   b. *Propithecus verreauxi verreauxi* resting on forked branches
   c. *Propithecus verreauxi coquereli* in a suspensory resting posture
   d. *Propithecus verreauxi verreauxi* female and infant sitting on a branch
   e. *Propithecus verreauxi coquereli* female and infant resting in a vertical clinging posture

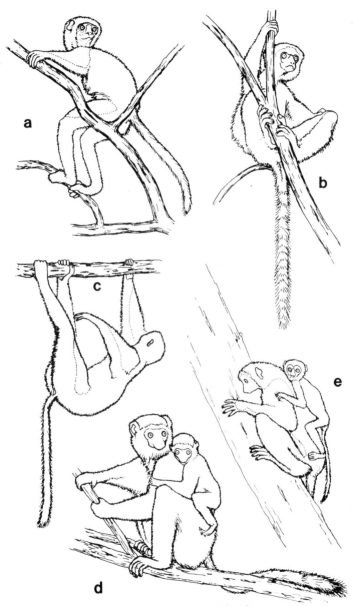

Fig. 6.44: *Propithecus* postural and behavioral drawings.

PHOTO BY RUSSELL A. MITTERMEIER

Fig. 6.45: Milne-Edwards' sifaka *(Propithecus diadema edwardsi)* in Ranomafana National Park.

Key to illustrations on the following page (Fig. 6.46):
  a. *Propithecus diadema edwardsi* with infant in seated resting posture, using branches above as supports
  b. *Propithecus diadema edwardsi* with infant, about to leap from vertical clinging position
  c. *Propithecus diadema edwardsi* with infant in vertical clinging rest posture
  d. *Propithecus diadema edwardsi* in seated resting posture

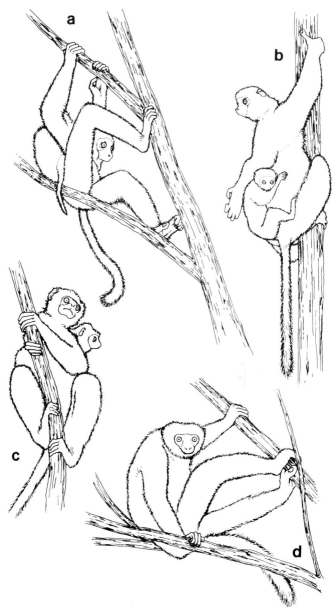

Fig. 6.46: *Propithecus* postural and behavioral drawings.

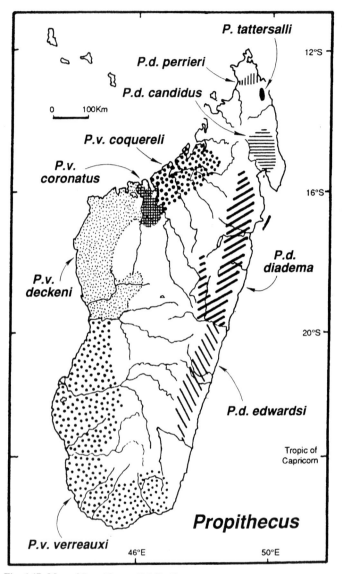

Fig. 6.47: Map of *Propithecus* distribution.

Propithecus verreauxi verreauxi   Color Plates 29,30
Verreaux's Sifaka   Pages 346, 347

French: Propithèque de Verreaux
German: Kronensifaka, Kappensifaka
Malagasy: Sifaka, Sifaka-bilany (Isalo area)

Identification
The fur of Verreaux's sifaka is predominantly white, with the top of the head black or chocolate brown. The ears are white, slightly tufted and only moderately prominent. Silver gray or goldish tints may exist on the back and flanks, and the base of the tail. A reddish-brown gland is visible at the base of the throat in males. The mean weight for four captive animals was 3.4 kg, both sexes being of similar size (Kappeler, 1991). *P. v. verreauxi* is impossible to confuse with other lemurs in its range.

A distinctive variant (previously given the name *P. v. "majori"*) is sometimes seen in troops containing typical Verreaux's sifaka. Such individuals are predominantly white, but with a head cap of dark chocolate brown (with white cheeks, ears and forehead), brownish-black on the back and on the inside of the arms and legs, a brownish chest, and a dark brown tail with a white tip. All specimens of this *"majori"* type have been seen within the geographical range of *P. v. verreauxi*, and mixed groups occur at widely scattered localities, making it highly unlikely that *"majori"* is a distinct taxon. In addition to this darker type, entirely white individuals are also reported.

Geographic Range
Verreaux's sifaka is found in the remaining forests of southern and southwestern Madagascar, from the Tsiribihina River east to the area a little to the west of Fort-Dauphin (= Tolagnaro), with the eastern limit apparently being the dry portion (Parcels 2 and 3) of the Andohahela Nature Reserve (Petter *et al.*, 1977; Petter and Petter-Rousseaux, 1979; Tattersall, 1982; O'Connor *et al.*, 1986, 1987). It has the widest distribution of the four *P. verreauxi* subspecies, and indeed of all *Propithecus* taxa.

Natural History
P. v. verreauxi is a diurnal vertical clinger and leaper, living in small, mostly multimale groups of 2-12 individuals, averaging 5 (Jolly, 1966; Richard, 1974a, 1985). Richard (1974a) suggests that these are less reproductive units than they are semi-permanent foraging parties. Females appear to be dominant over

males. The subspecies occurs in dry, semi-arid spiny vegetation (Didiereaceae forests), brush-and-scrub thickets and deciduous gallery forests along watercourses, and also has been observed in a small patch of humid forest between Parcels 2 and 3 in the Andohahela Nature Reserve. Home ranges may be 10 ha or more, but are often very much smaller, and densities are reported to range from 47/km^2 in the disturbed forests of Bealoka (O'Connor, 1987) to about 150-200/km^2 at nearby Berenty (Jolly *et al.*, 1982; O'Connor, 1987) to the equivalent of 400-500/km^2 at Antseranomby (Sussman, 1972). The diet of *P. v. verreauxi* consists principally of leaves, fruit and flowers, but is highly variable seasonally. Leaves are the most important food item during the dry season and fruit during the wet season, when this sifaka also appears to utilize fewer plant species (Richard, 1977). The survival of Verreaux's sifaka in Didiereaceae forest suggests that it does not need to drink and can survive severe drought (Jolly, 1966). Richard (1974b) suggests that water may be obtained during the dry season by eating the bark and cambium of *Operculicarya decaryi*.

The ability of this species to leap from trunk to trunk on members of the cactus-like Didiereaceae plant family, such as *Alluaudia ascendens*, is one of the most spectacular wildlife phenomena of Madagascar. These trees are covered with very hard, very sharp spines, yet the sifakas are able to leap among them with abandon, without injuring themselves. How this is actually accomplished remains to be studied, but it is one of the most spectacular lemur behavior patterns. *P. v. verreauxi's* bipedal locomotion on the ground, consisting of a series of comical kangaroo-like hops and bounds with arms raised over the head, is also a highlight.

Breeding is seasonal, with most births occurring in August and September. Infants ride on their mother's belly until about three months of age, at which point they shift to her back. They are almost completely independent by six months (Jolly, 1966).

Conservation Status

Verreaux's sifaka is dependent on Didiereaceae bush and riparian forests. These slow-growing forests are threatened largely by cutting of trunks for house construction, and firewood and charcoal production, problems that become more serious every year. Although hunting of *P. v. verreauxi* is *fady* to several of the tribes living in its range (*e.g.,* Antandroy, Mahafaly), it is hunted by others and by immigrants to the region. It is also quite easy to hunt in the open, relatively low bush in which it lives, in contrast to the *Propithecus* of the eastern rain forest. In the Isalo area, this animal is known as *sifaka-bilany* or "sifaka of the cooking pot", either because of its popularity as a food item or because of the sooty black appearance of individuals from this part of its range (H. J. Ratsimbazafy, pers. comm., P.Wright, pers. comm. See Plate 30, p. 347).

This subspecies occurs in the Isalo National Park, the Andohahela and Tsimanampetsotsa Nature Reserves, the Andranomena and Beza-Mahafaly Special Reserves and the Analabe and Berenty Private Reserves (Rakotomanga *et al.*, 1987; Nicoll and Langrand, 1989; Harcourt and Thornback, 1990; Mittermeier *et al.*, 1992). There are no population figures available, but a reasonable order of magnitude estimate would be >100,000 (Mittermeier *et al.*, 1992). About two dozen *Propithecus verreauxi* are reported to be in captivity in the U.S. and Europe, but the subspecies in question is uncertain (ISIS, 1993).

Due to its widespread distribution, presumed large population and occurrence in at least seven protected areas, *P. v. verreauxi* was given a *Low Priority* rating (3) in the IUCN/SSC Primate Specialist Group's *Lemurs of Madagscar: An Action Plan for their Conservation* (Mittermeier *et al.*, 1992). However, given recent information on hunting from Malagasy scientists, it seems to be at higher risk than previously believed. Using the latest IUCN Red List criteria, we place this subspecies in the *Vulnerable* category.

Where To See It

Not only is this lemur one of the most appealing and attractive animals in Madagascar, it is also one of the easiest to see. It is most readily observed in the Berenty Private Reserve west of Fort-Dauphin (= Tolagnaro) and sightings are guaranteed even on a day trip. In Berenty it is usually seen in the gallery forests in the main part of the reserve, but also can be seen in the small patches of Didiereaceae bush in the surrounding area.

Two places to see Verreaux's sifaka in large, impressive stands of Didiereaceae bush are at Hazafotsy at the edge of the dry parcels of the Andohahela Nature Reserve (located some 4-5 hours by four-wheel drive vehicle from Berenty) and in the region surrounding the Beza-Mahafaly Special Reserve some 5-6 hours by car east of Tuléar (= Toliary). It can also be readily observed in the Analabe Private Reserve and adjacent forests, one hour north of Morondava, where it lives in dry deciduous forest rather than Didiereaceae bush or gallery forests. The easiest place to see it moving bipedally on the ground is Berenty, where it regularly crosses the road near the tourist facilities.

Propithecus verreauxi coquereli   **Color Plate 29**
Coquerel's Sifaka   **Page 346**

French: Propithèque de Coquerel
German: Coquerels Kronensifaka
Malagasy: Tsibahaka, Sifaka, Ankomba Malandy

Identification

The face of Coquerel's sifaka is black, but generally with a patch of short white hair across the muzzle. Its ears are naked and quite small, but visible. The dense body hair is mostly white, but extensive maroon patches occur on the chest and on the front of the thighs and forelimbs. Brownish or silvery patches often occur on the back. Eight males studied by Kappeler (1991) weighed an average of 3.70 kg; 10 females weighed an average of 3.76 kg.

As with other *Propithecus*, it is impossible to confuse this distinctive animal with other sympatric lemur species.

Geographic Range

P. v. coquereli is found throughout the forested areas of northwestern Madagascar to the north and east of the Betsiboka River. Its southern limit is the area of Ambato-Boéni, while in the north its limit extends from Antsohihy southeast to Befandriana Nord (Tattersall, 1982).

Natural History

This diurnal vertical clinger and leaper is most commonly found in mixed deciduous and evergreen forests, and often in brush-and-scrub and secondary formations as well.   In Ankarafantsika, it is seen in small groups of variable age and sex composition, ranging from 3-10 individuals and probably representing foraging units as in *P. v. verreauxi* (Petter, 1962; Richard, 1974a; Albignac, 1981a). Home ranges are typically 4-9 ha. *P. v. coquereli* feeds mostly on young leaves, flowers, fruit, bark and dead wood in the wet season, and on mature leaves and buds in the dry season (Richard, 1974b). As many as 98 different plant species have been recorded in its diet.

Births are clustered in the months of June and July, and studies in captivity suggest a gestation period of about 162 days (Richard, 1976, 1987). Infants cling to the mother's chest for the first month or so, then transfer to her back.   They become completely independent by about six months of age, and reach adult size by one year.

Conservation Status

Coquerel's sifaka may be the most threatened of the *P. verreauxi* subspecies because of habitat destruction. It is found only in the Ankarafantsika Nature Reserve and the Bora Special Reserve, and these have been damaged by yearly fires set to encourage the growth of new grass for livestock, and by tree cutting for charcoal (Nicoll and Langrand, 1989; Harcourt and Thornback, 1990). The Bora Special Reserve was subjected to exploitation by oil companies and then by local people, leaving little intact forest in the southern part of this reserve. A local *fady* in Ankarafantsika protects this lemur, so poaching is limited; however, as in most other parts of Madagascar, immigration by people from other ethnic groups may rapidly erode the conservation value of this *fady*.

There are no population figures available, but a reasonable order of magnitude estimate would be 1,000-10,000 (Mittermeier *et al.*, 1992) There are approximately 20 Coquerel's sifaka in captivity at the Duke University Primate Center and the Vincennes Zoo in Paris (Olney and Ellis, 1992; ISIS, 1993).

Based upon its presumed small population and occurrence in only two protected areas, Coquerel's sifaka was given a *High Priority* rating (5) in the IUCN/SSC Primate Specialist Group's *Lemurs of Madagascar: An Action Plan for their Conservation* (Mittermeier *et al.*, 1992). Using the latest IUCN Red List criteria, we place this subspecies in the *Endangered* category.

Where To See It

The best place to see Coquerel's sifaka in the wild is at the Ampijoroa Forest Station located right along the main road running through the Ankarafantsika Nature Reserve. This station can easily be reached from Majunga (=Mahajanga) by car in about two hours.

Propithecus verreauxi coronatus   **Color Plate 31**
Crowned Sifaka   **Page 348**

French: Propithèque Couronné
German: Kronensifaka, Kappensifaka
Malagasy: Sifaka, Tsibahaka

Identification

Many authors recognize this sifaka as a distinct subspecies of *P. verreauxi*, but recent observations suggest that no clear geographic distinction can be drawn between *P. v. deckeni* and *P. v. coronatus* (Tattersall, 1982, 1986), even though "typical" forms of the two are clearly distinguishable to the eye.

The muzzle of the crowned sifaka is somewhat blunt and rounded, and its face naked and black. The hair of the crown, forehead, cheeks and throat is dark chocolate brown or black, and there is sometimes a slight white tufting around the ears. The shoulders and back are variably tinted, ranging from yellow-gold to silver-brown. The tail and hindlimbs are white. The chest is dark, lightening toward and across the abdomen (Tattersall, 1982). Based upon two specimens, head plus body length ranges from 42.5-45 cm, and tail length from 56-60 cm, for an overall length of approximately 98-105 cm.

Geographic Range

Kaudern (1915), who collected extensively in northwestern Madagascar earlier this century, established the limits of the crowned sifaka's distribution as the Mahavavy River to the southwest (separating it from *P. v. deckeni*) and the Betsiboka River to the northeast (separating it from *P. v. coquereli*). Subsequently, Petter *et al.* (1977), although adopting the same distributional limits, suggested that the Mahavavy River did not appear to constitute an effective barrier between *P.v. coronatus* and *P.v. deckeni* and that some hybridization might occur in its upper reaches. Also, reliable reports of *P. v. coronatus* as far south as the Sakay River, east as far as Andanotongo, and southeast beyond Tsiroanomandidy, suggest that limits to the distributions of these subspecies are more complicated than originally believed. The taxonomy and status of *P. v. coronatus* and *P. v. deckeni* warrant further investigation.

Natural History

There have been no field studies of the crowned sifaka to date.

Conservation Status

The primary threat to the survival of the crowned sifaka is destruction of its forest habitat, principally to provide grazing land for livestock and wood for charcoal. *P. v. coronatus* is not known to occur in any protected areas, although it is possible that the Kasijy Special Reserve may harbor a population. There are no population figures available, but a reasonable order of magnitude estimate would be 100-1,000 (Mittermeier *et al.*, 1992). A captive breeding colony of five animals is maintained at the Vincennes Zoo in Paris (ISIS, 1993).

Based upon the crowned sifaka's presumably small population and the fact that it is not known to occur in any protected areas, it was given a *Highest Priority* rating (7) in the IUCN/SSC Primate Specialist Group's *Lemurs of Madagascar: An Action Plan for their Conservation* (Mittermeier *et al.*, 1992). Using the latest IUCN Red List criteria, we place this subspecies in the *Critically Endangered* category.

Where To See It

We know of no sites sites where this sifaka can easily be found, and do not recommend that the first time visitor to Madagascar try to find it. Those who might be willing to conduct detailed research on *P. v. coronatus* should investigate remaining forests between the Mahavavy and Betsiboka Rivers. The authors of this guide would be very interested in any distributional information, photographs or other data on this poorly known animal.

Propithecus verreauxi deckeni   **Color Plate 31**
Decken's Sifaka   **Page 348**

French: Propithèque de von der Decken
German: Decken's Kronensifaka
Malagasy: Tsibahaka, Sifaka

Identification

The typical Decken's sifaka has a completely white pelage, sometimes tinged with silver-gray or yellow-gold on the back and limbs. The face is black, but usually with a whitish patch of hair running across it, and has a rather blunt-nosed look caused by bony pockets at either side of the muzzle.

Geographic Range

Decken's sifaka is found in patches of the highly fragmented deciduous forests of western Madagascar, between the Betsiboka and Tsiribihina Rivers (Tattersall, 1982, 1986). As indicated under *P. v. coronatus*, there is considerable uncertainty regarding the status and boundaries of *Propithecus verreauxi deckeni* and *P. v. coronatus* populations between the Betsiboka and Mahavavy Rivers, the northern part of Decken's sifaka's distribution. The eastern limit of its distribution is unknown. Travellers in western Madagascar can add to our knowledge of lemur systematics by reporting their observations of sifakas in this region.

Natural History

No field studies of Decken's sifaka have been undertaken.

Conservation Status

Decken's sifaka is threatened by habitat destruction from annual fires set to provide fresh growth for livestock (Nicoll and Langrand, 1989). No information is available on possible hunting pressure. This subspecies is known to occur in the Tsingy de Bemaraha and Namoroka Nature Reserves and the Ambohijanahary Special Reserve (Nicoll and Langrand, 1989; Harcourt and Thornback, 1990; Mittermeier *et al.*, 1992). Its range also appears to encompass the Bemarivo, Maningozo and Kasijy Special Reserves, but information is lacking about its occurrence in these protected areas. There are no population figures available, but a reasonable order of magnitude estimate would be 1,000-10,000 (Mittermeier *et al.*, 1992).

Based upon its presumed small population and its uncertain presence in several protected areas within its range, Decken's sifaka was given a *High Priority* rating (5) in the IUCN/SSC Primate Specialist Group's *Lemurs of Madagascar: An Action Plan for their Conservation* (Mittermeier *et al.*, 1992). Using the latest IUCN Red List criteria, we place this subspecies in the *Vulnerable* category.

Where To See It

The most accessible locality at which to see this subspecies is in the forest around the lighthouse at Katsepy, near the ferry landing from Majunga (= Mahajanga). It also appears to be common in the Tsingy de Bemaraha Nature Reserve, where it can be easily spotted, but it is difficult to follow because of the ruggedness of the terrain.

Propithecus tattersalli   **Color Plate 31**
Golden-Crowned Sifaka   **Page 348**

Other English: Tattersall's Sifaka
French: Propithèque de Tattersall
German: Tattersall-Sifaka
Malagasy: Ankomba Malandy, Simpona

Identification
   The golden-crowned sifaka is a medium to small sifaka with
an average adult weight of about 3.5 kg. The head and body
length is about 50 cm and tail length about 40 cm, for an overall
length of approximately 90 cm. It is mostly white in coloration,
but with a cap of golden fur between the ears and often on the
shoulders as well. The face is black with some whitish hairs, and
the ears are prominent and tufted. The pelage is relatively short,
and the hairs lie flat against the skin. The most useful characters
in field identification are the golden cap and protruding ears.
Locomotion, postures and group sizes are as in other *Propithecus*.
Vocalizations are generally like those in other *Propithecus*, but
the "si-fak!" call is particularly clearly pronounced.
   This is a monotypic species first mentioned and depicted in a
photograph by Tattersall (1982), but not formally described until
1988 (Simons, 1988). As with the other species of sifaka, this
animal is impossible to confuse with other lemurs living in its very
small range.

Geographic Range
   P. tattersalli has a very restricted distribution, limited to
forest patches between the Loky and Manambato Rivers in
northeastern Madagascar, and centering around the town of
Daraina on Route National 5a, approximately 56 km west of
Vohémar (Iharana). It occurs in both deciduous and semi-
evergreen forest within this range.

Natural History
   The forests throughout the range of this species are remnant
patches isolated by human agriculture. Most are deciduous
formations similar in composition to dry western Malagasy forests, but semi-evergreen forest persists on higher hills (Meyers
and Ratsirarson, 1989). The average group size is about 5

individuals, varying from 3 to 10. Groups commonly contain two adults of each sex, but typically only one female reproduces each year. Males sometimes switch groups during the mating season.

Home range size is about 9-12 ha, and day ranges vary seasonally from 400-1200 m. Population density ranges from 60-70 individuals/ km^2. The golden-crowned sifaka is diurnal, but occasionally moves before dawn and after dark during the rainy season. It sleeps at night in high emergent trees. Mobbing calls are directed against avian predators, while the " si-fak!" call is directed against terrestrial predators such as boas, fossas and sometimes humans. The diet consists principally of seeds, unripe fruit, young and mature leaves and flowers. Bark is sometimes eaten in the dry season. Mating occurs in late January, births in late June, and weaning in December (D. Meyers, pers. obs.).

Conservation Status

This unique animal is probably one of the two or three most endangered lemurs in Madagascar (Harcourt and Thornback, 1990). Although its existence was noted by Tattersall in 1974 (see Tattersall [1982]) for the first photograph ever taken of the species), it was not formally described by science until 1988 (Simons, 1988). It also has one of the smallest ranges and documented populations of all lemurs. Furthermore, it is not yet found in any protected area, although Meyers and Ratsirarson (1989) recommend establishment of a national park of some 20,000 ha in the Daraina area.

The main threats to the survival of the golden-crowned sifaka are forest clearance for agriculture, periodic brush fires and hunting for food. Although the people from the Daraina area traditionally consider this species to be *fady*, this is not the case with those moving in from other parts of Madagascar. Daraina is on the only east-west road in this region, and the road between Ambilobe and Vohimarina (RN 5a) is due to be improved in the near future, thus facilitating access to the region as a whole. Gold is found in the Daraina area as well; although gold miners have thus far hunted mainly the smaller lemurs, this could easily change (Meyers and Ratsirarson, 1989). Hunting by people from Ambilobe has already exterminated populations of this animal from the Maromakotra area, 30 km northwest of Daraina, and the same could happen to other golden-crowned sifaka populations if steps are not taken to protect this species now (Meyers and

Ratsirarson, 1989; Harcourt and Thornback, 1990).

The wild population of this species is estimated to be 6,000-8,000 (Meyers and Ratsirarson, 1989).   There are only four golden-crowned sifakas in captivity in the world, all at the Duke University Primate Center (ISIS, 1993). Two were wild caught to establish this colony, which first produced offspring in 1988. An additional two animals were captured in 1993.

Based upon its small and restricted population and the fact that this species does not occur in any protected area, *P. tattersalli* was given the *Highest Priority* rating (6) in the IUCN/SSC Primate Specialist Group's *Lemurs of Madagascar: An Action Plan for their Conservation* (Mittermeier *et al.*, 1992).   Using the latest IUCN Red List criteria,we place this species in the *Critically Endangered* Category.

Where To See It

The golden-crowned sifaka is most easily seen south of the town of Antsahampano, 11 km east of Daraina. However, this area is relatively difficult to reach, and a visit there should be left to the seasoned lemur watcher on a second or third trip.

Propithecus diadema diadema   **Color Plate 32**
Diademed Sifaka   **Page 349**

Other English: Diademed Simpona
French: Propithèque à Diadème
German: Diademsifaka
Malagasy: Simpona, Simpony

Identification

The diademed sifaka is perhaps the most stunningly beautiful of all the lemurs. The long, silky fur is principally white, but the top of the head and the back of the neck are black, and this coloration sometimes extends down onto the shoulders and back. In some individuals, this color shades beyond the shoulders to a silvery gray, while in others it remains dark almost to the golden pygal region at the base of the tail. The hindquarters and hind limbs are commonly light golden. The tail is usually white, but may be golden in some individuals. The hands and feet are black.

The diademed sifaka is also one of the largest lemurs; weights of adult animals captured in the wild for the Duke University Primate Center ranged from 6-7.25 kg, the upper limit exceeding the heaviest *Indri indri* on record (K. Glander, pers. comm.). Tail length averages 46.5 cm and head plus body length 52 cm, for an average overall length of close to 100 cm.

There is little chance of confusing the diademed sifaka with any other sympatric species. The only lemur of comparable size within its range is the indri, and the indri is immediately distinguished by its very short tail.

Geographic Range

P. d. diadema is the most widely distributed of the diademed sifakas, inhabiting the eastern rain forest strip of Madagascar, north from the Mangoro River to somewhere below the Antainambalana River (south of Maroantsetra), though the precise limits of its range are unknown (Petter *et al.*, 1977; Petter and Petter-Rousseaux; 1979; Tattersall, 1982) .

Natural History

Despite its widespread distribution, little is known of the natural history of this subspecies. However, based upon observations in the forests around Analamazaotra, it seems to exist in low densities wherever it occurs and is most commonly seen in groups of two to five individuals with home ranges of 20 ha or larger (Pollock, 1979). It is currently being studied by Joyce Powzyk in the Mantady National Park near Périnet (= Andasibe).

Conservation Status

P. d. diadema is threatened by habitat destruction due to slash-and-burn agriculture, logging, and hunting for food, which appears to be a common practice even in forests within protected areas (Simons, 1984). This subspecies occurs in the Mantady and Verezanantsoro National Parks, the Betampona and Zahamena Nature Reserves, and the Ambatovaky and Analamazaotra Special Reserves (Pollock, 1975, 1984; Simons, 1984; Raxworthy, 1986, 1988; Nicoll and Langrand, 1989; Katz, 1991; Thompson and Evans, 1991; Mittermeier *et al.*, 1992). There are no population figures available, but a reasonable order of magnitude estimate would be 1,000-10,000 (Mittermeier *et al.*, 1992). There are currently three diademed sifakas in captivity at the Duke University Primate Center (ISIS, 1993).

Due to its presumed small population size, the continuing threat of habitat destruction even in existing protected areas, and the fact that it is hunted for food in most parts of its range, *P. d. diadema* was given a *High Priority* rating (5) in the IUCN/SSC Primate Specialist Group's *Lemurs of Madagascar: An Action Plan for their Conservation* (Mittermeier *et al.*, 1992). Using the latest IUCN Red List criteria, we place this subspecies in the *Endangered* category.

Where To See It

The diademed sifaka is one of the most difficult species to see in the wild because of its low density. Visitors occasionally see it in the Mantady National Park near Périnet (=Andasibe), but this is by no means guaranteed. It can also be seen in the Zahamena Nature Reserve, but this large protected area is difficult to reach and requires expedition-level preparations to visit.

If a visitor to Périnet (= Andasibe) has a few extra days, it is worth the effort to visit Mantady National Park to try and see this beautiful animal. Use of local guides from the Association des Guides d'Andasibe is essential.

Propithecus diadema edwardsi   **Color Plate 32**
Milne-Edwards' Sifaka   **Page 349**

Other English: Milne-Edwards' Simpona
French: Propithèque de Milne-Edwards
German: Edward's Diademsifaka
Malagasy: Simpona, Simpony

Identification

The dense pelage of Milne-Edwards' sifaka is almost entirely black or dark chocolate brown. Bilateral whitish patches of varying extent grade into the darker surrounding fur on the flanks and back, and sometimes meet in the midline. In some individuals, these patches are represented by only a few silvery hairs and, in the variant formerly known as *P. d. holomelas,* they are absent entirely. The upper part of the chest is usually relatively pale. Six females examined by Glander *et al.* (1992) weighed an average of 5.9 kg and had average head and body lengths of 48 cm and tail lengths of 46 cm; eight males averaged 5.6 kg in weight, 48 cm for head and body length and 44 cm for tail length. Individual weights fluctuate seasonally. This sifaka is easily distinguished from the comparably or slightly larger-sized *Indri indri* by its much smaller ears and shorter muzzle, by its long tail, and by the lack of a distinctive call like that of the indri.

Some recent authors have recognized another subspecies of *P. diadema, P. d. holomelas*. However, documented sympatry in the isolated Nandihizana forest during the nineteenth century (Cowan, 1882) makes it almost certain that this form (black on all of the upperparts, except for a dark brown patch at the base of the tail) is simply a variant of *P. d. edwardsi* (Tattersall, 1986). It is possible (indeed, likely) that all known specimens of this form were collected at Nandihizana, the remaining patches of which lie on the modern Route National 7 between km 292-296, some 50 km north of Fianarantsoa. Since no simponas survive today at Nandihizana, where the only remaining lemurs are *Microcebus,* and maybe also *Eulemur fulvus* and *Hapalemur griseus*, any further field research on simponas at this site is impossible. The *holomelas* form could occur elsewhere, but this is unlikely.

Geographic Range

Milne-Edwards' sifaka is found in the eastern rain forest, between the Mangoro and Mananara Rivers (Tattersall, 1982). There is one possible collecting record north of the Mangoro, but this is debatable. Inland, simponas occurred a century ago in the isolated forests of Nandihizana and Tsarafidy, between Ambositra and Fianarantsoa, but nowadays they are restricted to the rain forest strip.

Natural History

Studies of *P. d. edwardsi* have been carried out at Ranomafana National Park (Wright *et al.*, 1987). Group size ranges from three to nine individuals, and it appears that the basic social unit is something other than an adult male and female with offspring. Population densities are low (8 individuals/km^2) and home ranges are large (100-200 ha), with daily ranges of 1000 m or more. Territorial aggression between groups has not been observed. The diet of *P. d. edwardsi* is varied, with leaves, fruit and flowers alternating as the principal components.   Between 17 and 27 species of plants are reported to be eaten each day.

Infants are born in June-July, and begin to transfer from their mothers' bellies to their backs after about three or four weeks of age, riding principally on the back by about two months. Weaning takes place in September.

Conservation Status

Milne-Edwards' sifaka is threatened by habitat destruction due to slash-and-burn agriculture and logging, even in the forests surrounding and within protected areas. This subspecies is found in the Ranomafana National Park, the Andohahela Nature Reserve and the Pic d'Ivohibe Special Reserve (O'Connor *et al.*, 1986, 1987; Nicoll and Langrand, 1989; Harcourt and Thornback, 1990; Mittermeier *et al.*, 1992). There are no population figures available, but a reasonable order of magnitude estimate would be 1,000-10,000 (Mittermeier *et al.*, 1992). There are no Milne-Edwards' simponas in captivity at this time.

As a result of its limited range and probable small population, *P. d. edwardsi* was given a *High Priority* rating (5) in the IUCN/SSC Primate Specialist Group's *Lemurs of Madagascar: An Action Plan for their Conservation* (Mittermeier *et al.*, 1992). Using the latest IUCN/SSC Red List criteria, we place this subspecies in the *Endangered* category.

Where To See It

The only place where this species can be seen with certainty is the Ranomafana National Park. Finding it is relatively easy with the help of local guides, and a two-day stay in the forest at Ranomafana is likely to result in some sightings.

Propithecus diadema candidus   **Color Plate 33**
Silky Sifaka   **Page 350**

Other English: Silky Simpona
French: Propithèque Soyeux
Malagasy: Simpona, Simpony

Identification

The fur of this subspecies is long and silky, and completely white, except that in some individuals silver gray tints may appear on the crown, back, and limbs. The pygal region at the base of the tail is usually somewhat discolored. This distinctive animal cannot be confused with any other sympatric lemur species.

Geographic Range

P. d. candidus is apparently distributed throughout the northern part of the humid forest belt from Maroantsetra to the Andapa Basin and Marojejy Massif (Tattersall, 1982), though recently it has only been reported from the Marojejy Nature Reserve and the Anjanaharibé-Sud Special Reserve.

Natural History

Only brief observations have been made of this subspecies in the Marojejy Special Reserve (Safford *et al.*, 1989). An average group size of 4.3 individuals was recorded for 12 groups sighted, with a range of three to seven. Sixty percent of the groups contained immature offspring, all of them about the same size and born in the same time period.

Conservation Status

P. d. candidus is threatened primarily by habitat destruction, although it also is reported to be hunted for food in the Marojejy Special Reserve (Safford *et al.*, 1989). In addition to Marojejy, it also is found in the Anjanaharibe-Sud Special Reserve (Nicoll and Langrand, 1989). There are no population figures available, but a reasonable order of magnitude estimate would be 100-1,000 (Mittermeier *et al.*, 1992). There are none in captivity at this time.

Due to its presumably very small population size, its occurrence in only two special reserves and the threats that remain even to populations in these protected areas, *P. d. candidus* was one of the lemurs given a *Highest Priority* rating (6) in the IUCN/SSC Primate Specialist Group's *Lemurs of Madagascar: An Action*

Plan for their Conservation (Mittermeier *et al.*, 1992). Using the latest IUCN Red List criteria, we place this subspecies in the *Critically Endangered* category.

Where To See It

The silky sifaka is most often seen near the town of Doany, on the western border of the Marojejy Nature Reserve. However, this area is far off the tourist circuit, requires expedition-level preparations to visit, and sightings are by no means guaranteed. This is one of the lemurs best left to the seasoned lemur watcher on a second or third trip to Madagascar.

Propithecus diadema perrieri   **Color Plate 33**
Perrier's Sifaka   **Page 350**

**Other English: Perrier de la Bathie's Sifaka; Perrier's
            Simpona**
French: Propithèque de Perrier
German: Schwarzer Sifaka
Malagasy: Radjako, Ankomba Job

Identification

The fur of Perrier's sifaka is dense, long, and silky and
uniformly a deep, lustrous black except for a brownish chest and
belly. This sifaka is smaller than *P. d. edwardsi,* the other dark-
colored *P.diadema* subspecies, and occurs far to the north of its
relative. This animal is the largest lemur within its small range
and is very unlikely to be confused with sympatric *Eulemur* or any
other lemur species. This distinctive animal may warrant recognition as a separate species, but much further research would be
needed to determine this.

Geographic Range

This subspecies was initially identified from extremely dry
forests to the northeast of the Andrafiamena mountain chain, just
to the south and east of Anivorano Nord (Petter *et al.*, 1977;
Tattersall, 1982). It is now known to occur throughout the whole
Analamera Special Reserve west to the Ankarana Massif (Hawkins
et al., 1990).

Natural History

P. d. perrieri is an inhabitant of dry forests. Groups have
been reported to range in size from two to six, usually with only
one juvenile-sized individual, and home ranges approach 30 ha in
size (Meyers and Ratsirarson, 1989). During a one-month study,
the diet was found to consist of about equal quantities of mature
leaves, unripe fruit and petioles, young leaves, stems and flowers.

Conservation Status

Perrier's sifaka is considered to be one of the rarest of the
lemurs. Threats to its survival include habitat destruction due to
slash-and-burn agriculture, fires to clear pasture for livestock, and
the cutting of timber for charcoal production. Hunting for food is
also a threat for this subspecies in part of its range (Fowler *et al.*,

1989). The bulk of the *P. d. perrieri* population is found in the Analamera Special Reserve (Meyers and Ratsirarson, 1989), but it is also present in the Ankarana Special Reserve (Hawkins *et al.*, 1990). The most recent estimate of this subspecies' population is 2,000 individuals (Meyers and Ratsirarson, 1989). There are none in captivity at this time.

Based upon its extremely small population and the fact that it remains threatened even within the two protected areas in which it occurs, Perrier's sifaka was given the *Highest Priority* rating (6) in the IUCN/SSC Primate Specialist Group's *Lemurs of Madagascar: An Action Plan for their Conservation* (Mittermeier *et al.*, 1992). Using the latest IUCN Red List criteria, we place this subspecies in the *Critically Endangered* category.

Where To See It

Perrier's sifaka is best seen along the Bobankindro River, which bisects the Analamera Reserve. Seeing this subspecies in the wild requires expedition-level preparations and is best left to the seasoned lemur watcher on a second or third visit to Madagascar.

Indri: **Indri or Babakoto**

Only one species has been described for this genus, generally considered to be the largest of the surviving lemurs. *Indri indri* is distinguished from most other lemurs not only by its large size, but by its vestigial tail. It is a diurnal species of the eastern rain forests that lives in small, territorial family groups.

No subspecies are recognized, although there is considerable difference in coloration among indris from different localities. In general, there is a tendency toward slightly lighter coloration in the south of the species' range. The predominant fur color is black, contrasted in the darkest individuals by white patches on the crown, flanks, forelimbs or thighs, or any combination of these. The ears are always black, tufted and prominent.

PHOTO BY RUSSELL A. MITTERMEIER

Fig. 6.48: Indri *(Indri indri)* in the forest at Perinet (=Andasibe).

Key to illustrations on the following page (Fig. 6.49):
  a. **Close-up of *Indri* feeding on leaves**
  b. ***Indri* calling**
  c. ***Indri* looking up, about to leap from vertical clinging posture**
  d. ***Indri* with infant resting in vertical clinging posture**
  e. ***Indri* with infant resting in sitting posture**

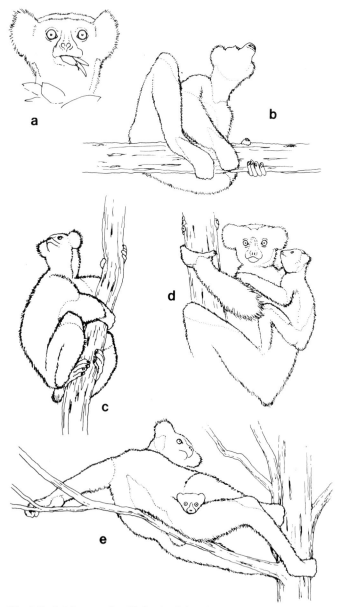

Fig. 6.49: *Indri* postural and behavioral drawings.

Fig. 6.50: Indri *(Indri indri)* in the forest at Perinet (=Andasibe).

Key to illustrations on the following page (Fig. 6.51):
   a. *Indri* suspended by its arms, using very simple arm-swinging
       locomotion
   b. *Indri* resting on horizontal branch
c-d.   *Indri* leaping
   e. *Indri* feeding from vertical clinging posture

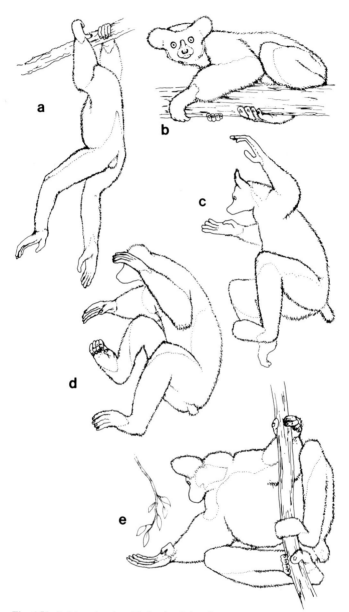

Fig. 6.51: *Indri* postural and behavioral drawings.

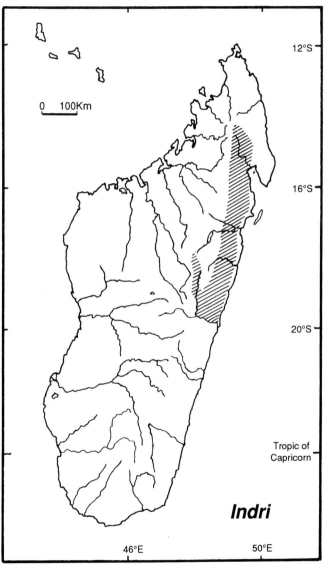

Fig. 6.52: Map of *Indri* distribution.

Indri indri   Color Plate 34
Indri   Page 351

French: Indri
German: Indri
Malagasy: Babakoto, Endrina, Amboanala

Identification

The indri is generally considered the largest-bodied living
lemur, averaging about 6-7 kg in body weight or possibly more,
but *Propithecus d. diadema* is a close competitor.   It is a typical
vertical clinger and leaper, with long hind limbs compared to the
trunk and forelimbs, and a preference for postures in which the
trunk is held vertically. The combined length of its head and body
averages slightly over 60 cm, but the tail is vestigial and only
about 5 cm long. Pelage coloration is highly variable. The fur is
predominantly black, with whitish patches that may be restricted
to the crown, neck or flanks, but which may also occur on the rear
and outside surfaces of the fore- and hindlimbs. Such paler areas
may be tinged with gray or gold. The face is black and may be
variably framed with paler fur. The ears are black, modestly
tufted, and highly visible. Darker individuals tend to be found at
the northern end of the species' range, lighter ones towards the
south.   The indri is easily located and identified by its eerie,
wailing loud song. It is also unlikely to be mistaken for any other
lemur species living in its range, except where it abuts with the
similarly proportioned and darkish-colored *Propithecus diadema
edwardsi*.   However, the indri is easily distinguished from this
animal and the lighter colored *P. diadema diadema*, with which
it is broadly sympatric, by its prominent ears, long muzzle and
especially by its vestigial tail, which contrasts strongly with the
long tail of the *Propithecus* species.

Geographic Range

This species inhabits the eastern rain forests of Madagascar,
from the Mangoro River north to near Sambava, but excluding the
Masoala Peninsula (Petter *et al.*, 1977; Tattersall, 1982). Its most
northerly occurrence appears to be in the reserve of Anjanaharibe-
Sud, just to the east of Andapa (Nicoll and Langrand, 1989).
Whether this range is even approximately continuous is not
known, and it has certainly shrunk in recent decades. Subfossil
evidence indicates that the indri once occurred in the interior of

Madagascar as far west as the Itasy Massif (Tattersall, 1982), and to the north on the Ankarana Massif (W. Jungers and E. Simons, pers. comm.). Its altitudinal range is up to 1500 m (Petter *et al.*, 1977).

Natural History

The indri has been studied in the wild by J. Pollock (1975, 1977, 1979) in the forests of Analamazaotra near Périnet (= Andasibe). It lives in groups of from three to five individuals, normally consisting of an adult pair and their offspring (Pollock, 1979). The female appears to be the dominant member of the pair, normally feeding higher in the trees than the male and having priority access to food sources. Its diet consists of leaves, flowers and fruit, which vary in their proportions according to season, and it also occasionally descends to the ground to eat earth. Home ranges of groups studied at Analamazaotra averaged about 18 ha, with day ranges of 300 to 700 m. Spacing between groups may be conditioned by the famous loud morning calls (which are answered from as far as 3 km away), accounting for a relatively small degree of range overlap between neighboring groups. Densities at Analamazaotra ranged from 9-16 individuals/km^2, both in primary and degraded forests (Pollock, 1975).

The indri seems to be the most strictly diurnal of all lemurs, its activity period occupying from 5-11 daylight hours, according to season (Pollock, 1979). It sleeps from 10-30 m above the ground, and no more than two animals ever sleep in contact with one another; distances between group members can be 100 m or more (Pollock, 1975).

Reproduction is highly seasonal, with births occurring in May after a gestation period of 120-150 days. Infants ride on the mother's ventrum up to the age of four to five months, then transfer to the back. By eight months they are moving independently, but they stay close to the mother until well into their second year (Pollock, 1975). Reproductive maturity is reached between seven and nine years of age (Pollock, 1977, 1984).

Conservation Status

The indri is threatened by loss of its eastern rain forest habitat for fuel, timber and slash-and-burn agriculture (Pollock, 1984), with destruction occurring even in protected areas. Although other lemur species are hunted within the indri's range, hunting of the indri itself is considered taboo by many local people. Nonetheless, there are reports that it is occasionally killed for food, especially by Chinese living in Madagascar. A small scandal erupted in 1984, when it came to light that Chinese workers on the road from Antananarivo to Tamatave (= Toamasina) were apparently buying indris as a delicacy.

The species is found in the Mantady and Verezanantsoro National Parks, the Betampona and Zahamena Nature Reserves, and the Ambatovaky, Analamazaotra and Anjanaharibe-Sud Special Reserves (Nicoll and Langrand, 1989; Harcourt and Thornback, 1990; Mittermeier *et al.*, 1992). There are no population figures available, but a reasonable order of magnitude estimate would be 1,000-10,000 (Mittermeier *et al.*, 1992). There are no indri in captivity anywhere in the world, and previous attempts to keep them were notably unsuccessful.

In recognition of the indri's taxonomic uniqueness, relatively small and probably discontinuous population, and the threats to its existence, even in protected areas, it was given the *Highest Priority* rating (6) in the IUCN/SSC Primate Specialist Group's *Lemurs of Madagascar: An Action Plan for their Conservation* (Mittermeier *et al.*, 1992). Using the latest IUCN Red List criteria, we place this species in the *Endangered* category.

Where To See It

The classic site for seeing the indri is the Analamazaotra Special Reserve near the train station at Périnet (= Andasibe). Seeing the animal there is almost guaranteed if one is willing to stay overnight, get up early the next morning, and stay in the forest until it starts calling. Indeed, the outside world's image of this unique species is based almost entirely on a single habituated group that has been seen daily for several decades. Employing a local guide, of which a number of excellent ones are available at low cost, makes finding the indri a virtual certainty. In fact, we strongly recommend using the local guides. They have organized themselves into a local organization called the Association des Guides d'Andasibe, and are a very positive force for conservation in the region.

No trip to Madagascar is complete without a visit to Périnet to see this spectacular animal, surely one of the most attractive, appealing and unusual creatures in the Animal Kingdom. Périnet can be reached by road from Antananarivo in 2-3 hours, or by train which departs early in the morning from the main train station in Antananarivo and takes about five hours to reach Périnet. Some people like to go by car or bus in one direction and by train in the other direction, to get somewhat different views of the local terrain and the villages through which one passes. Accommodations at the Hotel de la Gare in Périnet are quaint and part of the experience, and you very often meet other naturalists there from around the world.

It is possible to see (or more likely hear) the indri in other parts of Madagascar as well, especially in the protected areas mentioned above, but this is much more difficult and requires expedition-level preparations and a lot of time.

FAMILY DAUBENTONIIDAE

Daubentonia: Aye-Aye

This monotypic family is composed of one living species, the aye-aye, *Daubentonia madagascariensis*. This animal is separated from the other lemurs because it is highly specialized in many different ways, among them its unique dental formula (distinct from all other primates), its continuously growing incisor teeth (which led to its being considered a rodent during part of the 19th century), its large ears almost certainly used in locating insect larvae in dead wood, and its long skeleton-like middle finger used to extract larvae from holes. So unique is it among the lemurs that it has proven extremely difficult to determine which other lemurs are its closest relatives, although there is some suggestion that its affinities may lie with the indriids (Schwartz and Tattersall, 1985). The aye-aye is so unusual that it is not only strange within the context of the Order Primates, it is one of the most distinctive mammals on Earth.

Although only one living species of aye-aye is currently recognized, remains of a second, extinct species, *Daubentonia robusta*, are known from a few sites in the south of Madagascar. No skull has yet been found, but postcranial bones are larger and much more robust than those of the living form, suggesting that it was at least 2.5 times, and possibly as much as 5 times heavier. Teeth of *D. robusta* perforated for stringing provide one of the few direct evidences that any extinct lemur was hunted by humans, and it is virtually certain that this species was driven to extinction by human action (E. Simons, pers. comm.).

Key to illustrations on the following page (Fig. 6.53):
   a. Captive *Daubentonia* eating an egg using its long bony middle finger
   b. *Daubentonia* infant suckling
   c. *Daubentonia* in aggressive posture
   d. *Daubentonia* using its long incisor teeth to gnaw a hole in a branch
   e. *Daubentonia* listening and probing for grubs with its long bony middle finger (note the position of its ears)
   f. *Daubentonia* grooming its long bony middle finger

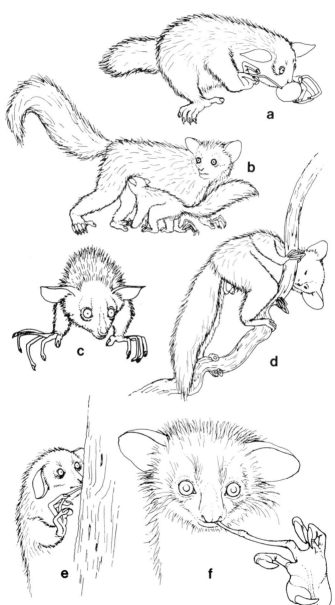

Fig. 6.53: *Daubentonia* postural and behavioral drawings.

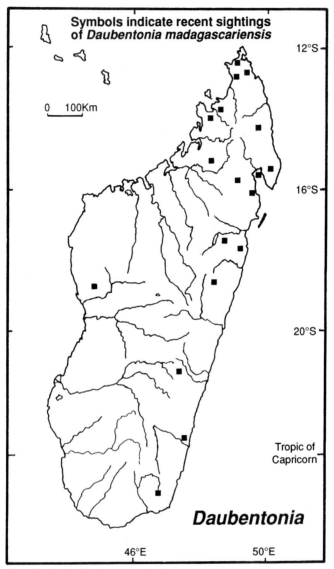

Symbols indicate recent sightings of *Daubentonia madagascariensis*

0   100Km

12°S

16°S

20°S

Tropic of Capricorn

Daubentonia

46°E   50°E

Fig. 6.54: Map of *Daubentonia* distribution.

Daubentonia madagascariensis
Aye-Aye

Color Plate 35, 36
Pages 352, 353

French: Aye-Aye
German: Fingertier
Malagasy: Hay-Hay, Ahay, Aiay

Identification

Due to the unique characters of the aye-aye, it is one of the easiest lemur species to identify. The head and body length is 40 cm, the tail is slightly longer, and the body weight is about 3 kg. Its hair is coarse in appearance but made from two layers, soft, short, off-white hair and long coarse white-tipped black hair. The ears are large and black and the nose is pink. The eyes are surrounded by dark rings while the rest of the face is pale, in some cases including the throat as well.

It is very difficult to confuse the aye-aye with any other lemur species, unless only the most superficial glance of the species is obtained in the forest at night. It is by far the largest nocturnal lemur, being more than double the size of *Lepilemur* and *Avahi*, and is easily distinguished from these by its huge ears, its long bushy tail, and its long coarse hair.

Geographic Range

Though it remains very sparsely distributed and presumably occurs at low densities wherever it is found, the aye-aye has been found in many new localities throughout the 1980's. It is known to occur along the entire east coast, in the Sambirano, the province of Antsiranana, and several locations in the northwest (Tattersall, 1982; Albignac, 1987; Simons, 1993). This is an incredible turn of events, as it was feared at one time that the species might be on the verge of extinction. Sightings are rare throughout its range, but it has been reported from a growing number of parks and reserves, and from other areas as well, including near Mananara and Maroantsetra and just south of Ambilobe and Ambanja (J. Andrews, pers. comm.).

Natural History

The preferred habitat of the aye-aye appears to be moist forest, as it is found throughout Madagascar's eastern rain forests. However, it occurs in some dry forest both to the north and south of the Sambirano. Signs of aye-aye presence include holes gnawed in dead trees or wood, which in drier forests can be easily attributed to this species due to lasting tooth marks. Other signs include *ramy* nuts (*Canarium madagascariensis*), which have been cracked open from the apex and again show distinctive large parallel tooth marks.

Practically all known information on the aye-aye in the wild comes from a two-year study by Yale University graduate student Eleanor Sterling (1992, 1993) on the island reserve of Nosy Mangabe. The diet of the aye-aye is dominated by very few items: insect larvae, the cotyledon (interior) of the *ramy* nut, nectar (or larvae) from the traveler's palm (*Ravenala madagascariensis*), fungus, and a recurrent growth on *Intsia* sp. Aye-ayes are nocturnal, solitary foragers and spend up to 80% of the night traveling and feeding. The average nightly journey at Nosy Mangabe was about 1500 m, and travel on the ground was not uncommon. In this study, eight individuals were seen to utilize some 100 nests, and different individuals would use the same nest on different days. Nests are usually high and hidden well in vine tangles.

There appears to be no restricted mating season, and births may occur at any time during the year. Recently, a pregnant female was brought into captivity and gave birth in late April (practically all other lemur species give birth from July through December). In the wild, infants are weaned after 7 months. Indications are that the aye-aye may give birth only once every 2-3 years (Petter and Peyrieras, 1970b).

Conservation Status

Once considered to be one of the most endangered mammals in the world, the aye-aye has recently been shown to be more widespread and abundant than previously believed, mainly as a result of in-depth fieldwork by several international teams (Pollock, 1984; Pollock *et al.*, 1985; Constable *et al.*, 1985; Ganzhorn, 1986; O'Connor *et al.*, 1986; Albignac, 1987; Raxworthy and Rakotondraparany, 1988; Petter and Andriatsafara, 1987; Nicoll and Langrand, 1989). Part of the problem was that no one really knew how to look for this elusive nocturnal species and identify nests and other signs. However, as researchers developed a "search image" for the animal, it has turned up in many new sites and is apparently quite adaptable in choice of habitats.

Nonetheless, we should not become complacent about the

aye-aye. It probably never occurred at very high densities and is still killed on sight in some areas as a harbinger of evil. It is also killed as a crop pest in coconut and lychee plantations but, fortunately, is rarely hunted for food because of its evil reputation (Albignac, 1987; Simons, 1993). Furthermore, as with all other species in Madagascar, its habitat continues to be destroyed.

The aye-aye is found in at least 16 protected areas, which bodes well for its survival, and several of these locations appear to have healthy populations. They include the Mantady, Montagne d'Ambre, Ranomafana and Verezanantsoro National Parks, the Andohahela, Betampona, Marojejy and Zahamena Nature Reserves, and the Ambatovaky, Analamazaotra, Analamera, Ankarana, Forêt d'Ambre, Manombo, Manongarivo and Nosy Mangabe Special Reserves (Nicoll and Langrand, 1989; Harcourt and Thornback, 1990; Mittermeier *et al.*, 1992). Also, although rarely kept in zoos, it has recently bred in captivity at the Duke University Primate Center and the Jersey Wildlife Preservation Trust (Simons, 1993), and there are small colonies at the Vincennes Zoo in Paris and Zoo Ivoloina and Parc Tsimbazaza in Madagascar (Olney and Ellis, 1992; ISIS, 1993).

Although no population figures are available, an order of magnitude estimate for the species would be 1,000 - 10,000 (Mittermeier *et al.*, 1992). Given its status as the only living representative of an entire, very unusual primate family (a distinction it shares only with *Homo sapiens* and with the South American Goeldi's monkey, *Callimico goeldii*, which is not nearly as distinct from its relatives as is the aye-aye), the aye-aye is not only a very high conservation priority for Madagascar, it rates among the highest global wildlife conservation priorities. Accordingly, it was given the *Highest Priority* rating (7) in the IUCN/SSC Primate Specialist Group's *Lemurs of Madagascar: An Action Plan for their Conservation* (Mittermeier *et al.*, 1992). Using the latest IUCN Red List criteria, we place this species in the *Endangered* category. It is *not* listed as *Critically Endangered* in spite of its very high numerical rating in the IUCN/SSC PSG Action Plan because this rating system gives extra heavy weight to the aye-aye's taxonomic uniqueness as a monotypic primate family. In spite of its great interest, it is not considered nearly as endangered as a number of other lemurs with much more restricted ranges and under more immediate threat (especially *Hapalemur simus*, *Hapalemur aureus* and *Propithecus tattersalli*).

Where To See It

Although seeing the aye-aye in the wild requires great patience and diligence, visitors to Madagascar now stand a fair
chance of seeing this bizarre animal, once considered one of
Nature's greatest rarities. The best place to see the aye-aye is in
the Verezanantsoro National Park (part of the Mananara-Nord
Biosphere Reserve) in the eastern rain forest, where the possibili-
ties of getting a nocturnal peek at this animal are apparently
reasonably high. Several tour companies in Madagascar now
include Mananara on their itinerary, especially for aye-aye viewing, so definitely give it a try if you have the time. There are few
species in the world that can compare.

The next best choice is the island of Nosy Mangabe, near
Maroantsetra in the Bay of Antongil in northeast Madagascar.
Nine aye-ayes were introduced there in 1966 (WWF, 1969;
Constable *et al.*, 1985), and they apparently took hold and thrived.
Although by no means guaranteed, you have a chance of seeing
an aye-aye on this small island if you stay for two or three nights,
and you also get to see plenty of *Varecia variegata variegata*,
Lemur fulvus albifrons and *Microcebus rufus*. Cross the bay to the
Masoala Peninsula, and you may also get a look at *Varecia
variegata rubra*. The chances of seeing aye-ayes on Nosy
Mangabe are now better than they were in the early 1980s, since
Eleanor Sterling conducted her study there and has several of
them habituated. Nosy Mangabe is also included in several tour
circuits, or you can get there by yourself by flying to Maroantsetra
and booking a room on the mainland and a boat to the island with
the Hotel Antongil.

Although there is also a chance of seeing aye-ayes elsewhere
within their range (*e.g.*, Montagne d'Ambre, Ranomafana and
Périnet (=Andasibe), you would have to spend several weeks (or
even months) searching before catching a glimpse of these elusive
creatures.

APPENDIX 1

LEMURS PRESENT
IN PROTECTED AREAS

In the preceding chapter, we have listed the protected areas in which the presence of each lemur taxon has been documented, as well as selected unprotected areas of Madagascar where lemurs can also be seen. In this chapter, to alert lemur watchers to the various taxa that may be seen at a particular location, we provide lemur lists for Madagascar's national parks, nature reserves and special reserves, together with country maps showing the location of these different protected areas.

We begin with a description of Madagascar's biogeographic regions, which provides the environmental framework for presentation of the different protected areas and their faunas (Table A.1). This is followed by maps showing the location of national parks, nature reserves and special reserves, and a table of lemur species to be found in each. Finally, we provide two more maps to show the location of the vast network of poorly known classified forests and forest reserves.

Biogeographic Regions of Madagascar

According to White in *The Vegetation of Africa* (1983), Madagascar can be divided into two major biogeographic regions - Eastern and Western (Fig. A.1). The Eastern Region includes four floristic domains: Eastern, Central, High Mountain and Sambirano. The Western Region is divided into two domains: Western and Southern. Each domain is characterized by specific types of vegetation (Guillaumet, 1984; Langrand, 1990; Nicoll and Rathbun, 1990). Several of these vegetation types are illustrated in Color Plates 1 and 2.

Eastern Region

Eastern Domain
Lowland rain forest, the natural vegetation between sea level and 800 m altitude, extends along the east coast from north of Samabava to Fort-Dauphin (= Tolagnaro). Average annual precipitation is between 2,000-3,000 mm and there is no dry season. The height of the evergreen

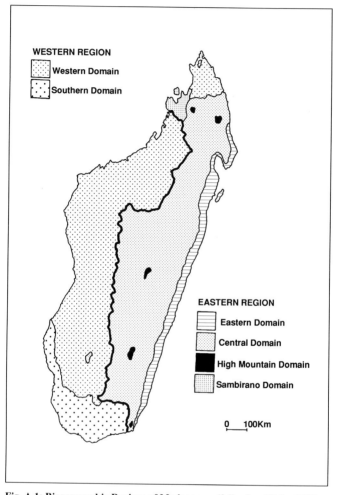

Fig. A.1: Biogeographic Regions of Madagascar (following White, 1983).

canopy averages between 20-30 m, with no emergent trees. This region is characterized by high species diversity and endemism. Eastern lowland forest represents one of the most endangered vegetation types in Madagascar (only the less extensive Sambirano and High Mountain Domains are more at risk), most of it having already been cleared. The largest remaining tracts are found in the northeastern and southeastern parts of the island. This and the Central Domain are the areas commonly referred to as the "Eastern Rain Forest Region" of Madagascar.

Central Domain

Forests of the Central Domain parallel those of the Eastern Domain and extend westward to Madagascar's central plateau above 800 m to altitudes of 1,300 m, and occasionally to 2,000 m. The average rainfall exceeds 1,500 mm and there is no dry season. Species diversity is as high as in the Eastern Domain; the level of endemism, however, is higher. The forest canopy is lower, averaging between 20-25 m. Epiphytic vegetation is more plentiful and the herbaceous stratum more developed. Most rain forest has disappeared in the Central Domain, but it remains Madagascar's most extensive biogeographic formation. The chief threats to this region are slash-and-burn cultivation (*tavy*) and exploitation for firewood.

High Mountain Domain

The High Mountain Domain comprises five distinct components: Tsaratanana in the northwest, Marojejy in the northeast, Ankaratra in the central east, Andringitra in the central southeast, and Andohahela in the southeast. Forests of the High Mountain Domain grow at altitudes of 2,000-2,867 m. Rainfall is substantial throughout the year and there is marked diurnal and seasonal variation in temperature. Species diversity is lower here than in previously mentioned domains, but species endemism is high. Fire is the chief threat to this vegetation type. The two largest intact blocks remaining are those at Marojejy and Andohahela.

Sambirano Domain

This domain consists of a small enclave of seasonal moist forest in the northwest. Together with the Tsaratanana Massif, it constitutes the northern end of Madagascar's central mountain range. Annual rainfall exceeds 2,000 mm. The Sambirano is characterized by high species diversity and a high level of endemism, and it represents something of a transition zone between Madagascar's Eastern and Western Regions. Forest canopy height is about 30 m, with some emergents. The chief threat to this vegetation type is cultivation of rice and coffee.

Western Region

Western Domain

This is the area popularly referred to as the "Western Dry Forest Region" or the "Western Dry Deciduous Forest Region" of Madagascar. The vegetation of the Western Domain now consists of discontinuous patches of dry deciduous forests on the coastal plains and limestone plateaux, ranging from sea level to 800 m. It covers the area from Antsiranana in the north to Morombe in the southwest. Annual rainfall ranges from 500-2,000 mm, being lightest in the south and heaviest in the north. There is a marked dry season of almost seven months during which many trees of the canopy layer shed their leaves. The shrub layer is well developed and vines are common. Plant species diversity is lower than forests of the Eastern Region , but the level of endemism is higher; lemur species diversity is comparable. This and the Eastern Domain are the most endangered forests in Madagascar. The principal threats to this type of vegetation are slash-and-burn cultivation, fire and uncontrolled use by livestock.

Southern Domain

The Southern Domain is characterized by deciduous thicket or thorn scrub, and is perhaps the least disturbed of Madagascar's biogeographic areas. It runs southward from Morombe along the coast, covering much of the island's southern tip from sea level to 400 m. Rainfall in this region is sparse and irregular, ranging from 300-800 mm. The dry season is marked and very long. Forest height is low and the formations are usually impenetrable due to a high incidence of thorny vegetation. The Didiereaceae, a plant family endemic to the Southern Domain, and various species of *Euphorbia* are the dominant plant groups. Species diversity and levels of endemism are very high. This is the region popularly referred to as the "Southern Spiny Desert Region" of Madagascar.

The primary threats to forests of the Southern Domain are charcoal and firewood production, the uncontrolled collection of ornamental and medicinal plants, and the overexploitation of the land by livestock, especially cattle and goats. Slash-and-burn agriculture is not a significant threat due to the poor quality of the soils.

Protected Areas of Madagascar

As discussed in Chapter 5, Madagascar has several different categories of protected areas. The traditional protected areas that have been the focus of national and international conservation efforts include six national parks totalling 175,340 ha, 11 strict nature reserves covering 569,542 ha, and 23 special reserves with an area of 376,600 ha - for a grand total of 1,121,482 ha or 1.91% of the country (Figs. A.2, A.3). These are the areas that you are most likely to visit in your search for lemurs, and the ones on which the most information is available (Table A.1).

In addition to these, there exists a huge network of classified forests and forest reserves, some 267 in all totalling more than 4,000,000 ha, or an additional 7% of the country. These have been almost entirely overlooked in conservation efforts of the last two decades. A recent study by Conservation International (1994) unearthed records of these areas from government archives and listed and identified all of them, but virtually nothing is known of the lemur fauna in these forests. Needless to say they are of great importance for biodiversity conservation, and should be a focus for future efforts. Their locations are indicated in Figs. A.5 and A.6, but we are unable to provide lemur lists for them at this time.

Key to illustration on the following page (Fig. A.2):

National Parks (Parcs Nationaux)

Legislation establishing national parks was passed in 1958 and 1962. Madagascar's National Parks are open to visitation by the public, but access is controlled. Rights of access and permission to use certain forest products may be provided to villagers, but restrictions are imposed.

Isalo National Park	81,540 ha
Ranomafana	41,600
Verezanantsoro	23,000
Montagne d'Ambre	18,200
Mantady	i0,000
Nosy Atafana (marine)	1,000
	175,340 ha

Strict Nature Reserves (Réserves Intégrales)

Legislation establishing the category of strict nature reserve was passed in 1966. Access to nature reserves is limited to officials of the Water and Forests Department and to researchers who have obtained permission from the appropriate government ministries.

Tsingy de Bemaraha Nature Reserve	152,000 ha
Andohahela	76,020
Zahamena	73,160
Ankarafantsika	60,520
Marojejy	60,150
Tsaratanana	48,622
Tsimanampetsotsa	43,200
Andringitra	31,160
Namoroka	21,742
Betampona	2,228
Lokobe	740
	569,542 ha

Private Reserves

In addition to the system of governmentally-protected areas, provision for private reserves is also made in Madagascar. Three such reserves currently exist, one at Analabe (north of Morondava in the southwest), one at St. Luce (on the east coast north of Fort-Dauphin) and one at Berenty (in the far south to the east of Fort-Dauphin).

Analabe Private Reserve	2,000 - 12,000 ha (?)
Berenty	265
St. Luce	200

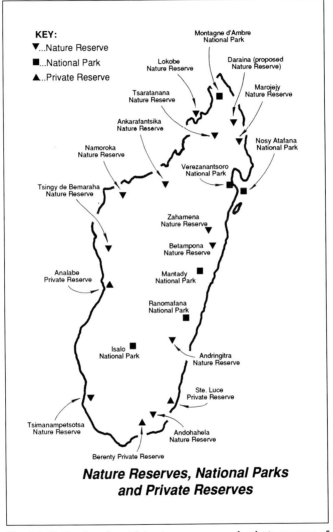

Fig. A.2: National parks, strict nature reserves and private reserves of Madagascar.

Key to illustration on the following page (Fig. A.3):

Special Reserves (Réserves Spéciales)

Various laws have been passed to establish special reserves in Madagascar. In most cases, these reserves have been created to protect a particular species of plant or animal. Permission must be obtained to enter Special Reserves, but allowances are made for certain traditional rights of use. There currently are 23 special reserves, only some of which are guarded by officials of the Water and Forests Department.

Ambatovaky	60,050 ha
Marotandrano	42,200
Manongarivo	35,250
Analamera	34,700
Anjanaharibe-Sud	32,100
Kalambatrita	28,250
Ambohijanahary	24,750
Kasijy	18,800
Ankarana	18,220
Analamaitso	17,150
Mangerivola	11,900
Bemarivo	11,570
Maningozo	7,900
Andranomena	6,420
Ambohitantely	5,600
Manombo	5,020
Forêt d'Ambre	4,810
Bora	4,780
Pic d'Ivohibe	3,450
Cap Sainte-Marie	1,750
Analamazaotra	810
Beza-Mahafaly	600
Nosy Mangabe	520
	376,600 ha

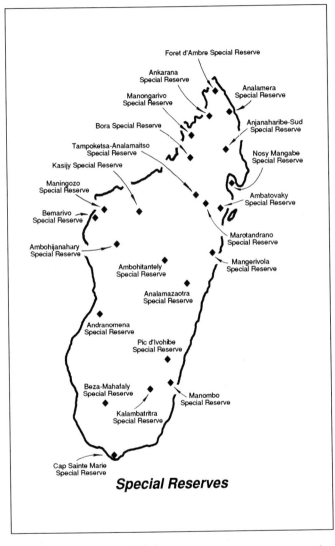

Fig. A.3: Special reserves of Madagascar.

Table A.1

Lemur Taxa Present
in the Protected Areas of Madagascar *

Eastern Region

Protected Area	Domains (ha)	Lemurs Present
Ambatovaky Special Reserve (60,050 ha)	Eastern - 51,050 Central - 9,000	*Microcebus rufus* *Cheirogaleus major* *Eulemur f. fulvus* *Eulemur rubriventer* *Lepilemur* sp. *Hapalemur g. griseus* *Varecia variegata variegata* *Avahi laniger* *Propithecus d. diadema* *Indri indri* *Daubentonia madagascariensis*
Verezanantsoro National Park (23,000 ha)	Eastern - 23,000	*Microcebus rufus* *Cheirogaleus major* *Allocebus trichotis* *Eulemur fulvus* sspp. *Varecia variegata variegata* *Hapalemur g. griseus* *Propithecus d. diadema* *Indri indri* *Daubentonia madagascariensis*

* Note that this list includes national parks, nature reserves and special reserves, together with a handful of private reserves. The many classified forests and forest reserves shown in the maps on pp. 288-291 have not yet been surveyed and are not included in this table. They represent a great opportunity and a challenge for future field research. Please note also that protected areas are listed according to size within the different domains, the largest areas coming first.

Protected Area	**Domains (ha)**	**Lemurs Present**
Mangerivola **Special Reserve** (11,900 ha)	Eastern - 11,900	?
Manombo **Special Reserve** (5,020 ha)	Eastern - 5,020	*Microcebus rufus* *Cheirogaleus* sp. *Hapalemur g. griseus* *Eulemur fulvus albocollaris*
Betampona **Nature Reserve** (2,228 ha)	Eastern - 2,228	*Microcebus rufus* *Cheirogaleus major* *Phaner f. furcifer* *Lepilemur mustelinus* *Hapalemur g. griseus* *Eulemur fulvus* sspp. *Varecia variegata variegata* *Avahi laniger* *Propithecus d. diadema* *Indri indri* *Daubentonia madagascariensis*
Nosy Mangabe **Special Reserve** (520 ha)	Eastern - 520	*Microcebus rufus* *Cheirogaleus major* *Eulemur fulvus albifrons* *Varecia variegata variegata* *Daubentonia madagascariensis*
Isalo **National Park** (81,540 ha)	Central - 81,540	*Lemur catta* *Eulemur fulvus rufus* *Propithecus v. verreauxi*

Protected Area	Domains (ha)	Lemurs Present
Zahamena	Central - 68,040	*Microcebus rufus*
Nature Reserve	Eastern - 5,124	*Cheirogaleus major*
(73,160 ha)		*Phaner f. furcifer*
		Lepilemur mustelinus
		Hapalemur g. griseus
		Eulemur fulvus sspp.
		Eulemur rubriventer
		Varecia variegata variegata
		Avahi laniger
		Propithecus d. diadema
		Indri indri
		Daubentonia madagascariensis
Andohahela	Central - 56,800	*Microcebus rufus*
Nature Reserve	Eastern - 6,300	*Cheirogaleus major*
Parcel 1		*Lepilemur mustelinus*
(63,100 ha)		*Lemur catta*
		Eulemur fulvus collaris
		Eulemur rubriventer
		Varecia variegata variegata
		Avahi laniger
		Propithecus d. diadema
		Indri indri
		Daubentonia madagascariensis
Marotandrano	Central - 42,200	?
Special Reserve		
(42,200 ha)		
Marojejy	Central - 42,105	*Microcebus rufus*
Nature Reserve	Eastern - 12,030	*Cheirogaleus major*
(60,150 ha)	High Mountain - 6,015	*Lepilemur mustelinus*
		Hapalemur g. griseus
		Eulemur fulvus albifrons
		Eulemur rubriventer
		Avahi laniger
		Propithecus diadema candidus
		Daubentonia madagascariensis

Protected Area	Domains (ha)	Lemurs Present
Ranomafana National Park (41,600 ha)	Central - 41,600	*Microcebus rufus* *Cheirogaleus major* *Lepilemur* sp. *Hapalemur g. griseus* *Hapalemur aureus* *Hapalemur simus* *Eulemur fulvus rufus* *Eulemur rubriventer* *Varecia variegata variegata* *Avahi laniger* *Propithecus diadema edwardsi* *Daubentonia madagascariensis*
Tsaratanana Special Reserve (48,622 ha)	Central - 36,952 Eastern - 8,270 High Mountain - 3,400	*Cheirogaleus major* *Phaner furcifer* sspp. *Lepilemur mustelinus* *Hapalemur g. griseus* *Eulemur f. fulvus* *Eulemur m. macaco* *Eulemur rubriventer*
Anjanaharibe-Sud Special Reserve (32,100 ha)	Central - 30,500 Eastern - 1,600	*Microcebus rufus* *Cheirogaleus major* *Hapalemur g. griseus* *Eulemur fulvus albifrons* *Avahi laniger* *Propithecus diadema candidus* *Indri indri*
Kalambatritra Special Reserve (28,250 ha)	Central - 28,250	*Eulemur fulvus rufus*
Ambohijanahary Special Reserve	Central - 24,750	*Propithecus verreauxi deckeni*

Protected Area	Domains (ha)	Lemurs Present
Andringitra **Nature Reserve** (31,160 ha)	Central - 21,860 High Mountain - 7,700 Eastern - 1,600	*Microcebus rufus* *Lepilemur microdon* *Lemur catta* *Eulemur fulvus rufus* *Eulemur rubriventer* *Varecia variegata variegata* *Avahi laniger*
Montagne d'Ambre **National Park** (18,200 ha)	Central - 18,200	*Microcebus rufus* *Cheirogaleus major* *Phaner furcifer electromontis* *Lepilemur septentrionalis* *Eulemur fulvus sanfordi* *Eulemur coronatus* *Daubentonia madagascariensis*
Tampoketsa- **Analamaitso** **Special Reserve** (17,150 ha)	Central - 17,150	?
Mantady **National Park** (10,000 ha)	Central - 10,000	*Microcebus rufus* *Cheirogaleus major* *Lepilemur microdon* *Hapalemur g. griseus* *Eulemur f. fulvus* *Eulemur rubriventer* *Varecia variegata variegata* *Avahi laniger* *Indri indri* *Daubentonia madagascariensis*
Ambohitantely **Special Reserve** (5,600 ha)	Central - 5,600	*Microcebus rufus* *Eulemur f. fulvus* *Avahi laniger*

Protected Area	Domains (ha)	Lemurs Present
Forêt d'Ambre **Special Reserve** (4,810 ha)	Central - 4,810	*Microcebus rufus* *Cheirogaleus major* *Phaner furcifer electromontis* *Lepilemur septentrionalis* *Eulemur fulvus sanfordi* *Eulemur coronatus* *Daubentonia* *madagascariensis*
Analamazaotra **Special Reserve** (= Périnet; = Andasibe) (810 ha)	Central - 810	*Microcebus rufus* *Cheirogaleus major* *Lepilemur microdon* *Hapalemur g. griseus* *Eulemur f. fulvus* *Eulemur rubriventer* *Varecia variegata variegata* *Avahi laniger* *Indri indri* *Daubentonia* *madagascariensis*

Manongarivo
Special Reserve
(35,250 ha)
	Sambirano -
	35,250
		Microcebus rufus
		Cheirogaleus major
		Phaner furcifer ssp.
		Lepilemur dorsalis
		Hapalemur g. griseus and/or
		  occidentalis
		Eulemur f. fulvus
		Eulemur m. macaco
		Daubentonia
		  madagascariensis

Lokobe **Nature Reserve** (740 ha)	Sambirano - 740	*Microcebus rufus* *Lepilemur dorsalis* *Eulemur m. macaco*
Pic d'Ivohibe **Special Reserve**	High Mountain - 3,450	*Eulemur fulvus rufus* *Propithecus diadema* *edwardsi*

Western Region

Protected Area	Domains (ha)	Lemurs Present
Tsingy de Bemaraha Nature Reserve (152,000 ha)	Western - 152,000	*Microcebus murinus* *Mirza coquereli* *Phaner furcifer pallescens* *Lepilemur edwardsi* *Hapalemur griseus occidentalis* *Eulemur fulvus rufus* *Propithecus verreauxi deckeni*
Ankarafantsika Nature Reserve (60, 520 ha)	Western - 60,520	*Microcebus murinus* *Cheirogaleus medius* *Lepilemur edwardsi* *Eulemur f. fulvus* *Eulemur mongoz* *Avahi occidentalis* *Propithecus verreauxi coquereli*
Analamera Special Reserve (34,700 ha)	Western - 34,700	*Microcebus murinus* *Phaner furcifer electromontis* *Lepilemur septentrionalis* *Eulemur fulvus sanfordi* *Eulemur coronatus* *Propithecus diadema perrieri* *Daubentonia madagascariensis*
Namoroka Nature Reserve (21,742 ha)	Western - 21,742	*Microcebus murinus* *Lepilemur edwardsi* *Eulemur fulvus* sspp. *Propithecus verreauxi deckeni*
Kasijy Special Reserve (18,800 ha)	Western - 18,800	?

Protected Area	**Domains(ha)**	**Lemurs Present**
Ankarana Special Reserve (18,200 ha)	Western - 18,200	*Microcebus murinus* *Microcebus rufus* *Cheirogaleus medius* *Phaner furcifer electromontis* *Lepilemur septentrionalis* *Hapalemur griseus occidentalis* *Eulemur fulvus sanfordi* *Eulemur coronatus* *Avahi occidentalis* *Propithecus diadema perrieri* *Daubentonia madagascariensis*
Bemarivo Special Reserve (11,570 ha)	Western - 11,570	?
Maningozo Special Reserve (7,900 ha)	Western - 7,900	?
Andranomena Special Reserve (6,420 ha)	Western - 6,420	*Microcebus murinus* *Mirza coquereli* *Cheirogaleus medius* *Phaner furcifer pallescens* *Lepilemur ruficaudatus* *Eulemur fulvus rufus* *Propithecus v. verreauxi*
Bora Special Reserve (4,780 ha)	Western - 4,780	*Eulemur f. fulvus* *Propithecus verreauxi (?)*
Analabe Private Reserve (2,000-12,000 ha)	Western	*Microcebus murinus* *Mirza coquereli* *Cheirogaleus medius* *Phaner furcifer pallescens* *Lepilemur ruficaudatus* *Eulemur fulvus rufus* *Propithecus v. verreauxi*

Protected Area	Domains (ha)	Lemurs Present
Tsimanampetsotsa **Nature Reserve** (43,200 ha)	Southern - 43,200	*Microcebus murinus* *Lemur catta* *Propithecus v. verreauxi*
Andohahela **Nature Reserve** Parcels 2 and 3 (12,920 ha)	Southern - 12,920	*Microcebus murinus* *Cheirogaleus medius* *Phaner furcifer* sspp. *Lepilemur leucopus* *Lemur catta* *Propithecus v. verreauxi*
Cap Sainte Marie **Special Reserve** (1,750 ha)	Southern - 1,750	*Microcebus murinus*
Beza-Mahafaly **Special Reserve** (600 ha)	Southern - 600	*Microcebus murinus* *Cheirogaleus medius* *Lepilemur leucopus* *Lemur catta* *Propithecus v. verreauxi*
Berenty **Private Reserve** (265 ha)	Southern - 265	*Microcebus murinus* *Cheirogaleus medius* *Lepilemur leucopus* *Lemur catta* *Eulemur fulvus rufus* *Propithecus v. verreauxi*

PHOTO BY RUSSELL A. MITTERMEIER

Fig. A.4: Village boy and female *Eulemur m. macaco* on the island of Nosy Komba, a popular tourist destination in NW Madagascar.

Key to illustration on the following page (Fig. A5):

Forest Reserves
Forest reserves are similar to classified forests in their administration and the degree of protection afforded to them.

Antsirana Province: 1) Peuplement de Mahabibo, 2) Baobab, 3) Ilôt du Pain de Sucre, 4) Ilôt de Sépulcre, 5) Territoire de protection RNI 6, 6) Ilôt des Aigrettes, 7) Lac Mahery, 8) Lac Texier, 9) Au Sud de Sambava, 10) Andranomanato, 11) Montagne des Français, 12) Massif Forestier d'Ambre

Toamasina Province: 1) Vohimena, 2) Sahavolamena, 3) Namandrahana, 4) Sandrangato, 5) Zone de Protection de la RNI 1, 6) Fénérive, 7) Fierenana

Fianarantsoa Province: 1) Mahavelona-Ambodihasinga, 2) Befalo et Analamaizina, 3) Amboapaka, 4) Antoetra 1, 5) Amparibe, 6) Ifanadiana 1, 7) Antoetra 2, 8) Ifanirea 1, 9) Ambohimahasoa et Ifanadiana, 10) Itendroka et Tsiatokana, 11) Fort-Carnot et Manapatrana, 12) Fort-Carnot 1, 13) Ifanirea 2, 14) Ifanirea 3, 15) Ambohimanga du Sud 1, 16) Ambohimanga du Sud 2, 17) Ifanirea 4, 18) Ifanirea et Ilakatra, 19) Ankarimbelo 1, 20) Ranomafana et Tsaratanana, 21) Ifanadiana et Tsaratanana, 22) Ampasinambo 1, 23) Ifanadiana 2, 24) Maromandia et Ambodiara, 25) Fort Carnot 2, 26) Analanana, 27) Ankarimbelo 2, 28) Ankarimbelo 3, 29) Analamarina, 30) Ankarimbelo 4, 31) Ampasinambo 2, 32) Ambohimiera 1, 33) Tsaratanana, 34) Fanantara, 35) Nosy Varika, 36) Ampasinambo 3, 37) Ampasinambo 4, 38) Manampatrana 1, 39) Fort Carnot 3, 40) Tolongoina, 41) Mahabako et Manampatrana, 42) Manampatrana 2, 43) Mahabako, 44) FCE voie ferrée, 45) Ifanadiana et Androrangavola, 46) Ambohimahamasina, 47) Ampasinambo 5, 48) Manakara 1, 49) Ambodinonoka, 50) Mananjary 1, 51) Mananjary 2, 52) Vondrozo et Ivohibe 1, 53) Vondrozo et Ivohibe 2, 54) Manakara 2,55) Maropaika, 56) Ivongo, 57) Nosivelo, 58) Mahazoarivo, 59) Mahaditra et Andomotra, 60) Ambatovaky et Mahatsinjony, 61) Ambatovaky, 62) Ambohimiera 2, 63) Vondrozo et Ivohibe 3, 64) Vondrozo et Ivohibe 4, 65) Antsindra 1, 66) Antsindra 2, 67) Fasintsara 1, 68) Ambohimanga du Sud 3, 69) Antsindra 3, 70) Fasintsara 2, 71) Anjorozoro, 72) Ambatovaky et Fandrandava, 73) Manakara 3, 74) Andomotra, 75) Ivongo, 76) Ihorombe, 77) Efasy, 78) Ivohibe et Ivongo, 79) Iakora, 80) Vohibola, 81) Befotaka, 82) Vohimary Vondronzo et Ivohibe, 83) Sakalalina et Ivohibe, 84) Lavaraty, 85) Vohitrafeno, 86) Ranotsara Sud, 87) Lopary

Toliary Province: 1) Betsako, 2) Isosa et Zazavery, 3) Mandena

Mahajanga Province: 1) Ankarafantsika, 2) Bora, 3) Tsinjoarivo, 4) Iles Fleuve Betsiboka, 5) Zone de protection de la RNI 7

Antananarivo Province: 1) Mandraka

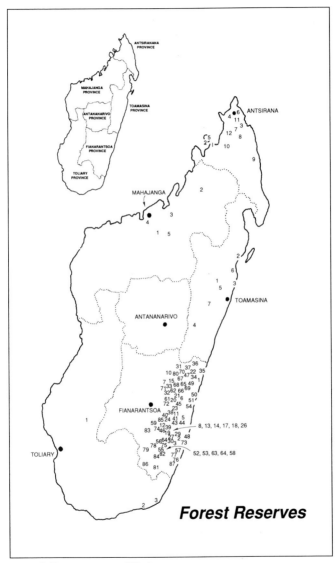

Fig. A.5: Forest reserves of Madagascar.

Key to illustration on the following page (Fig. A.6):

Classified Forests

Classified forests are created by individual ministerial decrees, and are administered at the provincial level. Exploitation is illegal, exceptions being made only for the use of traditional forest products. Protection is not necessarily permanent, and is often is weak or nonexistent.

Antsiranana Province: 1) Amporaha et Ambohidravy, 2) Ankify, 3) Ambato, 4) Sanhafary, 5) Ambre, 6) Antafondro, 7) Ambohitrakongona et Ambory, 8) Leviky et Ambohipiraka, 9) Antsakay Kalobenono, 10) Bezavona, 11) Tsialaindray et Andasiambe, 12) Andravory, 13) Bezavona et Sakatia, 14) Analalava, 15) Ambohimirahavavy, 16) Bezavona Atsima, 17) Haute Ramena, 18) Besariaka, 19) Andranomatavy et Anjanazanom-bandrany, 20) Ambodivohitra, 21) Cap Masoala, 22) Antrafonaomby, 23) Andavakoera

Toamasina Province: 1) Anjiabe, 2) Iofa, 3) Lokaitra, 4) Anjiro, 5) Haute Rantabe, 6) Mahakiry, 7) Vohitaly, 8) Vohitrambo, 9) Bemavo, 10) Tampolo, 11) Mangaika, 12) Ankeniheny, 13) Manamandrozana, 14) Sahivo, 15) Andranobe, 16) Tanamalaza, 17) Ambatomalana, 18) Anandrivola, 19) Anjahanaribe, 20) Ambalahady, 21) Ambalavato-Nord, 22) Sahatavy Ouest, 23) Vohidrazana, 24) Manohilany, 25) Sandravololona, 26) Antokobe, 27) Mahalina, 28) Amparafana, 29) Ankarahaka, 30) Vohinala, 31) Beheloka, 32) Andiamilalo, 33) Betamotamo, 34) Andranobe I, 35) Nankinana, 36) Namolazana, 37) Sahamalala, 38) Saharongana, 39) Voronkidiana-Behengitra, 40) Sahasina, 41) Befanenitra, 42) Andavakimenarana, 43) Farankaraina, 44) Ambalahady-Ambohidava, 45) Lakato, 46) Lempona, 47) Ambalorirana, 48) Mandanivatsy, 49) Marotoko, 50) Raboana, 51) Andravarahina, 52) Ampiadianombalany, 53) Andrevabe, 54) Haute Rianila, 55) Haute Teza, 56) Ambalavato-Sud, 57) Ambatoila, 58) Ambohilero, 59) Betampona, 60) Anjolokato, 61) Kambolaza, 62) Vohibe, 63) Vohidramontsona, 64) Ambolosy, 65) Sivora, 66) Haute Vohitra, 67) Savarindrano, 68) Antarandravalona, 69) Saranindona, 70) Tsinjoarivo, 71) Andasira, 72) Andonabe, 73) Ankerana, 74) Fanantenana, 75) Anjolovato-Marohitabe, 76) Sahanotra, 77) Manerinerina-Ambalahady, 78) Onive, 79) Ankazonaomby et Andrangotra, 80) Madioranobe, 81) Sarongana atsimo, 82) Tantavona et Anjiro, 83) Vohittrakolahy, 84) Beroranga, 85) Antrafonomy, 86) Bezavona, 87) Betrafo et Andranokobaka, 88) Verezanantsoro et Ivontaka, 89) Sahanody, 90) Sandrangato, 91) Andriantantely, 92) Matsitsirano, 93) Bidia, 94) Vohibary, 95) Ambalahady, 96) Pointe à Larrée, 97) Tsiazombazaha, 98) Finariana, 99) Bekotro

Fianarantsoa Province: 1) Fenoamby Sud, 2) Manambondro Nord, 3) Ankazomivady, 4) Faliarivo, 5) Itremo

Toliary Province: 1) Zombitse, 2) Marofihitra, 3) Ampataka, 4) Anadabolava, 5) Tsitongambarika I, 6) Bevona, 7) Taviala, 8) Tsitongambarika II, 9) Ankoadava

Mahajanga Province: 1) Antsangabe, 2) Anjiamangarina, 3) Tsiombikibo, 4) Mangrove Betsiboka, 5) Bongolava, 6) Ambiha, 7) Befotaka Tsimembo, 8) Antsinjomorona, 9) Manongarivo, 10) Amboromailala, 11) Masiaposa, 12) Tongay, 13) Ambereny-Ankavitra, 14) Tsitondroindahy, 15) Andongonambo, 16) Antsakoamileka, 17) Ampahatsiarovana, 18) Sandrakota, 19) Betafo, 20) Andranoboka, 21) Tsitanandro, 22) Bora

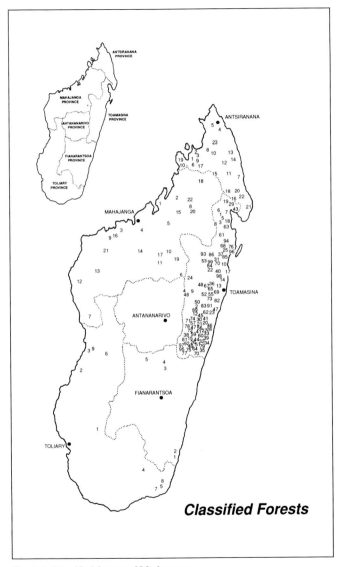

Fig. A.6: Classified forests of Madagascar.

APPENDIX 2

ALTERNATIVE NAMES FOR TOWNS & SITES IN MADAGASCAR

A number of cities, towns and localities have several names, the French names that have wider use internationally, and the Malagasy names that are official, and are used by the Malagasy government and most of the Malagasy populace. In a few cases, there are actually three names, one French and two Malagasy. Although both French and Malagasy names are usually given in the text, we provide a partial listing of the most commonly used here for your convenience.

French	Malagasy
Tananarive	Antananarivo
Tamatave	Toamasina
Majunga	Mahajanga
Fort-Dauphin	Tolagnaro or Tolanaro
Diégo-Suarez	Antsiranana
Tuléar	Toliary
Périnet*	Andasibe (also Analamazaotra)
Cap d'Ambre	Tanjona Bobaomby
Cap Sainte-Marie	Tanjona Vohimena
Ile Sainte-Marie	Nosy Boraha
Presque' île de Masoala (Masoala Peninsula)	Tanjona Masoala

*Perinet is the widely known French name for the train stop and the small town near which the indri may be seen, Andasibe is the Malagasy name for the same town, and Analamazoatra is the official name for the Special Reserve located about 2 km from the Périnet (= Andasibe) train station and hotel. Périnet is most often used to refer to this area, but you may see both of the other names in the literature as well.

References

Albignac, R. 1981a. Lemurine social and territorial organization in a northwestern Malagasy forest (restricted area of Ampijoroa). Pp. 25-29 in: Chiarelli, A. B. and R. S. Corruccini (eds.), *Primate Behavior and Sociobiology*. Springer Verlag, Berlin.

Albignac, R. 1981b. Variabilité dans l'organisation territoriale et l'écologie de *Avahi laniger* (Lémurien nocturne de Madagascar). *Compte Rendus Academie Science Paris* 292 Série III: 331-334.

Albignac, R. 1987. Status of the aye-aye in Madagascar. *Primate Conservation* 8: 44-45.

Andrews, J. 1989. Black lemur survey 1988: A survey of the distribution and habitat of black lemurs, *Lemur macaco*, in northwest Madagascar. Unpublished preliminary report.

Andriampianina, J. 1981. Les réserves naturelles et la protection de la nature à Madagascar. In: Oberlé (ed.), *Madagascar, un Sanctuaire de la Nature*, Kintana, Riedisheim, France.

Andriampianina, J. and A. Peyrieras. 1972. Les réserves naturelles intégrales de Madagascar. Pp. 103-123 in: *Comptes Rendus de la Conférence Internationale sur la Conservation de la Nature et de ses Resources à Madagascar, Tananarive, Madagascar 7-11 Octobre 1970*. IUCN, Gland, Switzerland and Cambridge, U.K.

Andrianarivo, A. J. 1981. Etude comparée de l'organisation sociale chez *Microcebus coquereli*. Unpublished dissertation, University of Madagascar, Antananarivo.

Andriatsarafara, R. 1988. Note sur les rythmes d'activité et sur le régime alimentaire de *Lemur mongoz* Linnaeus 1766 à Ampijoroa. Pp. 103-106 in: Rakotovao, L., V. Barre and J. Sayer (eds.), *L'Equilibre des Ecosystèmes Forestiers à Madagascar: Actes d'un Sèminaire International*. IUCN, Gland, Switzerland and Cambridge, UK.

Arbelot-Tracqui, V. 1983. Étude Ethoécologique de Deux

Primates Prosimiens: *Lemur coronatus* Gray et *Lemur fulvus sanfordi* Archbold, Contribution à l'Étude des Mécanismes d'Isolement Reproductif Intervenant dans la Spéciation. Unpublished PhD thesis. University of Rennes, France.

Ausilio, E. and G. Raveloarinoro 1993. Statut et densités des especes de lemuriens de la région d'Antsalova (ouest de Madagascar) (Forêts de l'Antsingy, de Tsimembo et de la région de Tsiandro). Unpublished report to UNESCO - Project 507/INT/40. Antananarivo, Madagascar.

Barnes, C. 1986. *Social Analysis and Program Recommendations: Madagascar CDSS Update.* Report to REDSO/ESA, U.S. Agency for International Development.

Barre, V., A. Lebac, J.-J. Petter and R. Albignac 1988. Etude du Microcèbe par radiotracking dans la forêt de l'Ankarafantsika. Pp. 61-71 in: Rakotavao, L., V. Barre and J. Sayer (eds.), *L'Equilibre des Ecosystémes Forestiers à Madagascar: Actes d'un Seminaire International.* IUCN, Gland, Switzerland and Cambridge, UK.

Bauchot, R. and H. Stephan. 1966. Données nouvelles sur l'encéphalisation des insectivores et des prosimiens. *Mammalia* 30(1): 160-196.

Birkel, R. 1987. 1987 International Studbook for the Black Lemur, *Lemur macaco* Linnaeus, 1766. St. Louis Zoo, St. Louis, Missouri.

Bogart, M. H., R. W. Cooper and K. Benirschke 1977. Reproductive studies of black and ruffed lemurs, *Lemur macaco macaco* and *L. variegatus* ssp. *International Zoo Yearbook* 17: 177-182.

Boskoff, K. J. 1977. Aspects of reproduction in ruffed lemurs (*Lemur variegatus*). *Folia Primatologica* 28: 241-250.

Brisson, M. J. 1756. *Regnum Animale in Classes IX Distributum.* J. B. Bauche, Paris.

Budnitz, N. and K. Dainis 1975. *Lemur catta*: ecology and behavior. Pp. 219-235 in: Tattersall, I. and R. W. Sussman (eds.), *Lemur Biology.* Plenum Press, New York

Buffon 1789. *Histoire Naturelle Générale et Particulière Servant de Suite à l'Histoire des Animaux Quadrupèdes.* Paris, France.

Buttner-Janusch, J. and A. E. Hamilton 1979. Chromosomes of Lemuriformes, IV: karyotype evolution in *Lemur fulvus collaris. American Journal of Physical Anthropology* 50(3): 363-365.

Ceska, V., H.-U. Hoffman and K.-H. Winkelsträter 1992. *Lemuren im Zoo.* Verlag Paul Parey, Berlin.

Charles-Dominique, P. and C. M. Hladik 1971. Le *Lepilemur* du sud de Madagascar: Ecologie, alimentation et vie sociale. *La Terre et la Vie* 25: 3-66.

Charles-Dominique, P. and J.-J. Petter 1980. Ecology and social life of *Phaner furcifer.* Pp. 191-203 in: P. Charles-Dominique, H. M. Cooper, A. Hladik, C. M. Hladik, E. Pagés, G. F. Pariente, A. Petter-Rousseaux, J.-J. Petter and A. Schilling (eds.), *Nocturnal Malagasy Primates: Ecology, Physiology and Behavior.* Academic Press, New York.

Commerson, P. 1771. *Voyage à Madagascar en 1770.* Muséum National d'Histoire Naturelle, Paris.

Conservation International 1990. *The Rain Forest Imperative.* Conservation International, Washington, D.C. 15 pp.

Conservation International 1993. *Repertoire et Carte de Distribution-Domaine Forestièr National de Madagascar.* Direction des Eaux et Forêts Service des Ressources Forestières.

Constable, I. D., R. A. Mittermeier, J. I. Pollock, J. Ratsirarson and H. Simons 1985. Sightings of aye-ayes and red-ruffed lemurs on Nosy Mangabe and the Masoala Peninsula. *Primate Conservation* 5: 59-62.

Cowan, W. D. 1882. Notes on the natural history of Madagascar. *Proceedings of the Royal Society of Edinburgh* 7: 133-150.

Dague, C. and J.-J. Petter 1988. Observations sur le *Lemur rubriventer* dans son milieu naturel. In: L. Rakotavao., V. Barre, and J. Sayer (eds.), *L'Equilibre des Ecosystèmes Forestiers à Madagascar: Actes d'un Séminaire International*. IUCN, Gland, Switzerland and Cambridge, U.K.

Daniels, P. 1991. A first look at the Zahamena Reserve. *Tropicus* (Conservation International) 5(2): 8-9.

Edwards, G. 1758. *Gleanings of Natural History*. Royal College of Physicians, London.

Flacourt, E. de 1658. *Histoire de la grande Isle Madagascar composé par le Sieur de Flacourt*, 2 vols. Chez G. de Lvyne, Paris.

Foerg, R. 1982. Reproduction in *Cheirogaleus medius*. *Folia Primatologica* 39: 49-62.

Forsyth Major, C. I. 1894. On *Megaladapis madagascariensis*, an extinct gigantic lemuroid from Ambolisatra. *Proceedings of the Royal Society of London*, pp. 176-179.

Fowler, S. V., P. Chapman, D. Checkley, S. Hurd, M. McHale, G.-S. Ramangason, J.-E. Randriamasy, P. Stewart, R. Walters and J. M. Wilson 1989. Survey and management proposals for a tropical deciduous forest reserve at Ankarana in northern Madagascar. *Biological Conservation* 47: 297-313.

Ganzhorn, J. U. 1986. The aye-aye (*Daubentonia madagascariensis*) found in the eastern rainforest of Madagascar. *Folia Primatologica* 46: 125-126.

Ganzhorn, J. U. 1987. A possible role of plantations for primate conservation in Madagascar. *American Journal of Primatology* 12: 205-215.

Ganzhorn, J. U. 1988. Food partitioning among Malagasy primates. *Oecologia* (Berlin) 75: 436-450.

Ganzhorn, J. U., J. P. Abraham and M. Razanahoera-Rakotomalala 1985. Some aspects of the natural history and food selection of *Avahi laniger*. *Primates* 26(4): 452-463.

Geoffroy, E. St.-Hilaire 1812. Suite au tableau des quadrumanes. *Ann. Mus. Nat. Hist., Paris* 19:156-175.

Glander, K. E., P. Wright, D. S. Seigler and B. Randrianasolo 1989. Consumption of cyanogenic bamboo by a newly discovered species of bamboo lemur. *American Journal of Primatology* 19: 119-124.

Glander, K. E., P. C. Wright, P. S. Daniel and A. M. Merenlender 1992. Morphometrics and testicle size of rainforest lemur species from southeastern Madagascar. *Journal of Human Evolution* 22: 1-17.

Godfrey, L. and M. Vuillaume-Randriamanatena 1986. *Hapalemur simus*: endangered lemur once widespread. *Primate Conservation* 7:92-96.

Goodman, S. M. O. Langrand and C. J. Raxworthy 1993. Food habits of the long-eared owl, *Asio madagascariensis*, in two habitats in southern Madagascar. *Ostrich* 64: 79-85.

Grandidier, A. 1875-1921. *Histoire physique, naturelle, et politique de Madagascar.* 32 vols. Hachette, Paris.

Grandidier, G. 1905. Recherches sur les lémuriens disparus et en particulier ceux qui vivaient à Madagascar. *Nouv. Arch. Mus. Natl. Hist. Nat. Paris* (4th Series) 7: 1-142.

Green, G. M. G. and R. W. Sussman 1990. Deforestation history of the eastern rain forests of Madagascar from satellite images. *Science* 248: 212-215.

Groves, C. P. and R. H. Eaglen. 1988. Systematics of the Lemuridae (Primates, Strepsirhini). *Journal of Human Evolution* 17: 513-538.

Groves, C. P. and I. Tattersall 1991. Geographical variation in the fork-marked lemur *Phaner furcifer* (Primates, Cheirogaleidae). *Folia Primatologica* 56: 39-49.

Guillaumet, J. L. 1984. The vegetation: an extraordinary diversity. In: Jolly, A., Oberlé, P. and Albignac, R. (eds.), *Key*

Environments: Madagascar, IUCN and Pergamon Press.

Hamilton, A., I. Tattersall, R. W. Sussman and J. Buettner-Janusch 1980. Chromosomes of Lemuriformes, VI. Comparative karyology of *Lemur fulvus*: a G-banded karyotype of *Lemur fulvus mayottensis* Schlegel, 1866. *International Journal of Primatology* 1: 81-93.

Harcourt, C. S. 1987. Brief trap/retrap study of the brown mouse lemur (*Microcebus rufus*). *Folia Primatologica* 49: 209-211.

Harcourt, C. S. In press. A study of the diet and behaviour of a nocturnal lemur, *Avahi laniger*, in the wild. *Journal of Zoology*.

Harcourt, C. and J. Thornback. 1990. *Lemurs of Madagascar and the Comoros*. The IUCN Red Data Book, compiled by C. Harcourt. IUCN, Gland, Switzerland and Cambridge, U.K.

Harper, F. 1945. *Extinct and Vanishing Mammals of the Old World*. Special publication, American Committee for International Wildlife Protection, New York, 12: 1-850.

Harrington, J. E. 1975. Field observations of social behavior of *Lemur fulvus fulvus* E. Geoffroy 1812. In: Tattersall, I. and Sussman, R. W. (eds), *Lemur Biology*. Plenum Press, New York. Pp. 259-279.

Harrington, J. E. 1978. Diurnal behavior of *Lemur mongoz* at Ampijoroa, Madagascar. *Folia Primatologica* 29: 291-302.

Hawkins, A. F. A., P. Chapman, J. U. Ganzhorn, Q. M. C. Bloxam, S. C. Barlow and S. J. Tonge 1990. Vertebrate conservation in Ankarana Special Reserve, northern Madagascar. *Biological Conservation* 54: 83-110.

Hick, U. 1976. The first year in the new lemur house at the Cologne Zoo. *International Zoo Yearbook* 16: 141-145.

Hladik, C. M. 1979. Diet and ecology of prosimians. Pp. 307-357 in: G. A. Doyle and R. D. Martin. *The Study of Prosimian Behavior*. Academic Press, New York.

Hladik, C. M. and P. Charles-Dominique 1974. The behavior and ecology of the sportive lemur (*Lepilemur mustelinus*) in relation to its dietary peculiarities. Pp. 23-37 in: R. D. Martin, G. A. Doyle and A. C. Walker (eds.), *Prosimian Biology*. Duckworth, London.

Hladik, C. M., P. Charles-Dominique and J.-J. Petter 1980. Feeding strategies of five nocturnal prosimians in the dry forest of the west coast of Madagascar. Pp. 41-73 in: Charles-Dominique, P., H. M. Cooper, A. Hladik, C. M. Hladik, E. Pages, G. F. Pariente, A. Petter-Rousseaux, J.-J. Petter and A. Schilling (eds.), *Nocturnal Malagasy Primates: Ecology, Physiology and Behavior*. Academic Press, New York.

ISIS 1993. ISIS Species Distribution Report Abstract for Mammals, 31 December 1993. International Species Inventory System, 12101 Johnny Cake Ridge Road, Apple Valley, Minnesota, USA.

Jenkins, P. D. 1987. *Catalogue of Primates in the British Museum (Natural History) and elsewhere in the British Isles. Part IV: Suborder Strepsirrhini, including the subfossil Madagascan Lemurs and the Family Tarsiidae*. British Museum (Natural History), London.

Jenkins, P. D. and G. Albrecht 1991. Sexual dimorphism and sex ratios in Madagascar prosimians. *American Journal of Primatology* 24: 1-14.

Joint Nature Conservation Committee 1993. *A Preliminary Review of the Status and Distribution of Reptile and Amphibian Species Exported from Madagascar*. Joint Nature Conservation Committee Report No. 155, 77 pp.

Jolly, A. 1966. *Lemur Behavior*. University of Chicago Press, Chicago.

Jolly, A. 1980. *A World Like Our Own: Man and Nature in Madagascar*. Yale University Press, New Haven, Connecticut.

Jolly, A., R. Albignac and J.-J. Petter 1984. The lemurs. Pp. 183-202 in: Jolly, A., P. Oberlé and R. Albignac (eds.), *Key Environments: Madagascar.* Pergamon Press, Oxford.

Jolly, A., H. Gustafson, W. L. R. Oliver and S. M. O'Connor 1982. *Propithecus verreauxi* population and ranging at Berenty, Madagascar, 1975 and 1980. *Folia Primatologica* 39: 124-144.

Jolly, A., W. L. R. Oliver and S. M. O'Connor 1982. Population and troop ranges of *Lemur catta* and *Lemur fulvus* at Berenty, Madagascar: 1980 census. *Folia Primatologica* 39: 115-123.

Jolly, A., R. Albignac and J.-J. Petter 1984. The lemurs. Pp. 183-203 in: Jolly, A., P. Oberlé and R. Albignac (eds.), *Key Environments: Madagascar.* Pergamon Press, Oxford.

Kappeler, P. M. 1987. Reproduction in the crowned lemur (*Lemur coronatus*) in captivity. *American Journal of Primatology* 12: 497-503.

Kappeler, P. M. 1991. Patterns of sexual dimorphism in body weight among prosimian primates. *Folia Primatologica* 57: 132-146.

Katz, A. 1990. Letter from the edge. *On the Edge* (Wildlife Preservation Trust International) 42: 4-5.

Kaudern, W. 1915. Säugetiere aus Madagaskar. *Arkiv für Zoologie* 9 (18): 1-101.

Klopfer, P. H. and K. J. Boskoff 1979. Maternal behavior in prosimians. Pp. 123-156 in: G. A. Doyle and R. D. Martin (eds.), *The Study of Prosimian Behavior.* Academic Press, London.

Klopfer, P. H. and J. Dugard 1976. Patterns of maternal care in lemurs: III: *Lemur variegatus. Zeitschrift für Tierpsychologie* 48: 87-99.

Koechlin, J., J. L. Guillaumet and P. Morat. 1974. *Flore et Végétation de Madagascar.* V. Cramer, Vaduz.

Koenders, L., Y. Rumpler, J. Ratsirarson and A. Peyrieras 1985. *Lemur macaco flavifrons* (Gray, 1867): a rediscovered subspecies of primate. *Folia Primatologica* 44: 210-215.

Langrand, O. 1990. *Guide to the Birds of Madagascar*. Yale University Press, New Haven.

Lindsay, N. B. D. and H. J. Simons 1986. Notes on *Varecia* in the northern limits of its range. *Dodo* 23: 19-24.

Linnaeus, C. 1758. *Systema Naturae*, 10th ed. Salvius, Stockholm.

Linnaeus, C. 1766. *Systema Naturae*, 11th ed. Salvius, Stockholm.

Mace, G. M. and R. Lande 1991. Assessing extinction threats: toward a re-evaluation of IUCN threatened species categories. *Conservation Biology* 5: 148-157.

Mack, D. and R. A. Mittermeier 1984. *The International Primate Trade, Vol. 1, Legislation, Trade and Captive Breeding*. TRAFFIC (USA) and the International Union for the Conservation of Nature, Washington, D.C.

Martin, R. D. 1972. A preliminary field study of the lesser mouse lemur (*Microcebus murinus* J. F. Miller 1777). *Zeitschrift für Tierpsychologie*, Supplement 9: 43-89.

Martin, R. D. 1973. A review of the behaviour and ecology of the lesser mouse lemur (*Microcebus murinus* J. F. Miller 1777). Pp. 1-68 in: R. P. Michael and J. H. Crook (eds.), *Comparative Ecology and Behaviour of Primates*. Academic Press, London.

Marsh, C. W., A. D. Johns and J. M. Ayres 1987. Effects of habitat disturbance on rain forest primates. Pp. 83-107 in: Marsh, C. W. and R. A. Mittermeier (eds.), *Primate Conservation in the Tropical Rain Forest*, Alan R. Liss, New York.

Mast, R. B. 1993. *Lemur News*. Vol. 1, No. 1. Newsletter of the Madagascar Section of the IUCN/SSC Primate Specialist Group. Conservation International, Washington, D.C.

Mast, R. B., J. V. Rodriguez and R. A. Mittermeier 1993. The Colombian cotton-top tamarin in the wild. In: Clapp, N. K. (ed.), *A Primate Model for the Study of Colonic Carcinoma: The Cotton-top Tamarin (Saguinus oedipus)*. CRC Press, Boca Raton, Florida.

McNeely, J. A., K. R. Miller, W. V. Reid, R. A. Mittermeier and T. B. Werner (eds.) 1990. *Conserving the World's Biological Diversity*. International Union for the Conservation of Nature and Natural Resources, World Resources Institute, Conservation International, World Wildlife Fund - US, and the World Bank. Gland, Switzerland and Washington , D.C.

Meier, B. 1987. Preliminary report of a field study on *Lemur rubriventer* and *Hapalemur simus* (nov. subspecies) in Rano-mafana-Ifanadiana 312 Faritany Fianarantsoa, Madagascar, July 1986-January 1987. Unpublished report to Ministry of Scientific Research, Antananarivo.

Meier, B. and R. Albignac 1989. Hairy-eared dwarf lemur rediscovered (*Allocebus trichotis*). *Primate Conservation* 10: 30.

Meier, B. and R. Albignac 1991. Rediscovery of *Allocebus trichotis* Günther 1875 (Primates) in North East Madagascar. *Folia Primatologica* 56(1): 57-63.

Meier, B. and Y. Rumpler 1987. Preliminary survey of *Hapalemur simus* and of a new species of *Hapalemur* in eastern Betsileo, Madagascar. *Primate Conservation* 8:40-43.

Meier, B., R. Albignac, A. Peyrieras, Y. Rumpler and P. Wright 1987. A new species of *Hapalemur* (Primates) from southeast Madagascar. *Folia Primatologica* 48: 211-215.

Meyers, D. 1988. Behavioral ecology of *L. f. rufus* in rain forest in Madagascar. *American Journal of Physical Anthropology* 75(2): 250.

Meyers, D. and J. Ratsirarson 1989. Distribution and conserva-tion of two endangered sifakas in northern Madagascar. *Primate Conservation* 10: 82-87.

Meyers, D., C. Rabarivola and Y. Rumpler 1989. Distribution and conservation of Sclater's lemur: implications of a morphological cline. *Primate Conservation* 10: 78-82.

Mittermeier, R. A. 1987. Effects of hunting on rain forest primates. Pp. 109-146 in: Marsh, C. W. and R. A. Mittermeier (eds.), *Primate Conservation in the Tropical Rain Forest*. Alan R. Liss, New York.

Mittermeier, R. A. 1988. Primate diversity and the tropical forest: case studies from Brazil and Madagascar and the importance of the megadiversity countries. Pp. 145-154 in: Wilson, E. O. and F. M. Peters (eds.), *Biodiversity*. National Academy Press, Washington, D.C.

Mittermeier, R. A. and A. F. Coimbra-Filho 1977. Primate conservation in Brazilian Amazonia. Pp. 117-166 in: Prince Rainier and G. H. Bourne (eds.), *Primate Conservation*. Academic Press, New York.

Mittermeier, R. A. and C. Goettsch de Mittermeier 1992. La importancia de la diversidad biologica en Mexico. Pp. 63-73 in: Sarukhan, J. and R. Dirzo (eds.), *Mexico ante los Retos de la Bioversidad*. Comision Nacional para el Conocimiento y uso de la Biodiversidad, Mexico.

Mittermeier, R. A., L. H. Rakotovao, V. Randrianasolo, E. J. Sterling and D. Devitre 1987. *Priorités en Matière de Conservation des Espèces à Madagascar*. Occasional Papers of the IUCN Species Survival Commission, Number 2. Gland, Switzerland.

Mittermeier, R. A., W. G. Kinzey and R. B. Mast 1989. *Neotropical primate conservation*. Journal of Human Evolution 18: 597-610.

Mittermeier, R. A., W. R. Konstant, M. E. Nicoll and O. Langrand 1992. *Lemurs of Madagascar: An Action Plan for their Conservation. 1993-1999*. IUCN/SSC Primate Specialist Group, Gland, Switzerland.

Morland, H. S. 1990. Parental behavior and infant development in ruffed lemurs (*Varecia variegata*) in a northeast Madagascar rain forest. *American Journal of Primatology* 20: 253-265.

Morland, H. S. 1991. Preliminary report on the social organization of ruffed lemurs (*Varecia variegata variegata*) in a northeast Madagascar rain forest. *Folia Primatologica* 56: 157-161.

Morland, H. S. 1993. Seasonal behavioral variation and its relation to thermoregulation in ruffed lemurs. Pp. 193-203 in: Kappeler, P. M. and J. Ganzhorn (eds.), *Lemur Social Systems and Their Ecological Basis*. Plenum Press, New York.

Mundy, P. 1907-1936. The Travels of Peter Mundy in Europe and Asia, 1608-1667. Vol. 1, 1907; vol. 2, 1914; vol. 3, 1919; vol. 4, 1924; vol. 5; 1936. R. C. Temple (ed.), The Hakluyt Society, Cambridge.

Mutschler, T. and U. Thalmann 1990. Sighting of *Avahi* (woolly lemur) in western Madagascar. *Primate Conservation*, 11: 9-11.

Myers, N. 1988. Threatened biotas: "hotspots" in tropical forests. *Environmentalist* 8(3): 1-20.

Myers, N. 1990. The biodiversity challenge: expanded hot-spots analysis. *Environmentalist* 10(4): 243-256.

Nicoll, M. E. and O. Langrand 1989. *Madagascar: Revue de la Conservation et des Aires Protégées.* World Wide Fund for Nature, Gland, Switzerland, xvii + 374 pp.

Nicoll, M. E. and G. B. Rathbun 1990. *African Insectivora and Elephant-Shrews: An Action Plan for their Conservation.* IUCN/SSC Insectivore, Tree-Shrew and Elephant-Shrew Specialist Group, Gland, Switzerland.

O'Connor, S. S. M. 1987. The effect of human impact on vegetation and the consequences to primates in two riverine forests, southern Madagascar. Unpublished PhD thesis, University of Cambridge, U.K.

O'Connor, S., M. Pidgeon and Z. Randria 1986. Conservation program for the Andohahela Reserve, Madagascar. *Primate Conservation* 7: 48-52.

O'Connor, S., M. Pidgeon and Z. Randria 1987. Un programme de conservation pour la Réserve d'Andohahela. Pp. 31-36 in: R. A. Mittermeier, L. H. Rakotovao, V. Randrianasolo, E. J. Sterling and D. Devitre (eds.), *Priorités en Matière de Conservation des Espèces à Madagascar.* Occasional Papers of the IUCN Species Survival Commission, Number 2, Gland, Switzerland.

Olney, P. J. S. and P. Ellis (eds.) 1992. Census of Rare Animals in Captivity 1991. *International Zoo Yearbook* (Vol. 31). Zoological Society of London, U. K.

Overdorff, D. J. 1988. Preliminary report on the activity cycle and diet of the red-bellied lemur (*Lemur rubriventer*) in Madagascar. *American Journal of Primatology* 16: 143-153.

Overdorff, D. 1990. Flower predation and nectarivory in *Lemur fulvus rufus* and *Lemur rubriventer*. *American Journal of Physical Anthropology* 81(2): 276.

Overdorff, D. J. 1991. Ecological correlates of social structure in two prosimian primates: *Eulemur fulvus rufus* and *Eulemur rubriventer* in Madagascar. Unpublished Ph. D. Thesis, Duke University, Durham, North Carolina.

Pagès, E. 1978. Home range, behaviour and tactile communication in a nocturnal Malagasy lemur *Microcebus coquereli*. Pp. 171-177 in: D. A. Chivers and K. A. Joysey (eds), *Recent Advances in Primatology*, Vol. 3. Academic Press, London.

Pagès, E. 1980. Ethoecology of *Microcebus coquereli* during the dry season. Pp. 97-116 in: P. Charles-Dominique, H. M. Cooper, A. Hladik, C. M. Hladik, E. Pagès, G. F. Pariente, A. Petter-Rousseaux, J.-J. Petter and A. Schilling (eds.), *Nocturnal Malagasy Primates: Ecology, Physiology and Behavior.* Academic Press, New York.

Pereira, M. E., Macedonia, J. M., D. M. Haring and E. L. Simons 1989. Maintenance of primates in captivity for research: the need for naturalistic environments. Pp. 40-60 in: E.Segal (ed.), *Housing, Care and Psychological Wellbeing of Captive and Laboratory Primates.* Noyes, Park Ridge.

Petter, A. and J.-J. Petter 1971. Part 3.1 Infraorder Lemuriformes. Pp. 1-10 in: J. Meester and H. W. Setzer (eds.), *The Mammals of Africa: An Identification Manual.* Smithsonian Institution Press, Washington, D.C.

Petter, J.-J. 1962. Recherches sur l'écologie et l'éthologie des lémuriens malgaches. *Mémoires Museum National Histoire Naturelle*, Paris (A) 27: 1-146.

Petter, J.-J. 1978. Contribution à l'étude du *Cheirogaleus medius* dans la forêt de Morondava. Pp. 57-60 in: L. Rakotovao, V. Barre and J. Sayer (eds.), *L'Equilibre des Ecosystèmes Forestiers à Madagascar: Actes d'un Séminaire International.* IUCN, Gland, Switzerland and Cambridge, U. K.

Petter, J-J. and S. Andriatsarafara 1987. Conservation status and distribution of lemurs in the west and northwest of Madagascar. *Primate Conservation* 7: 169-171.

Petter, J-J. and A. Petter-Rousseaux 1960. Remarques sur la systématique du genre *Lepilemur*. *Mammalia* 24: 76-86.

Petter, J.-J. and A. Petter-Rousseaux 1964. Première tentative d'estimation des densités de peuplement des lémuriens malgaches. *La Terre et la Vie* 18: 427-435.

Petter, J.-J. and A. Petter-Rousseaux 1979. Classification of the prosimians. Pp. 359-409 in: G. A. Doyle and R. D. Martin (eds.), *The Study of Prosimian Behavior.* Academic Press, London.

Petter, J-J. and A. Peyrieras 1970a. Observations éco-éthologiques sur les lémuriens malgaches du genre *Hapalemur*. *La Terre et la Vie* 24:356-382.

Petter, J-J. and A. Peyrieras 1970b. Nouvelle contribution a l'étude d'un lémurien malgache, le aye-aye (*Daubentonia madagascariensis* E. Geoffroy). *Mammalia* 34(2): 167-193.

Petter, J-J. and A. Peyrieras 1975. Preliminary notes on the behavior and ecology of *Hapalemur griseus*. Pp 281-286 in: I.

Tattersall and R. W. Sussman (eds.), *Lemur Biology*. Plenum Press, New York,

Petter, J.-J., R. Albignac and Y. Rumpler 1977. Mammifères: lémuriens (Primates prosimiens). *Faune de Madagascar No. 44*. ORSTOM-CNRS, Paris.

Petter, J.-J., A. Schilling and G. Pariente 1971. Observations éco-éthologiques sur deux lémuriens malagaches nocturnes: *Phaner furcifer* et *Microcebus coquereli*. *La Terre et la Vie* 25: 287-327.

Petter, J-J., A. Schilling and G. Pariente 1975. Observations on the behavior and ecology of *Phaner furcifer*. Pp. 209-218 in: I. Tattersall and R. W. Sussman (eds.), *Lemur Biology*. Plenum Press, New York,

Petter-Rousseaux, A. 1964. Reproductive physiology and be-havior of the Lemuroidea. Pp. 91-132 in: Buettner-Janusch, J. (ed.), *Evolution and Genetic Biology of the Primates*. Academic Press, New York.

Petter-Rousseaux, A. 1980. Seasonal activity rhythms, reproduc-tion, and body weight variations in five sympatric nocturnal prosimians, in simulated light and climatic conditions. Pp. 137-152 in: P. Charles-Dominique, H. M. Cooper, A. Hladik, C. M. Hladik, E. Pagés, G. F. Pariente, A. Petter-Rousseaux, J.-J. Petter and A. Schilling (eds.), *Nocturnal Malagasy Primates: Ecology, Physiology and Behavior*. Academic Press, New York.

Pollock, J. I. 1975. Field observations on *Indri indri*: A prelimi-nary report. Pp. 287-311 in: I. Tattersall and R. W. Sussman (eds.), *Lemur Biology*. Plenum Press, New York.

Pollock, J. I. 1977. The ecology and sociology of feeding in *Indri indri*. Pp. 37-69 in: T. Clutton-Brock, (ed.), *Primate Ecology: Studies of Feeding and Ranging Behavior in Lemurs, Monkeys and Apes*. Academic Press, London.

Pollock, J. I. 1979. Spatial distribution and ranging behavior in lemurs. Pp. 359-409 in: G. A. Doyle and R. D. Martin (eds.), *The Study of Prosimian Behavior*. Academic Press, New York.

Pollock, J. I. 1984. Preliminary report on a mission to Madagascar by Dr. J. I. Pollock in August and September 1984. Unpublished report to WWF-US Primate Program.

Pollock, J. I. 1986. A note on the ecology and behavior of *Hapalemur griseus. Primate Conservation* 7: 97-100.

Pollock, J. I., I. D. Constable, R. A. Mittermeier, J. Ratsirarson and H. Simons 1985. A note on the diet and feeding behavior of the aye-aye, *Daubentonia madagascariensis. International Journal of Primatology* 6(4): 435-447.

Porton, I. (ed.) 1993. *Prosimian Taxon Advisory Group Regional Collection Plan for Lemurs.* AAZPA.

Preston-Mafham, K. 1991. *Madagascar: A Natural History.* Facts on File, Oxford and New York.

Purchas, S. 1625. *Hakluytus Posthumus, or Purchas His Pilgrimes* (5 vols.). Henry Fetherston, London.

Quansah, N. (ed.) 1988. Conclusions and recommendations. Manongarivo Special Reserve (Madagascar): 1987/88 Expedition Report. Madagascar Environmental Research Group, U.K.

Rabarivola, C., D. Meyers and Y. Rumpler 1991. Distribution and morphological characters of intermediate forms between the black lemur (*Eulemur macaco macaco*) and Sclater's lemur (*E. m. flavifrons*). *Primates* 32(2): 269-273.

Rakotomanga, P., A. F. Richard and R. W. Sussman 1987. Beza-Mahafaly: formation et mesures de conservation. Pp. 41-43 in: R. A. Mittermeier, L. H. Rakotovao, V. Randrianasolo, E. J. Sterling and D. Devitre (eds.), *Priorités en Matière de Conservation des Espèces à Madagascar.* Occasional Papers of the IUCN Species Survival Commission, Number 2, Gland, Switzerland.

Ratsirarson, J. and Y. Rumpler 1988. Contribution à l'étude comparée de l'éco-éthologie de deux espèces de lémuriens, *Lepilemur mustelinus* (I. Geoffroy 1850), et *Lepilemur septentrionalis* (Rumpler and Albignac 1975). Pp. 100-102 in: L.

Rakotovao, V. Barre and J. Sayer (eds.), *L'Equilibre des Ecosystèmes Forestiers à Madagascar, Actes d'un Séminaire International.* IUCN, Gland, Switzerland and Cambridge, U.K.

Ratsirarson, J., J. Anderson, S. Warter and Y. Rumpler 1987. Notes on the distribution of *Lepilemur septentrionalis* and *L. mustelinus* in northern Madagascar. *Primates* 28(1): 119-122.

Raxworthy, C. 1986. The lemurs of Zahamena Reserve. *Primate Conservation* 7:46-48.

Raxworthy, C. 1988. Expedition dans la Réserve de Zahamena. Pp. 320-323 in: L. Rakotovao, V. Barre and J. Sayer (eds.), *L'Equilibre des Ecosystèmes Forestiers à Madagascar: Actes d'un Séminaire International.* IUCN, Gland, Switzerland and Cambridge, U.K.

Raxworthy, C. J. and F. Rakotondraparany 1988. Mammals report. In: N. Quansah, N. (ed.), Manongarivo Special Reserve (Madagascar), 1987/88 Expedition Report. Madagascar Environmental Research Group, U.K.

Razanahoera-Rakotomalala, M. 1981. Les adaptations alimentaires comparés de deux lémuriens folivores sympatriques: *Avahi* Jourdan, 1834 - *Lepilemur* I. Geoffroy, 1851. Unpublished PhD thesis, University of Madagascar, Antananarivo.

Richard, A. F. 1973. Social organisation and ecology of *Propithecus verreauxi*, Grandidier 1867. Ph. D. Thesis. University of London.

Richard, A. F. 1974a. Patterns of mating in *Propithecus verreauxi verreauxi.* Pp. 49-74 in: R. D. Martin., G. A. Doyle and A. C. Walker (eds.), *Prosimian Biology.* Duckworth, London.

Richard, A. F. 1974b. Intra-specific variation in the social organization and ecology of *Propithecus verreauxi. Folia Primatologica* 22: 178-207.

Richard, A. F. 1976. Preliminary observations on the birth and development of *Propithecus verreauxi* to the age of six months.

Primates 17: 357-366.

Richard, A. F. 1977. The feeding behavior of *Propithecus verreauxi*. Pp. 71-96 in: T. Clutton-Brock (ed.), *Primate Ecology: Studies of Feeding and Ranging Behavior in Lemurs, Monkeys and Apes*. Academic Press, London.

Richard, A. F. 1978. Variability in the feeding behavior of a Malagasy prosimian, *Propithecus verreauxi*: Lemuriformes. Pp. 519-533 in: G.G. Montgomery (ed.), *The Ecology of Arboreal Folivores*, Smithsonian Institution, Washington, D.C.

Richard, A. F. 1985. Social boundaries in a Malagasy prosimian, the sifaka (*Propithecus verreauxi*). *International Journal of Primatology* 6(6): 553-568.

Richard, A. F. 1987. Malagasy prosimians: female dominance. Pp. 25-33 in: Smuts, B. B., D. L. Cheny, R. M. Seyfarth, R. W. Wrangham and T. T. Struhsaker (eds.), *Primate Societies*, University of Chicago Press, Chicago.

Rumpler, Y. 1975. The significance of chromosomal studies in the systematics of the Malagasy lemurs. Pp. 25-40 in: I. Tattersall and R. W. Sussman (eds.), *Lemur Biology*. Plenum Press, New York.

Rumpler, Y. and Albignac, R. 1975. Intraspecific chromosome variability in a lemur from the north of Madagascar: *Lepilemur septentrionalis*, species nova. *American Journal of Physical Anthropology* 42: 425-429.

Russell, R. J. 1977. The behavior, ecology, and environmental physiology of a nocturnal primate, *Lepilemur mustelinus* (Strepsirhini, Lemuriformes, Lepilemuridae). Unpublished Ph. D. thesis, Duke University, Durham, North Carolina.

Russell, R. J. 1980. The environmental physiology and ecology of *Lepilemur ruficaudatus* (= *L. leucopus*) in arid southern Madagascar. *American Journal of Physical Anthropology* 52: 272-274.

Safford, R. J. and J. W. Duckworth 1990. *A Wildlife Survey of*

Marojejy Nature Reserve, Madagascar. International Council of Bird Preservation, Study Report. 40: 1-184.

Safford, R. J., J. C. Durbin and J. W. Duckworth 1989. Cambridge Madagascar rainforest expedition to R.N.I. No. 12 - Marojejy. Unpublished preliminary report.

Sauther, M. 1991. Reproductive behavior of free-ranging *Lemur catta* at Beza-Mahafaly Special Reserve, Madagascar. *American Journal of Physical Anthropology* 463-478.

Schmid, J. and P. M. Kappeler 1994. Sympatric Mouse Lemurs (*Microcebus* spp.) in Western Madagascar. *Folia Primatologica*. In press.

Schmidt, C. R. 1986. A review of zoo breeding programmes for primates. *International Zoo Yearbook* 24/25: 107-123.

Schwarz, E 1931. A revision of the genera and species of Madagascar Lemuridae. *Proceedings of the Zoological Society of London* 1931: 399-428.

Schwartz, J. H. and I. Tattersall 1985. Evolutionary relationships of living lemurs and lorises (Mammalia, Primates) and their potential affinities with European Eocene Adapidae. *Anthropological Papers of the American Museum of Natural History*, 60 (1). New York, 100 pp.

Seyler, J. R., C. A. Pryor, J. G. Gaudet and C. Barnes 1986. *Energy/Natural Resources Sub-sector Strategy Update.* Report to REDSO/ESA, U.S. Agency for International Development.

Simons, E. L. 1988. A new species of *Propithecus* (Primates) from northeast Madagascar. *Folia Primatologica* 50: 143-151.

Simons, E. L. and Y. Rumpler 1988. *Eulemur:* new generic name for species of *Lemur* other than *Lemur catta. C. R. Acad. Science* Paris, Ser. 3 307: 547-551.

Simons, H. J. 1984. Report on a survey expedition to Natural Reserve No. 3 of Zahamena. Unpublished report.

Simons, H. J. and N. B. D. Lindsay 1987. Survey work on ruffed lemurs (*Varecia variegata*) and other primates in the northeastern rain forests of Madagascar. *Primate Conservation* 8: 88-91.

Simons, E. L., L. R. Godfrey, M. Vuillaume-Randriamanantena, P. S. Chartrath, and M. Gagnon 1990. Discovery of new giant subfossil lemurs in the Ankarana Mountains of northern Madagascar. *Journal of Human Evolution* 19(3): 311-319.

Sonnerat, C. 1782. *Voyage aux Indes Orientales et à la Chine*, vol. 2. Paris.

Sterling, E. 1992. Timing the reproduction of aye-ayes (*Daubentonia madagascariensis*) in Madagascar. *American Journal of Primatology* 27(1): 59-60.

Sterling, E. 1993. Patterns of range use and social organization in aye-ayes. Pp. 1-10 in: Kappeler, P. M. and J. Ganzhorn (eds.), *Lemur Social Systems and Their Ecological Basis*. Plenum Press, New York.

Sussman, R. W. 1972. An ecological study of two Madagascan primates: *Lemur fulvus rufus* Audebert and *Lemur catta* Linnaeus. Unpublished PhD thesis, Duke University, Durham, North Carolina.

Sussman, R. W. 1974. Ecological distinctions in sympatric species of lemur. Pp. 75-108 in: R. D. Martin, G. A. Doyle and A. C. Walker (eds.), *Prosimian Biology*. Duckworth, London.

Sussman, R. W. 1975. A preliminary study of the behavior and ecology of *Lemur fulvus rufus* Audebert 1800. Pp. 237-258 in: I. Tattersall and R. W. Sussman (eds.), *Lemur Biology*. Plenum Press, New York.

Sussman, R. W. 1977. Distribution of Malagasy lemurs. Part 2: *Lemur catta* and *Lemur fulvus* in southern and western Madagascar. *Annals of the New York Academy of Sciences* 293: 170-183.

Sussman, R. W. 1991. Demography and social organization of free-ranging *Lemur catta* in Beza Mahafaly Reserve. *American Journal of Physical Anthropology* 84: 43-58.

Sussman, R. W. and A. Richard 1986. Lemur conservation in Madagascar: the status of lemurs in the south. *Primate Conservation* 7: 85-92.

Sussman, R. W. and I. Tattersall 1976. Cycles of activity, group composition and diet of *Lemur mongoz* Linnaeus 1766 in Madagascar. *Folia Primatologica* 26: 270-283.

Sussman, R. W., A. F. Richard and P. Rakotomanga 1987. La conservation des lémuriens à Madagascar: leur statut dans le sud. Pp. 75-81 in: R. A. Mittermeier, L. H. Rakotovao, V. Randrianasolo, E. J. Sterling and D. Devitre (eds.), *Priorités en Matière de Conservation des Espèces à Madagascar*. Occasional Papers of the IUCN Species Survival Commission, No. 2. Gland, Switzerland.

Tattersall, I. 1976a. Group structure and activity rhythm in *Lemur mongoz* (Primates, Lemuriformes) on Anjouan and Mohéli Islands, Comoro Archipelago. *Anthropological Papers of the American Museum of Natural History* 53(4): 369-380.

Tattersall, I. 1976b. Notes on the status of *Lemur macaco* and *Lemur fulvus* (Primates, Lemuriformes). *Anthropological Papers of the American Museum of Natural History* 53(2): 257-261.

Tattersall, I. 1977a. Distribution of the Malagasy lemurs, Part 1: The lemurs of northern Madagascar. *Annals of the New York Academy of Sciences* 293: 160-169.

Tattersall, I. 1977b. The lemurs of the Comoro Islands. *Oryx* 13(5): 445-448.

Tattersall, I. 1977c. Behavioural variation in *Lemur mongoz* (=*L. m. mongoz*). Pp. 127-132 in: D. J. Chivers and K. A. Joysey (eds), *Recent Advances in Primatology*, Vol. 3. Academic Press, London. 382 pp.

Tattersall, I. 1982. *The Primates of Madagascar*. Columbia University Press, New York.

Tattersall, I. 1983. Status of the Comoro lemurs: A reappraisal. *IUCN/SSC Primate Specialist Group Newsletter* 3: 24-26.

Tattersall, I. 1986. Notes on the distribution and taxonomic status of some species of *Propithecus* in Madagascar. *Folia Primatologica* 46: 51-63.

Tattersall, I. 1989. The Mayotte lemur: cause for alarm. *Primate Conservation* 10: 26-27.

Tattersall, I. and J. H. Schwartz 1991. Phylogeny and nomenclature in the *Lemur*-group of Malagasy Strepsirhine primates. *Anthropological Papers of the American Museum of Natural History* 69: 1-18.

Tattersall, I. and R. W. Sussman 1975. Observations on the ecology and behavior of the mongoose lemur *Lemur mongoz mongoz* Linnaeus (Primates, Lemuriformes) at Ampijoroa, Madagascar. *Anthropological Papers of the American Museum of Natural History* 52(4): 195-216.

Thompson, P. and M. I. Evans 1991. Unpublished report to the Madagascar Environmental Research Group. London, U.K.

Van Horn, R. N. and G. G. Eaton 1979. Reproductive physiology and behavior in prosimians. Pp. 79-122 in: Doyle, G. A. and R. D. Martin (eds.), *The Study of Prosimian Behavior*. Academic Press, New York.

Vick, E. G. and M. E. Pereira 1989. Episodic targeting aggression and the histories of *Lemur* social groups. *Behavior, Ecology and Sociobiology* 25: 3-12.

Warter, S., G. Randrianasolo, B. Dutrillaux and Y. Rumpler 1987. Cytogenetic study of a new subspecies of *Hapalemur griseus*. *Folia Primatologica* 48: 50-55.

White, F. 1983. *The Vegetation of Africa*. UNESCO, Paris, France.

White, F. J. 1989. Diet, ranging behavior and social organization of the black-and-white ruffed lemur, *Varecia variegata variegata*, in southeastern Madagascar. *American Journal of Physical Anthropology* 78(2): 323.

White, P. T. 1994. Rice: the essential harvest. *National Geographic* 185(5): 48-79.

Wilde, J., M. H. Schwibbe and A. Arsène 1988. A census for captive primates in Europe. *Primate Report* 21: 1-120.

Wilson, J. M., P. D. Stewart and S. V. Fowler 1988. Ankarana - a rediscovered nature reserve in northern Madagascar. *Oryx* 22: 163-171.

Wilson, J. M., P. D. Stewart, G.-S. Ramangason, A. M. Denning, and M. S. Hutchings 1989. Ecology and conservation of the crowned lemur, *Lemur coronatus*, at Ankarana, N. Madagascar, with notes on Sanford's lemur, other sympatrics and subfossil lemurs. *Folia Primatologica* 52: 1-26.

World Bank, U. S. Agency for International Development, Cooperation Suisse, UNESCO, United Nations Development Program, and Worldwide Fund for Nature 1988. *Madagascar Environmental Action Plan, Vol. 1 (Synthesis and Proposed Actions)*, Washington, D.C.

Wright, P. 1986. Diet, ranging behavior and activity pattern of the gentle lemur (*Hapalemur griseus*) in Madagascar. *American Journal of Physical Anthropology* 69(2): 283.

Wright, P. 1988. IUCN Tropical Forest Program, Critical Sites Inventory. Report to the World Conservation Monitoring Centre, Cambridge, U. K.

Wright, P. 1989. Comparative ecology of three sympatric bamboo lemurs in Madagascar. *American Journal of Physical Anthropology* 78(2): 327.

Wright, P., P. S. Daniels, D. M. Meyers, D. J. Overdorff and J. Rabesoa 1987. A census and study of *Hapalemur* and *Propithecus* in southeastern Madagascar. *Primate Conservation* 8: 84-87.

WWF 1969. Conservation Program in Madagascar 1969. *World Wildlife Fund Yearbook 1969*. Morges, Switzerland.

Color Plates

318

PLATE 1

a. Baobab tree at Hazafotsy village, at the edge of the spiny desert portion of the Andohahela Nature Reserve, southern Madagascar. *Propithecus v. verreauxi* is easily seen here.

b. Trail through dry forest at Ampijoroa Station, Ankarafantsıka Nature Reserve, in northwestern Madagascar. This station is on the road from Mahajanga to Antananarivo.

c. Waterfall in the rain forest of Montagne d'Ambre National Park in extreme northern Madagascar. Montagne d'Ambre is easily reached from Diégo-Suarez.

d. Rain forest on the island of Nosy Mangabe, in the Bay of Antongil, near Maroantsetra, northeastern Madagascar. *Daubentonia* and *Varecia v. variegata* are both introduced here.

PLATE 2

a. Southern spiny desert portion of the Andohahela Nature Reserve, southern Madagascar.

b. Close-up view of southern spiny desert at Hazafotsy village, Andohahela Nature Reserve.

c. Grove of *Alluaudia ascendens*, a Didiereaceae endemic to southern Madagascar.

d. Grove of *kili* trees, *(Tamarindus indica)* which occur in narrow strips of gallery forest, southern Madagascar.

e. Giant baobab trees *(Adansonia grandidieri)* near Morondava, southwestern Madagascar.

f. Dry forest of the Montagne des Français, near Diégo-Suarez, extreme northern Madagascar.

g. Rain forest at Périnet (= Andasibe), home of *Indri indri* and only two hours drive east of Antananarivo.

h. Rain forest on the island of Nosy Mangabe, Bay of Antongil, eastern Madagascar.

PLATE 3

a. Color plate of the indri (*Indri indri*) from Audebert, *Histoire Naturelle des Singes et des Makis* (1799), a classic work on primates of the late 18th century.

b. 'The Mongooz' (*Eulemur mongoz*), from George Edwards' *Gleanings of Natural History* (1758-64), another classic work of zoology.

c. *Lemur catta*, from *General and Particular Descriptions of the Vertebrated Animals - Order Quadrumania,* (1821) by Edward Griffith.

d. Plate of *Propithecus d. diadema* from Grandidier's monumental work on Madagascar, Volume IX, the book of plates of the Indriidae.

PLATE 4

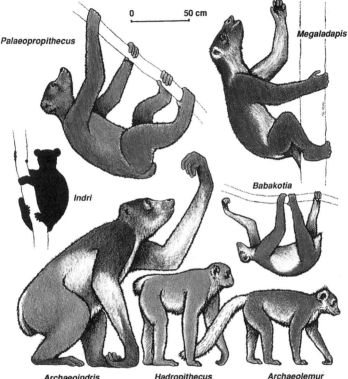

0   50 cm

Palaeopropithecus

Megaladapis

Indri

Babakotia

Archaeoindris   *Hadropithecus*   *Archaeolemur*

ILLUSTRATION BY STEPHEN D. NASH

Reconstructions of 6 of the 8 subfossil lemur genera that have already gone extinct in Madagascar. The indri, largest of the living genera, is included in silhouette to show scale.

Note that all these extinct genera were larger than the extant species, and include some of the largest primates that ever lived.

Archaeoindris, for example, was a huge terrestrial animal probably similar in niche to the giant ground sloths of South America and reached 160-200 kg in weight, as large as a male gorilla.

It is believed that *Hadropithecus* was a behaviorally baboon-like lemur, with powerful jaws and a terrestrial lifestyle.

PLATE 5

a. *Microcebus myoxinus* from Analabe, near Morondava.

b. *Hapalemur aureus* in the Ranomafana National Park.

c. *Lepilemur dorsalis* from the Lokobe Nature Reserve, Nosy Be.

d. *Lepilemur edwardsi*, Ampijoroa Station, Ankarafantsika Reserve.

e. *Propithecus v. verreauxi* in spiny *Alluaudia*, Beza Mahafaly Reserve.

f. *Indri indri* and infant in the Périnet (=Andasibe) Special Reserve.

ALL PHOTOS BY RUSSELL A. MITTERMEIER

PLATE 6

a. Female *Eulemur rubriventer*, Ranomafana National Park.

b. Male *Eulemur rubriventer*, Ranomafana National Park.

c. Male *Eulemur m. macaco*, Nosy Komba island.

d. Female *Eulemur m. macaco*, Nosy Komba island.

e. *Lemur catta*, on sisal plant, Berenty Private Reserve.

f. Male *Eulemur f. rufus*, Analabe Private Reserve.

324

PLATE 7

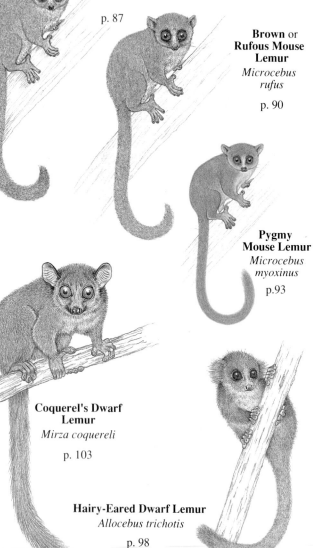

Gray Mouse Lemur
Microcebus murinus

p. 87

Brown or
**Rufous Mouse
Lemur**
*Microcebus
rufus*

p. 90

**Pygmy
Mouse Lemur**
*Microcebus
myoxinus*

p.93

**Coquerel's Dwarf
Lemur**
Mirza coquereli

p. 103

Hairy-Eared Dwarf Lemur
Allocebus trichotis

p. 98

PLATE 8

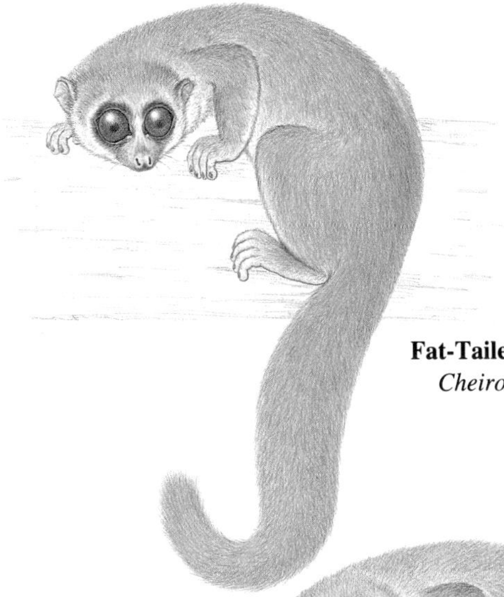

Fat-Tailed Dwarf Lemur
Cheirogaleus medius
p. 112

Greater Dwarf Lemur
Cheirogaleus major
p. 109

PLATE 9

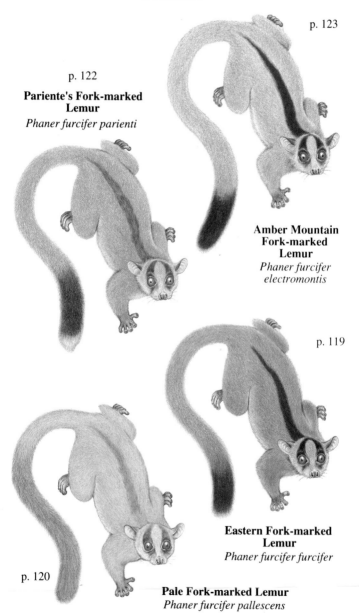

p. 123

p. 122

Pariente's Fork-marked Lemur
Phaner furcifer parienti

Amber Mountain Fork-marked Lemur
Phaner furcifer electromontis

p. 119

Eastern Fork-marked Lemur
Phaner furcifer furcifer

p. 120

Pale Fork-marked Lemur
Phaner furcifer pallescens

PLATE 10

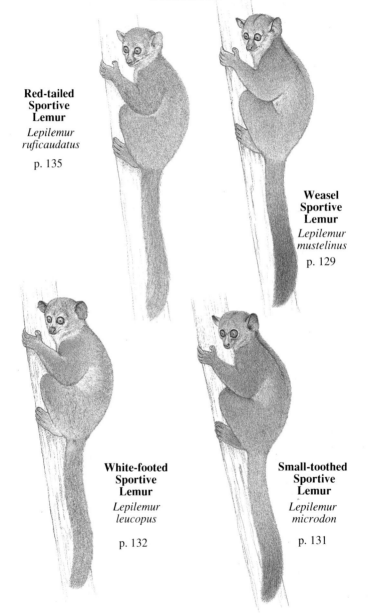

**Red-tailed
Sportive
Lemur**

*Lepilemur
ruficaudatus*

p. 135

**Weasel
Sportive
Lemur**

*Lepilemur
mustelinus*

p. 129

**White-footed
Sportive
Lemur**

*Lepilemur
leucopus*

p. 132

**Small-toothed
Sportive
Lemur**

*Lepilemur
microdon*

p. 131

PLATE 11

**Northern
Sportive
Lemur**

*Lepilemur
septentrionalis*

p. 141

**Gray-backed
Sportive
Lemur**

*Lepilemur
dorsalis*

p. 139

**Milne-Edwards'
Sportive Lemur**

*Lepilemur
edwardsi*

p. 137

PLATE 12

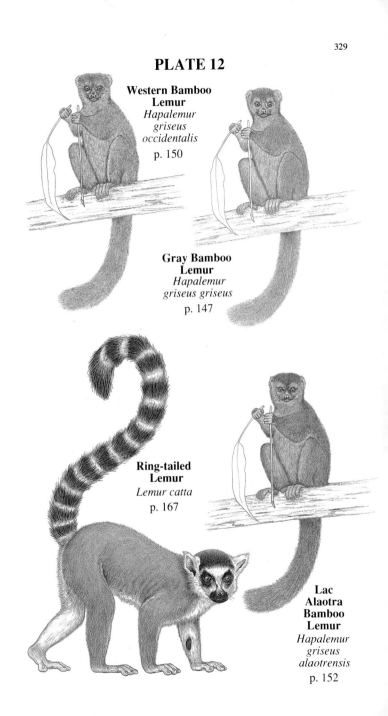

Western Bamboo Lemur
Hapalemur griseus occidentalis
p. 150

Gray Bamboo Lemur
Hapalemur griseus griseus
p. 147

Ring-tailed Lemur
Lemur catta
p. 167

Lac Alaotra Bamboo Lemur
Hapalemur griseus alaotrensis
p. 152

PLATE 13

**Greater Bamboo
Lemur**
Hapalemur simus

p. 157

Golden Bamboo Lemur
Hapalemur aureus

p. 155

PLATE 14

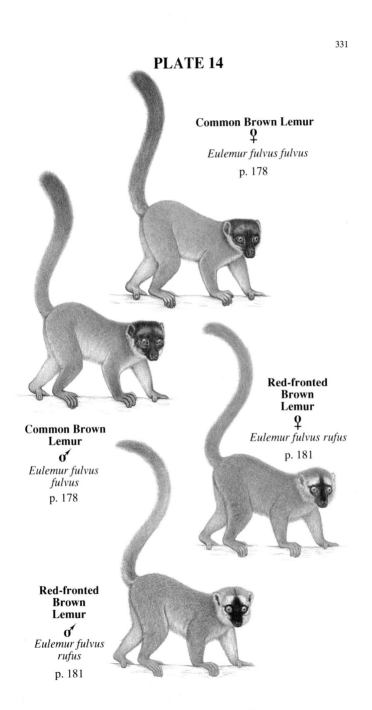

Common Brown Lemur
♀
Eulemur fulvus fulvus
p. 178

**Common Brown
Lemur**
♂
*Eulemur fulvus
fulvus*
p. 178

**Red-fronted
Brown
Lemur**
♀
Eulemur fulvus rufus
p. 181

**Red-fronted
Brown
Lemur**
♂
*Eulemur fulvus
rufus*
p. 181

PLATE 15

**White-fronted
Brown Lemur**
♀

Eulemur fulvus albifrons

p. 184

**White-fronted
Brown Lemur**
♂
*Eulemur fulvus
albifrons*

p. 184

**Sanford's
Brown Lemur**
♀
*Eulemur fulvus
sanfordi*

p. 186

**Sanford's
Brown Lemur**
♂
*Eulemur fulvus
sanfordi*

p. 186

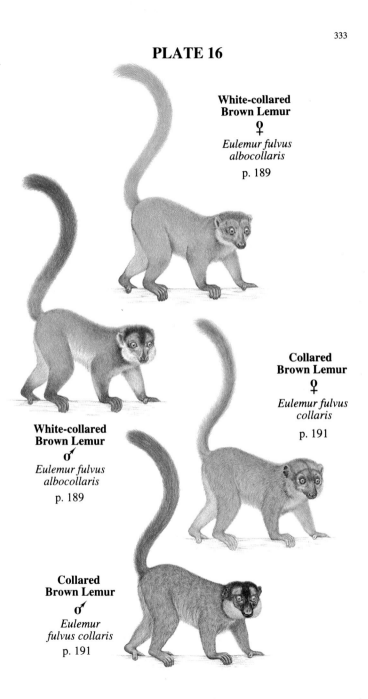

PLATE 16

**White-collared
Brown Lemur**
♀
*Eulemur fulvus
albocollaris*

p. 189

**White-collared
Brown Lemur**
♂
*Eulemur fulvus
albocollaris*

p. 189

**Collared
Brown Lemur**
♀
*Eulemur fulvus
collaris*

p. 191

**Collared
Brown Lemur**
♂
*Eulemur
fulvus collaris*

p. 191

PLATE 17

Common Brown Lemur ♂
(left) and ♀ (below)

Eulemur fulvus fulvus
p. 178

Red-fronted Brown Lemur
♂ (left) and ♀ (below)
Eulemur fulvus rufus
p. 181

White-fronted Brown Lemur
♂ (above) and ♀ (right)
Eulemur fulvus albifrons
p. 184

PLATE 18

Sanford's Brown Lemur
♂ (left) and ♀ (below)

Eulemur fulvus sanfordi

p. 186

White-collared Brown Lemur
♂ (left) and ♀ (below)

Eulemur fulvus albocollaris

p. 189

Collared Brown Lemur
♂ (above) and ♀ (right)

Eulemur fulvus collaris

p. 191

336

PLATE 19

Black Lemur
♀
Eulemur macaco macaco

p. 193

**Sclater's
Black Lemur**
♀
*Eulemur macaco
flavifrons*

p. 197

Black Lemur
♂
*Eulemur macaco
macaco*

p. 193

**Sclater's
Black Lemur**
♂
*Eulemur macaco
flavifrons*

p. 197

PLATE 20

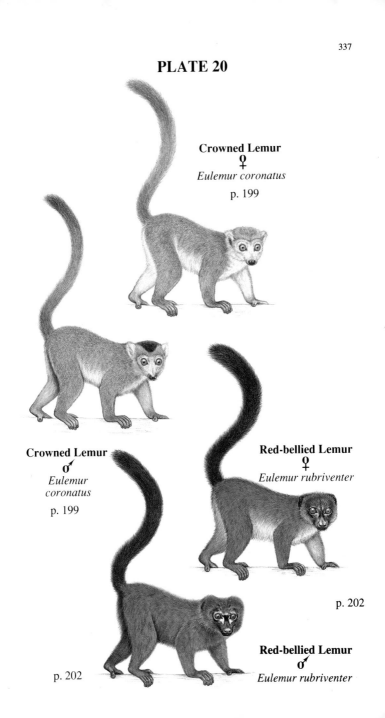

Crowned Lemur
♀
Eulemur coronatus
p. 199

Crowned Lemur
♂
Eulemur coronatus
p. 199

Red-bellied Lemur
♀
Eulemur rubriventer

p. 202

Red-bellied Lemur
♂
Eulemur rubriventer

p. 202

PLATE 21

**Black Lemur ♂ (left)
and ♀ (below)**

*Eulemur macaco
macaco*

p. 193

**Sclater's Black Lemur
♂ (above) and ♀ (right)**

Eulemur macaco flavifrons

p. 197

PLATE 22

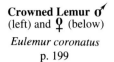

Crowned Lemur ♂
(left) and ♀ (below)

Eulemur coronatus
p. 199

Red-bellied Lemur ♂ (left)
and ♀ (below)   p. 202

Eulemur rubriventer

Mongoose Lemur ♂
(above) and ♀ (right)

Eulemur mongoz

p. 204

PLATE 23

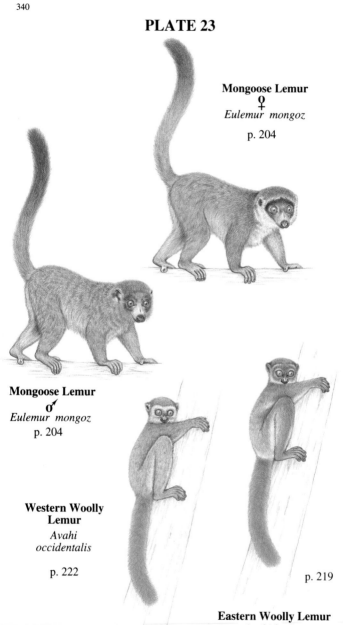

Mongoose Lemur
♀
Eulemur mongoz

p. 204

Mongoose Lemur
♂
Eulemur mongoz
p. 204

**Western Woolly
Lemur**
*Avahi
occidentalis*

p. 222

p. 219

Eastern Woolly Lemur
Avahi laniger

PLATE 24

**Black-and-white Ruffed
Lemur,** *"subcincta"* **group**
Varecia variegata variegata
p. 210

p. 210
**Black-and-white Ruffed
Lemur,** *"variegata"* **group**
Varecia variegata variegata

p. 210
**Black-and-white Ruffed
Lemur,** *"editorum"* **group**
Varecia variegata variegata

Red Ruffed Lemur
Varecia variegata rubra
p. 213

PLATE 25

**Varieties of Black-and-white Ruffed Lemurs
of the "subcincta" group**

Varecia variegata variegata

(Adapted from Ceska *et al.*, 1992)

PLATE 26

**Varieties of Black-and-white Ruffed Lemurs
of the "subcincta" group**

Varecia variegata variegata

(Adapted from Ceska *et al.*, 1992)

PLATE 27

"variegata" group
(left column)

"editorum" group
(right column)

**Varieties of Black-and-white Ruffed Lemurs
of the *"variegata"* and *"editorum"* groups**

Varecia variegata variegata

(Adapted from Ceska *et al.*, 1992)

PLATE 28

Varieties of Red Ruffed Lemur

Varecia variegata rubra

(Adapted from Ceska et al., 1992)

PLATE 29

Coquerel's Sifaka
Propithecus verreauxi coquereli

Verreaux's Sifaka
*Propithecus verreauxi
verreauxi*

p. 236

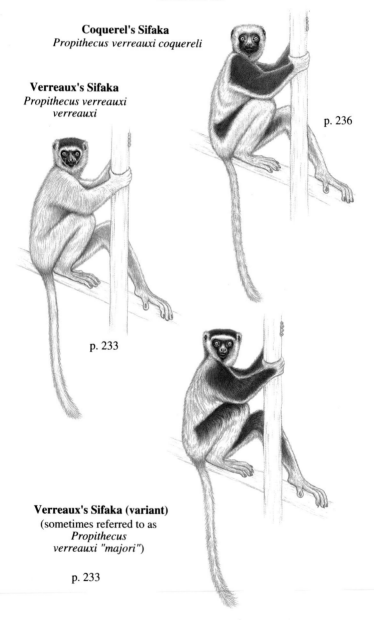

p. 233

Verreaux's Sifaka (variant)
(sometimes referred to as
*Propithecus
verreauxi "majori"*)

p. 233

PLATE 30

p. 233

**Verreaux's Sifaka
color variants**
*Propithecus verreauxi
verreauxi*

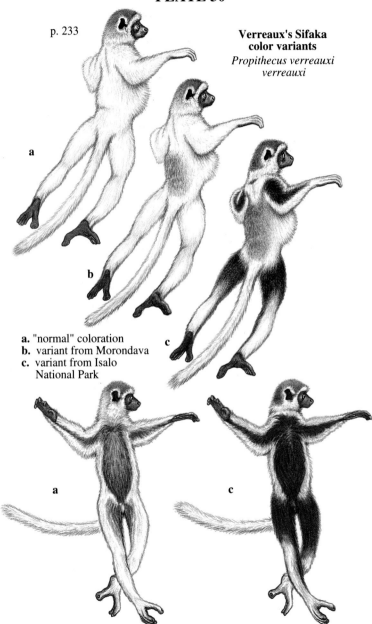

a

b

c

a. "normal" coloration
b. variant from Morondava
c. variant from Isalo
    National Park

a

c

PLATE 31

Golden-crowned Sifaka
Propithecus tattersalli

Decken's Sifaka
*Propithecus verreauxi
deckeni*

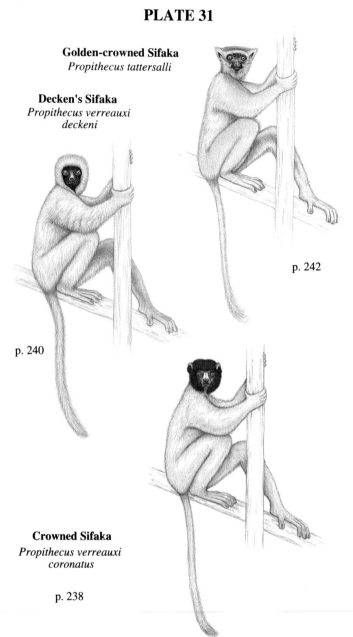

p. 242

p. 240

Crowned Sifaka
*Propithecus verreauxi
coronatus*

p. 238

PLATE 32

Diademed Sifaka
Propithecus diadema diadema

p. 245

Milne-Edwards' Sifaka
Propithecus diadema edwardsi

p. 247

PLATE 33

Perrier's Sifaka

Propithecus diadema perrieri

p. 251

Silky Sifaka

*Propithecus diadema
candidus*

p. 249

PLATE 34

Indri or Babakoto
Indri indri
p. 258

color variants of
Indri indri

PLATE 35

p. 265

Aye-aye
Daubentonia madagascariensis

Detailed views of the
face (above), and dorsal
(left) and ventral (right)
surfaces of the left hand of
Daubentonia. Note the
slender, elongate third digit.

PLATE 36

Aye-aye
Daubentonia madagascariensis
Skeletal structure of the most divergent of all primates

p. 265

LEMUR LIFE-LIST

✔	Name	Locality / Date
❏	*Microcebus murinus*	........................./............
❏	*Microcebus rufus*	........................./............
❏	*Microcebus myoxinus*	........................./............
❏	*Allocebus trichotis*	........................./............
❏	*Mirza coquereli*	........................./............
❏	*Cheirogaleus major*	........................./............
❏	*Cheirogaleus medius*	........................./............
❏	*Phaner furcifer furcifer*	........................./............
❏	*Phaner furcifer pallescens*	........................./............
❏	*Phaner furcifer parienti*	........................./............
❏	*Phaner furcifer electromontis*	........................./............
❏	*Lepilemur mustelinus*	........................./............
❏	*Lepilemur microdon*	........................./............
❏	*Lepilemur leucopus*	........................./............
❏	*Lepilemur ruficaudatus*	........................./............
❏	*Lepilemur edwardsi*	........................./............
❏	*Lepilemur dorsalis*	........................./............
❏	*Lepilemur septentrionalis*	........................./............
❏	*Hapalemur griseus griseus*	........................./............
❏	*Hapalemur griseus occidentalis*	........................./............
❏	*Hapalemur griseus alaotrensis*	........................./............
❏	*Hapalemur aureus*	........................./............
❏	*Hapalemur simus*	........................./............
❏	*Lemur catta*	........................./............

✔	Name	Locality / Date

❑ *Eulemur fulvus fulvus* ..../............

❑ *Eulemur fulvus rufus* ..../............

❑ *Eulemur fulvus albifrons* ..../............

❑ *Eulemur fulvus sanfordi* ..../............

❑ *Eulemur fulvus albocollaris* ..../............

❑ *Eulemur fulvus collaris* ..../............

❑ *Eulemur macaco macaco* ..../............

❑ *Eulemur macaco flavifrons* ..../............

❑ *Eulemur coronatus* ..../............

❑ *Eulemur rubriventer* ..../............

❑ *Eulemur mongoz* ..../............

❑ *Varecia variegata variegata* ..../............

❑ *Varecia variegata rubra* ..../............

❑ *Avahi laniger* ..../............

❑ *Avahi occidentalis* ..../............

❑ *Propithecus verreauxi verreauxi* ..../............

❑ *Propithecus verreauxi coquereli* ..../............

❑ *Propithecus verreauxi coronatus* ..../............

❑ *Propithecus verreauxi deckeni* ..../............

❑ *Propithecus tattersalli* ..../............

❑ *Propithecus diadema diadema* ..../............

❑ *Propithecus diadema edwardsi* ..../............

❑ *Propithecus diadema candidus* ..../............

❑ *Propithecus diadema perrieri* ..../............

❑ *Indri indri* ..../............

❑ *Daubentonia madagascariensis* ..../............

REQUEST FOR INFORMATION

As indicated in various places in the text, we would welcome hearing from you if you see lemurs in unusual places, or in unusual circumstances. If you think that you have seen something of scientific interest, please contact one of us at the addresses below. You may have made an observation worthy of publication in *Lemur News*, the newsletter of the IUCN/SSC Primate Specialist Group's Madagascan Section, or another primatological journal. Of particular interest are the following kinds of data:

1. Lemur sightings outside the geographical ranges given in this book (please provide place names and latitude and longitude where possible).
2. Photographs or videotape of the animals sighted to assist us in confirming identifications.
3. Cases in which lemurs have been kept as pets, or captured or shot for food; this would include situations in which lemurs or lemur body parts (skins, meat, skulls, etc.,) are being sold in markets, shops, etc., (again, photographs would be helpful).
4. Sites not mentioned in this book where lemurs are especially abundant or where observation conditions are really outstanding. We would like to add such sites to future editions of this book.
5. Any other information that you think might be useful in enhancing our knowledge of lemur conservation and biology.

Please write to:

Russell A. Mittermeier, President, Conservation International, 1015 Eighteenth Street NW, Washington, DC 20036, USA

Ian Tattersall, Curator, Department of Anthropology, American Museum of Natural History, Central Park West at 79th. Street, NewYork, NY 10024-5192, USA

William R. Konstant, Vice President for Conservation, The Philadelphia Zoo, 3400 West Girard Avenue, Philadelphia, PA 19104-1196, USA

Stephen D. Nash, Department of Anatomical Sciences, Health Sciences Center, State University of New York, Stony Brook, NY 11794-8081, USA

Are you interested in becoming more involved in the conservation of lemurs and their habitats on the unique island of Madagascar?

Join Conservation International.

❏ I want to become a member of Conservation International.

❏ I want to make an additional gift to CI's field projects.

❏ $35 (minimum annual membership dues)   ❏ $500
❏ $50   ❏ $1000+ Emerald Circle
❏ $100   ❏ Other $_____

Please charge $_____ to my ❏ Visa ❏ Mastercard

_____
Card No.   Exp. Date

_____
Name on Card

_____
Signiture

❏ My employer has a matching gift program and I will forward the forms to Conservation International.

_____
Employer

Your contributions are tax-deductible to the fullest extent allowed by law.

Please make your check payable to **Conservation International** and send to:
Conservation International, 1015 Eighteenth Street, NW, Suite 1000, Washington, DC 20036, USA
Tel. (202) 429-5660

_____
Name

_____
Address

_____
City

_____
State   Zip

_____ ❏ Please do not call me.
Telephone

LEMFG